AF716508

Geoffrey Simpson-Scott is a solicitor and partner at Hodge Jones & Allen. With a distinguished career that includes tenure at the Royal Court of Justice, Geoffrey specialises in clinical negligence offering invaluable expertise honed through over two decades of dedicated practice.

Geoffrey is also author of a book called 'A Practical Guide to Clinical Negligence' making him an expert in his field.

Ramune Mickeviciute is a solicitor at Hugh James. She has built her career at national law firms in London and qualified as a solicitor in July 2021. Clinical negligence has always been her main passion. She shares her considerable experience built over the past eight years in this area of law.

A Practical Guide to Fixed Costs in Clinical Negligence Cases

A Practical Guide to Fixed Costs in Clinical Negligence Cases

Geoffrey Simpson-Scott,
Solicitor and Partner at Hodge Jones & Allen

Ramune Mickeviciute,
Solicitor at Hugh James

Law Brief Publishing

© Geoffrey Simpson-Scott & Ramune Mickeviciute

All rights reserved. No part of this publication may be reproduced, stored in a retrieval system, or transmitted, in any form or by any means, electronic, mechanical, photocopying, recording or otherwise, without the prior permission of the publisher.

Excerpts from judgments and statutes are Crown copyright. Any Crown Copyright material is reproduced with the permission of the Controller of OPSI and the King's Printer for Scotland. Some quotations may be licensed under the terms of the Open Government Licence (http://www.nationalarchives.gov.uk/doc/open-government-licence/version/3).

Cover image © iStockphoto.com/Nelson Hernandez Chitiva

The information in this book was believed to be correct at the time of writing. All content is for information purposes only and is not intended as legal advice. No liability is accepted by either the publisher or author for any errors or omissions (whether negligent or not) that it may contain. Professional advice should always be obtained before applying any information to particular circumstances.

Published 2024 by Law Brief Publishing, an imprint of Law Brief Publishing Ltd
30 The Parks
Minehead
Somerset
TA24 8BT

www.lawbriefpublishing.com

Paperback: 978-1-916698-18-5

Thank you for purchasing this book.

This handbook is dedicated to the resilient and unwavering community of clinical negligence lawyers who tirelessly champion the cause of justice. In the face of evolving legal landscapes and the challenges posed by fixed recoverable costs, your dedication to upholding the rights of the vulnerable remains an inspiration to us all.

To those who navigate the intricate web of medical negligence cases with tenacity and compassion, this book is a tribute to your commitment and a testament to the indomitable spirit of the legal profession. Your pursuit of justice, even in the face of formidable challenges, embodies the highest ideals of our legal system.

May this handbook stand as a token of our appreciation for the invaluable work you do, and may it provide you with the guidance and insights needed to navigate the complexities of clinical negligence law in an era marked by change.

FOREWORD

As the doting human slave of a very vocal Bengal cat, I rarely get the first word at home, so it is not only an honour but a pleasure to provide the Foreword to 'A Practical Approach to FRC in Clinical Negligence'. In so doing, I hope the authors of do not mind if I begin by using their very own words *"Learning from others is our greatest resource, using their knowledge and lessons in order to use the same methods yourself whilst avoiding the same mistakes tips the odds in your favour ..."*. The expertise of the authors of this book is certainly to be learnt from.

In advance of April 2024 it is imperative that clinical negligence solicitors be familiar with the fixed recoverable costs regime and its potential impact on their practice, litigation efficiency and business model. This book comprehensively explains that regime as it relates to clinical negligence claims and analyses the ambiguities and pitfalls for the unwary. Most valuable of all, it is an insightful guide as to the practical steps to be taken to ensure that the new, (and for many unwelcome), dawn of fixed recoverable costs in clinical negligence cases can be made to work for you and your firm. I would be so bold as to say that no other resource is needed; which may give some comfort to the busy practitioner when a google search on 'fixed recoverable costs in clinical negligence cases' returns 165,000 results.

I will leave the reader with two medical/cost related thoughts, inspired by two quips:

(1) *"Any man who goes to a psychiatrist ought to have his head examined"* (per Samuel Goldwyn). The same could be said of any claimant clinical negligence solicitor who does not have this book as their go to guide; and

(2) *"A cynic is a man who knows the price of everything and the value of nothing"* (per Oscar Wilde). The practitioners that avail

themselves of this guide will not be cynics. Rather, where cases do fall within the fixed recoverable costs regime, those practitioners will be superbly placed to evaluate and understand the cost of every step in their litigation process, and the value it will bring to their client, and to their own profit margin.

Eva Ferguson
Hailsham Chambers
November 2023

PREFACE

It is our genuine pleasure to have been invited to write this handbook to the ever-increasing library of practitioner guides published by Law Brief Publishing Ltd. As we write this, the ecosystem we work in faces drastic changes. Those of you that watched the Civil Justice Council's 12th National Forum *"Improving Access to Justice in a Cost of Living Crisis"* (available on YouTube) will not have seen any mention of clinical negligence at all; we could be forgiven for seeing our area of law as a backwater where the consequences of imposing fixed recoverable costs have not been thought through.

More concerning is the possibility that they have. The Ministerial Foreword to the September 2023 *"Fixed Recoverable Costs in Lower Value Clinical Negligence Claims – Government Response"* entirely equates protecting access to justice with reducing costs.

These reforms are being imposed at a time when the NHS continues to face the worst crisis of its existence. There are continuing and egregious failures in being able to provide the care it wants to; overwhelmed GP, A&E and ambulance services; very poor staff morale; very long waiting times for specialist investigations; and increasing numbers of patients paying privately.

Yet actual examples of sub-standard care remain the exception and remain difficult to prove in practice. Again, one should be forgiven for thinking that reducing the amount negligently injured patients can recover for pursuing the compensation they need to live with these injuries is likely to reduce the amount of claims successfully brought and so make it appear that there is 'less negligence' in the NHS.

As our prehistoric ancestors once did, we stand at the head of a mountain pass looking down on the vista of new lands before us. Far from being green and fertile, we can see from our lofty vantage point that the lowlands are dry and arid although rivers and oases do pepper the landscape. These sources of water will likely be hard fought over and may not be as productive as they appear from afar. Caliginous bogs await the unwary; mirages trick the unobservant and we must be prepared to adapt our farming techniques for what we find when we arrive. The path is set, however – we cannot go back. We must go forward.

Our intention is to cover issues which arise in everyday practice and which have a tendency to cause delay and increased costs. A fixed costs regime essentially demands efficiency. The spectre of a fixed costs regime has long been with us and so some degree of planning has been possible. Whilst there are advantages to one, it is essential that downward costs pressures do not adversely affect access to justice, patient safety or full compensation. The reform proposals we have seen so far do not clearly identify how they achieve these aims which have underpinned successive legal systems since the Code of Hammurabi around 3,700 years ago.

Traditionally, clinical negligence lawyers on both sides of the profession have taken a considerable amount of time and effort to ensure that the complex issues in their clients' cases are explored properly. Anecdotally, downwards costs pressures still seem to be imposed arbitrarily too often. The middle ground remains for us to continue to become more knowledgeable about the underlying medicine and substantive law; good practice and procedure; more skilful and collaborative litigators; and more effective negotiators (as opposed to compromisers).

This book does not pretend to be the definitive guide to fixed recoverable costs in clinical negligence but our sincere hope remains that the issues covered in this book assist in striking a reasonable practical balance between cost effectiveness and effective litigation.

The case law referred to in this book shows the relevant underlying legal principles and illustrates how the courts apply them. We have endeavoured to correctly state the law as it is at the end of December 2023. However, any errors are ours alone.

So, allow us to be your guides. In this practitioner's handbook, we seek to provide in depth analyses of the new rules as they apply to clinical negligence across different damages bands; what lessons can be learned from those areas already affected by FRC; how funding and valuing cases are likely to be affected; how expert evidence will need to adapt; before considering how improvements in legal technology may assist us; what strategies we may want to employ; and how negotiations and settlement may proceed.

We sincerely hope that this helps you in continuing to provide your clients with the high-quality service which is focussed on their needs in the face of these very significant challenges. This remains an exciting and continually area of law and we sincerely hope that you enjoy practising it as much as we do.

Geoffrey Simpson-Scott, Solicitor and Partner at Hodge Jones & Allen

Ramune Mickeviciute, Solicitor at Hugh James

London, January 2024

AUTHOR'S NOTE

Without even thinking twice, I would get into a fight to prove that clinical negligence is one of the most interesting areas of law. And not to brag about any persuasion skills, but I am sure I would win. I would, however, avoid the subject of costs at all costs, let alone the unknown of fixed recoverable costs.

While one might have already gotten the impression that the costs subject is not why one is excited about clinical negligence, this was actually the main reason why I have decided to co-write this book.

I know that when something is less exciting, then it tends to be misunderstood. Therefore, I wanted to ensure that those who are less interested in the subject, opposite to my co-writer, would not be left in the dark. We read the rules over and over so you do not have to; we summarised a lot of them where we could so that you could skim through.

I hope that now no one's heart will skip a beat when they hear 'fixed recoverable costs', and we can all discuss the subject with confidence. And with a bit of luck, one day, costs might become the reason why clinical negligence is so priceless.

Ramune Mickeviciute, Solicitor at Hugh James

London, January 2024

CONTENTS

TABLE OF CASES

LEGISLATION AND OTHER SOURCES

CHAPTER ONE

NEW RULES:
WHAT IS CHANGING?

Current Position

To have a better understanding of the new rules that are coming into force regarding fixed recoverable costs (FRC), good practice would be to recap what the current rules are. For more detail, please see *'A Practical Approach to Clinical Negligence'* (3rd Edition) 2023, Law Brief Publishing Ltd.

It is easy to say that each one of us should be familiar with the rules, however, when it comes to better understanding things that easily become a part of our habitual routine, one would be surprised how difficult it gets to explain something that is so natural to us.

Without going into too much detail, it might be enough to say that despite the FRC changes having made its way into certain personal injury areas, clinical negligence has not been affected by any of the FRC before October 2023 and so those who work in the field have been dealing with their cases as per usual. In very simple terms, the usual process is to record your work and then negotiate your costs at the end of each successful claim. Costs recovery is based upon that work being objectively proportionate and reasonable using the criteria set out at *CPR 1998, Rule 44.3(5)*:

> *"(5) Costs incurred are proportionate if they bear a reasonable relationship to –*
>
> *(a) The sums in issue in the proceedings;*
>
> *(b) The value of any non-monetary relief in issue in the proceedings;*

> (c) *The complexity of the litigation;*
>
> (d) *Any additional work generated by the conduct of the paying party; and*
>
> (e) *Any wider factors involved in the proceedings such as reputation or public importance."*

In the FRC regimes considered in this book, the amount of recoverable costs are set. If they apply to your case, then they are assumed to be proportionate and necessary. These 5 criteria only remain relevant for multi-track cases or in the very limited circumstances where additional amounts of costs are permitted in excess of the FRC amounts.

One of the important reasons why clinical negligence has not been caught by FRC until now is the complex nature of the cases that we (clinician negligence lawyers) are dealing with. This additional complexity is well-recognised. In *Hobbs v Guy's & St Thomas' NHS Foundation Trust [2015] EWHC B20 (Costs), Master O'Hare* said *(at para. 35)* that *"Even in modest value clinical negligence claims it is necessary to incur costs … clinical negligence claims have more complexity and involve more work than do other claims of similar value."*

Citations such as this may still assist claimants' lawyers in persuading the court to apply FRC in a just fashion thereby helping to retain some degree of access to justice. As we will see in Chapters 2 & 3, clinical negligence does not, as of right, attract higher FRC amounts than other types of civil litigation notwithstanding its recognised greater complexity.

Clinical negligence cases tend to require long hours of work being done and an impressive amount of disbursements being proportionately and reasonably incurred. And so, it has been previously recognised that it would be difficult to justify a fixed amount for the same in the way the new rules impose (see Chapters 2 & 3). This is particularly so taking into account that each case is very different, and it becomes rather difficult to predict whether any other case, even of similar nature, might end up costing the same. Again, herein lies a potential avenue to assisting the courts in applying these rules fairly and justly (please see Chapters 5, 6 & 10).

Those working on the defendants' side will have their own arguments to make about costs related to clinical negligence claims and the proportionality of the same. However, this is an argument for another day (as this area develops). For now, we have provided assistance with what these might be based on our experience.

In this book, we shall discuss the actual changes that have been implemented for cases worth between £25,000 and £100,000, proposed for cases worth under £25,000 and how they will impact the existing rules which have been in place for clinical negligence lawyers for the years since the *Civil Procedure Rules 1998* were introduced in April 1999. Many practitioners will have never known any other system.

Some of the changes influencing our new attitudes, behaviours and habits, however, have already been implemented earlier in 2023 to introduce new rules on costs recoverability for the defendants. The change relates to new QOCS rules affecting all cases issued on and after 6th April 2023 where pre-existing *Part 36* offers had not been made by defendants. The new rules allow for any cost orders to be enforced against the claimant's damages and costs, whereas before this was not realistic in practice.

As a result of the interplay with FRC, lawyers will need to be more careful when dealing with *Part 36* offers. This includes providing much more structured advice to their clients about the risks and considering any offers more carefully. This is likely to impact on the recoverability of legal costs.

The FRC changes are further rules that initially came into force on 1st October 2023 and have an actual, measurable effect on the recoverability of legal costs. The rules are addressed to all civil claims and so, with some exceptions, to clinical negligence. This is considered further in Chapters 6 & 11.

The new rules are designed to expand FRC onto the claims higher in value and into new areas. There is a new intermediate track introduced to cover these cases that might no longer be suitable for the multi-track. The general thinking is that such unsuitable cases should not, just so that they can be dealt with under fixed costs, be transferred to the fast track. Therefore, as per new rules, all civil claims with value of up to £100,000 will be dealt with outside the multi-track, and so will be caught under FRC. With some exceptions applicable to clinical negligence cases, fewer of our cases will be caught up initially. However, currently from April 2024, introducing the light and standard track FRC for lower-value cases means that the majority of clinical negligence claims are likely to be infected with these reforms.

In the absence of suitable admissions, the majority of clinical negligence claims are likely to continue to be dealt with as multi-track claims post-issue, and so not caught by FRC. Nevertheless, there will be some exceptions and, currently from April 2024, pre-action FRC tracks apply to cases potentially valued at under £25,000. We will look at ways in which these rules might result in more clinical negligence cases being caught under these new rules too. Following that, our aim is to summarise the changes and explain their implications on clinical negligence.

This chapter will aim to summarise what the current rules are and what overall changes have been implemented. It is hoped that once this is clear, the next chapters will then explain in more detail the effects on clinical negligence claims and what we could do better in practice.

Implementation of New Rules

The first set of new rules on Fixed Recoverable Costs started to apply for cases where the cause of action arose on or after 1st October 2023.

Fast Track Claims

To remind ourselves, the fast track is very rarely appropriate for clinical negligence cases. It is the normal track for claims that meet the following criteria:

- value of the claim not higher than £25,000;
- the trial is likely to last for no longer than one day;
- oral expert evidence is limited to one expert per party in any expert field; and
- expert evidence is limited to two expert fields.

The majority of civil claims to date that fall under the fast track would be dealt with under FRC, and as per the new rules, all civil cases that will be dealt with under the fast track will be dealt with under the revised FRC rules.

You are right to think that most of the clinical negligence claims tend to be allocated to the multi-track regardless of their value. And so even if the case is allocated to the fast track, the parties would usually be able to demonstrate to the judge that the case should be allocated to the multi-track instead. That is usually associated with the complexity of each clinical negligence matter, and mostly for not meeting the criteria listed above.

It is anticipated that there will be little to add to the existing circumstances and so cases should continue to stay outside of the scope of this track and its rules. However, with further changes coming out related to low value clinical negligence claims in the near future, this might not stay the situation for long. The defendants might also start pushing for clinical negligence claims to meet the above criteria so that they could argue that the case is caught by FRC. As a result, unless one is sure that the case will not meet the above criteria, we should remain mindful about our costs.

Intermediate Track

Until 1st October 2023, any cases that were not suitable to be dealt with under the fast track (if the criteria above are not met, which was the case for the majority of clinical negligence claims) would be allocated to the multi-track.

However, according to new rules, there is now a new track that will cover all cases with a value of between £25,000 and £100,000. Instead of being allocated to the multi-track, they may end up in the intermediate track instead.

The intermediate track will be caught by the FRC regime, and so all cases that will be dealt with under this track will be caught by the new rules.

Once again, clinical negligence has been excluded from this track, unless certain criteria designed for clinical negligence claims are met. Therefore, most of the cases which would normally be allocated to the multi-track, will continue to be dealt with under the multi-track, with some exceptions.

Cases that fall under this exception are claims for clinical negligence where breach of duty and causation have been admitted. Following the *CPR Committee November 2023 Minutes*, these admissions should be made in the letter of response rather than later (i.e. before issuing proceedings or when the defence is served) for the intermediate track and FRC to apply.

For the claim to be allocated to the intermediate track, the case value would also need to be below £100,000, as otherwise it would proceed to be dealt with in multi-track due to its value.

There are some further nuances related to expert evidence and other criteria that we will discuss in this book. However, unless these criteria are met, clinical negligence cases are technically excluded from the intermediate track.

However, same as with fast track claims, the defendants might seek to implement different strategies and so not to be caught unawares at the end, it will remain our recommendation that we should stay cautious about the possible costs positions unless absolutely sure otherwise.

Multi-Track

The multi-track, has been the track that included all the claims where the value was below £25,000 where the case would not meet the criteria to be dealt with in fast track (most clinical negligence claims).

However, from now on, this would continue to cover only clinical negligence matters which in practice are not suitable for FRC tracks, and there is a risk that valuation issues become the major battleground where the value is not clearly above £100,000.

Therefore, it is expected that the majority of clinical negligence cases will initially continue to be allocated to the multi-track. This is because the criteria for the case to be allocated to intermediate track are not that easy to meet.

Nevertheless, as we should not expect that neither the system nor the defendants will make our job easy. We shall prepare for the worse and expect that some of our cases might end up in the FRC tracks and risk becoming unprofitable. Access to justice may reduce significantly. Accordingly, while it is good to stay optimistic, the message that we are trying to spread is that one should be prepared for the worse and remain careful about the cost consequences in this new era.

Tracks and FRC

The table below summarises whether FRC are going to be applicable based on the stage and then on the tract it is likely to be allocated to.

Clinical Negligence Claims		
Stages/Track	**FRC Applicable?**	**Comments**
Pre-Issue	Yes	Pre-Issued cases will be caught by the rules if in practice they would fall outside of the multi-track. This is particularly so once the <£25,000 FRC Standard & Light Tracks come into force.
Fast Track	Possibly	Clinical negligence claims will rarely be dealt with in fast track despite their value. However, if they are going to be, FRC are likely to apply. Our view is that the new rules do not preclude this.
Intermediate Track	Yes	Cases will be dealt with under this track. The main two things to note which will help to determine whether the claim will be caught are as follows: a) case value is between £25K & 100K, and b) breach of duty and causation needs to be admitted. If the above criteria is met, review chapter related to cases in value between £25-100k for further exceptions.
Multi-Track	No	Cases where the value is above £100,000, and cases which are lower in value but liability has not been admitted in full will remain in multi-track. Some lower value cases may also remain unsuitable for other tracks. Limited exclusions apply in any event.

Things to Consider

The main concern will be all cases valued at less than £100,000. While not all cases that fall below £100,000 in value will be caught under FRC, these cases should receive specific treatment right at the start of the case in light of the new risks.

The fact that FRC can apply to both pre-litigated and post-litigated cases will result in different management to all cases that can potentially fall outside of the multi-track. All cases that will be treated as suitable for multi-track will be 'protected' from FRC and the usual rules will apply. Therefore, all those that are unclear/uncertain of being suitable for a multi-track should be treated with caution.

Cases where it is unclear whether these fall within the multi-track (and this situation might not be clear until later in the case), should be treated as being dealt with under FRC; anything else that can be recovered would be a bonus. Doing otherwise risks turning a strong case into an unprofitable one.

Working this way will require some adaptation, especially that some or even the majority of cases will remain to be dealt with under the standard rules. Nevertheless, one can only see this as an opportunity to be more reasonable with the time and costs spent on each case and the silver lining is that perhaps such methods will be adapted when dealing with higher value claims too.

The table below compares old rules and new rules when it comes to the implication of FRC.

		Old Rules		New Rules	
Stage	**Track**	**FRC applies?**	**Conditions**	**FRC applies?**	**Conditions**
Pre- Issue	-	No	-	Maybe	If the case, if issued, would be considered to fall outside of multi-track.
Post-Issue	Fast Track	Yes	Case will unlikely to end up in fast track	Yes	Case will unlikely to end up in fast track (subject to the new rules being clarified)
	Intermediate track	-	-	Yes	The following criteria needs to be met: a) case value is between £25 – 100K, and b) breach of duty and causation needs to be admitted.
	Multi track	No	Most of the cases will end up in multi track.	No	-
Summary	No fixed recoverable costs (FRC) implications in clinical negligence			Any case in value less than £100k should be treated as if it falls under the fixed costs, until it is clear that it does not.	

Pre-Issue

Even if some might have experience dealing under certain cost implications when it comes to litigated cases, this has never been the case with those dealt with pre-issue. While we of course have to stay reasonable and think about the proportionality etc. we still to date have not had to worry about any fixed costs.

Nevertheless, the situation has changed and FRC might kick in right at the start, even before we know it. This is because while the rules are clear that only an exceptional amount of cases that meet certain criteria would be dealt with outside of the multi-track, it will not be clear whether the case might fall outside of the multi-track until later.

While there are two main conditions that will need to be met (one regarding the case value and then another one regarding liability status), ambiguity persists and the case value might not mean that the case would automatically be considered outside of the multi-track or within the FRC tracks. The defendant's position will usually not become clear until a letter of response is received, which is when a lot of proportionate and reasonable investigative work has already been done.

As a result, any cases that are potentially worth below £100,000 should be dealt with as they might fall within intermediate track in order to avoid any unpleasant surprises.

There can be strategic and tactical movements implemented, which we will touch base on in later chapters. However, regardless of anything else, we should ensure that we are aware of all of the potential costs implications in order to maximising the chances of benefitting from the situation irrespective of the outcome.

The table below summarises how high the risk is that the case might fall outside of the multi-track and so should be dealt with some caution.

<table>
<tr><th colspan="6">New Rules – Pre-Issued Cases</th></tr>
<tr><td colspan="3">Value £100,000 or below</td><td colspan="3">Value above £100,000</td></tr>
<tr><td colspan="3">Firstly, consider how confident you are regarding the case value being below £100,000.
If you are confident, proceed with considering below.</td><td colspan="3">Firstly, consider how confident you are regarding the case value being above £100,000.
If you are confident that the value is much higher then potentially no need to consider anything else.
If not confident, and/or case value/any future offers might be lower, then proceed with considering below.</td></tr>
<tr><td colspan="3">Defendant's Position regarding Liability</td><td colspan="3">Defendant's Position regarding Liability</td></tr>
<tr><td>Indication for an early admission</td><td>Remaining issues with Causation</td><td>Everything has been admitted</td><td>Indication for an early admission</td><td>Remaining issues with Causation</td><td>Everything has been admitted</td></tr>
<tr><td>High chance of being caught by FRC.</td><td>Low chance by being caught under FRC.</td><td>High chance of being caught by FRC.</td><td>High chance of being caught by FRC.</td><td>Low chance by being caught under FRC.</td><td>High chance of being caught by FRC.</td></tr>
</table>

Post-Issue

When it comes to post-issued cases, the situation should be much clearer. The main reason is because full liability investigations would have already been undertaken and the defendant's liability status would also be clear by this point.

Therefore, if the case meets the criteria of case value being below £100,000, and liability was admitted in full, then the case will most likely be allocated to the intermediate track. It appears that the intention is that only a very small minority of cases worth under £25,000 will be issued justifiably.

However, unless this criterion above applies, then one should be more confident of the case being allocated to the multi-track, but also more inspired to argue that it should be allocated to the multi-track if for whatever reason this has not been done so.

Practical Advice

We will attempt to cover any strategic actions that can be undertaken to protect both yourself and the client throughout the book. However, in a short summary, there are a few things that one might want to consider before we take a deeper look into the issues.

More than ever, we will need to start thinking about the rules and their implementation right at the start. This will involve us making a note of the following to determine whether the FRC costs can be applicable and to protect ourselves from any such severe costs that we might not receive:

a) **Key dates** – as the rules will apply to call cases where the cause of action happened on or after 1st October 2023, it will be important to consider your limitation dates very carefully. Cases potentially worth under £25,000 should have suitable letters of claim (or notification) sent before 1st April 2024.

b) **Case value** – while the case value is rather difficult to detriment at the start, we will need to be even more careful when trying to predict how much the case might be worth.

c) **Funding documents** – ensure that the retainer/funding documents address this issue and an explanation is given to the client if the recovery of costs from the client is going to be sought in case the case falls under FRC.

We should also remain cautious of any changes to the case value as the case progresses, and/or any Part 36 offers due to both new QOCS rules and the change of case value if the lower offer is accepted etc.

Where possible, and where the signs suggest that this might be achieved, an indication of liability should be sought from the defendant as soon as possible. Even if no response is received, such attempts/communications should be recorded and could be used as evidence when it comes to the argument of the case being allocated to one track or another based on the defendant's position.

Under the current rules it is not clear whether liability should be admitted at the earliest opportunity and/or pre-issue (subject to the CPR Committee's proposals being implemented). However, if there are several attempts made (within the reason) to seek a clear confirmation regarding the defendant's position, then one can more persuasively argue that an opportunity to make a full admission as per the relevant criteria has not been achieved within a timely manner.

Conclusion

We understand that there is a lot to take in, following which we will discuss each aspect in more detail in this book. The problem we see is that current rules have some gaps and it is not always clear what might happen in practice.

Therefore, and until we know better from letting the rules embed into the clinical negligence world first, we will try to prepare you for the worst first. Our approach is that unless you are 100% sure that the case is suitable for multi-track and multi-track only, then you should treat your case as benign caught by FRC. If at the end, you manage to get your full costs back, then we consider this to be the cherry on top.

CHAPTER TWO

CASES OF £25K TO £100K VALUE

Introduction

From 1st October 2023, fixed recoverable costs (FRC) are introduced for clinical negligence cases. Not all cases will be affected but, for those that are, there is a fundamental change of approach: the costs are not based on the amount of work done – instead, you get a prescribed amount based on the stage the case has reached.

The cases that will fall under the FRC will be those that would be considered suitable for a new intermediate track, instead of the usual multi-track. As we already know, most clinical negligence cases are considered to be suitable for the multi-track, but the situation is no longer as certain as it was.

The multi-track remains the usual track for clinical negligence cases (*CPR 1998, Rule 26.9(10)(b)*), and therefore, only a very limited cohort of cases will qualify for allocation to the intermediate track. Cases that are most vulnerable to fall outside of the multi-track are those of a value under £25,000 and up to £100,000 (taking these new rules in isolation).

Nevertheless, it is very important to understand which cases will be subject to the intermediate track because this will be the only way when you can then ensure that the cases you are dealing with are ineligible for it.

As a result, in this chapter we will talk about the cases which would fall into this bracket and discuss whether, based on the new rules, there is a risk for them to be dealt with outside of the multi-track (which would then mean that the case would be caught by FRC).

This chapter looks at what these rules are and what they do and might mean in practice.

Intermediate Track

In order to understand the position, it is important to understand what are the cases that will fall under the intermediate track, and the criteria are as follows:

1. The cause of action must have arisen after 1st October 2023 (*The Civil Procedure (Amendment) Rules 2023, Rule 2.2(a)*);

2. Breach of duty and causation of damage must be admitted (*CPR 1998, Rule 26.9(10)(b)*);

3. The value must be between £25,000 and £100,000 (*CPR 1998, Rule 26.9(7)*)

4. There must be 1 or 2 experts giving oral evidence at trial (*CPR 1998, Rule 28.14(2)*;

5. The trial length must be less than 3 days;

6. The claim may be justly and proportionately managed in the intermediate track;

7. There are no other factors making the intermediate track inappropriate; and

8. There are no more than two claimants or defendants against one opponent.

Initially, you are unlikely to have a case with an accrued cause of action too soon after 1st October 2023. How many cases do you currently have in your caseload which meet the remaining criteria? Of those, how many settle pre-action? Judging from our respective caseloads, not enough.

What happens if we reframe the question? How many of your qualifying cases would you feel confident of settling within the FRC limits? Under the new rules, the leeway given by proportionality and reasonableness is lost because there is now a direct correlation between the amount of permitted recoverable costs and the value of the case.

Other Things to Consider

Unfortunately, in our view, the new rules appear to allow several other potential entry points for FRC. The extent to which exceptions apply is considered below. The extent to which the FRC rules are subject to the other parts of the *CPR 1998* is considered in later chapters.

What constitutes an admission?

The plain reading of *CPR 1998, Rule 26.9(10)(b)* is that a full admission on breach of duty and causation of damage is required. However, the rules do not state that the admission must be 'full'. They just refer to an admission. This leaves open the possibility that lesser admissions will result in cases being allocated to the intermediate track. Possible scenarios include:

a) Where there is an admission on breach and a very limited admission on causation of damage;

b) Where multiple allegations are made and only some of these are admitted;

c) Where there is an admission of one allegation on breach of duty and an admission on causation of damage but other allegations remain disputed; and

d) Where admissions on breach and causation have been made but are not linked to each other;

When must the admission be made?

Originally, the rules did not state when the admission must be made. Following the publication of the *CPR Committee Minutes November 2023 (para. 13),* it is probable that this will be clarified by an amended rule requiring the admissions to be made in the letter of response. This followed the September 2023 consultation response which sought additional submissions on this issue. If so, then the admission should be made in the letter of response. If not, the practical effect of the new rules is that the defendant can make the admissions as late as its defence and the case would then be allocated to the intermediate track if the other qualifying criteria were met.

Conceivably, and for completeness, it is also possible that suitable admissions could be made after service of the defence and before allocation if, for example, an effective *Part 18 Request* was made and there was a delay in allocating the case. It is possible that a court could be persuaded to allocate a case to the intermediate track in these circumstances.

Before the admissions on breach and causation are made, there is uncertainty as to whether the case will or will not be allocated to the intermediate track. During this period, liability remains disputed and so must be investigated. There is no express provision preventing the defendant contesting breach and causation until the defence is served in the hope that it can reach a final decision then and automatically limit the claimant's recoverable costs.

Who makes the decision?

A court officer will make the provisional allocation decision once the defence has been received. As such, there is no judicial input involved in what is essentially an administrative decision. This creates a risk that the court officer to allocate the case to a different track than you were anticipating and of you having to apply to the court to change this. We discuss the allocation mechanism more fully below.

What happens after allocation? (i.e. reallocation)

The new rules also permit cases to be reallocated (*CPR 1998, Rule 26.18*; please see further below). Accordingly, it is possible that the court could reallocate a case from the multi-track to the intermediate track either of its own initiative or upon the application of either party if suitable admissions are made after allocation.

If so, then the costs of the new track apply to all stages (*CPR 1998, Rule 45.14(1)*) and so there is a risk that you move from budgets costs to fixed costs retrospectively.

Costs arguments on the multi-track

Even where no application to reallocate the case from the multi-track to the intermediate track is made, there is no express provision preventing a party from raising the issue in its points of dispute. For example, it might be argued that it was disproportionate to apply for reallocation but, but nonetheless, the settlement value shows that the proportionate and reasonable costs should be nearer to the FRC limits than the budgeted costs.

Whilst this may not be the intention of the rule drafters, there is a commercial incentive on the part of defendants to limit the costs payable and a professional obligation to act in their clients' best interests. Court officers are not necessarily legally trained and so may understandably misunderstand whether a 'qualifying' admission has been made.

How Does Allocation Work?

The provisional allocation decision is made by a court officer (*CPR 1998, Rule 26.4(1)(a)*) when the defence is received. At this point, they will send the parties the notice of proposed allocation. *CPR 1998, Rule 26.4(2)* sets out what information this notice should include and, apart from the proposed track, the most important piece of information is the date for filing directions (*CPR 1998, Rule 26.4(2)(v)*).

This date should be 28 days from the date of the notice (*CPR 1998, Rule 26.4(6)*) and not the date of receipt. This date cannot be varied by the consent of the parties (*CPR 1998, Rule 26.4(7)*). If one party does not file its DQ within this prescribed time limit, then the court should issue a follow-up notice giving them a further 7 days to do so or else have their statement of case struck out.

Since we are all likely to have experienced unfortunate delays with the courts, there is at least the possibility that we may have considerably less time than 28 days to consider the provisional allocation and file the DQ. It would certainly appear to be imprudent to assume that 'no news is good news' if you have not received the notice within a reasonable period of the defence being served on you and so diarising one or more enquiries to the court may be sensible (even if it increases your and the court's workloads).

You may be able to use the DQ to explain why the provisional allocation is incorrect. Once the DQs have been received, the court will allocate the case to the appropriate track and assign it to a complexity band (*CPR 1998, Rule 26.7(1)*). A complexity band is a new concept in clinical negligence; in essence cases with greater complexity attract higher FRC than simpler ones. Where a stay has been requested to allow for settlement, the allocation decision will be made at the end of the stay (*CPR 1998, Rule 26.7(2)*). *CPR 1998, Rule 26.7(4)* allows the court to request more information from the parties before allocating and hold a specific hearing if needed (*CPR 1998, Rule 26.7(5)*). The rules do not state that this hearing has to be at the same time as the CMC

Although the current wording of *CPR 1998, Rule 28.12* requires the court to set a CMC date, the *CPR Committee's October 2023 Minutes* stated that this is likely to become optional and this was confirmed in their *November 2023 Minutes (para. 12)*. Thus, this means that there is no guarantee that we will be given CMCs and that allocation, assignment and directions may all be done on paper. This means that we need to be ready to pre-empt this by submitting our case on these issues before the notice of proposed allocation is made. Given how busy procedural judges are, providing them with a succinct summary with the relevant documents (perhaps identified in a pithy witness statement and paginated exhibit) would probably be of considerable assistance to them.

The Possible Tracks

As indicated above, the usual track for clinical negligence cases remains the multi-track (*CPR 1998, Rule 26.9(10)(b)*). The only exception should be those cases which fall into the intermediate track. However, since we have seen examples of county courts allocating cases to the fast or small claim tracks based on value under the pre-October 2023 regime, we cover all the tracks here to help practitioners try to head this off. The new rules do not expressly prohibit allocating clinical negligence cases to these other tracks.

The seed for this lies in cases qualifying for the multi-track by exclusion. Although *CPR 1998, Rule 26.9(10)(b)* clearly states that the multi-track must be used, the exception in *CPR 1998, Rule 26.9(10)(b)(i) is "the claim is one which would normally be allocated to the intermediate track"*. This means that we need to understand which cases would normally be allocated to the intermediate track where breach and causation have been admitted.

CPR 1998, Rule 26.9(7) provides that one of the criteria is that cases are suitable for the intermediate track if they are unsuitable for the small or fast claims tracks. Therefore, we must also be prepared to exclude our case from these tracks. The other criteria are as set out above.

CPR 1998, Rule 26.9(5) & *(6)* provides that the fast track is the normal track for cases with a value less than £25,000; as long as the trial length is 1 day or less and if there is one oral expert per party and in no more than 2 different disciplines. Although likely to be rare, cases worth under £25,000 could be allocated to the intermediate track if liability is admitted but multiple experts are required on causation of consequential losses and quantum. Likewise, it is conceivable that a case worth under £25,000 could be allocated to the fast track if the other criteria are not met or the court accepted that the 'allocation by exclusion' is a reasonable interpretation of the new rules. It is also possible that a contested case could fall into this track because the fast track does not require that breach and causation be admitted as one of its qualifying criteria and the intermediate track requires that a case must be unsuitable for the fast track.

Similarly, *CPR 1998, Rule 26.9(1)(a)* provides that the small claims track is the normal track for a PI claim with general damages are less than or equal to £1,500 and the overall value is less than or equal to £10,000. It is not outside of the realms of possibility that some very low value, single issue clinical negligence claims could meet these criteria. It should be noted that the small claims track criteria do not refer to trial length or number of experts. If expert evidence is required on breach or causation, then it is difficult to see how the case is suitable for the small claims track. However, would you need expert evidence for quantum in such a low value case? Given the myriad possibilities practitioners encounter, this cannot be completely excluded.

However, the rest of this book proceeds on the basis that the case will be allocated to the intermediate track.

Assignment to Complexity Bands

In addition to the *track*, cases must also be assigned to a *complexity band* within it (*CPR 1998, Rule 26.14)*). There are four tracks within the intermediate track: 1, 2, 3 & 4. These reflect the assumed complexity of cases within each track. If cases appear to fit the pre-defined generic categories of cases within a complexity band, then that is the starting point for assigning them. There is no specific complexity band for clinical negligence cases.

As indicated above, the court officer will provisionally assign the case to its complexity band at the same time as provisionally allocating it (*CPR 1998, Rule 26.7(1)*). Likewise, the court request further information or hold a hearing (*CPR 1998, Rules 26.7(4)* & *(5)*, respectively). The hearing can just deal with assignment (i.e. where allocation is agreed). The notice of proposed allocation will state the proposed assignment. The parties must include the complexity band they feel is appropriate in the DQ and also say whether this is agreed (although the court can override this (*CPR 1998, Rule 26.14*)). Once allocated & assigned, the court sends out a notice of allocation & assignment (*CPR 1998, Rule 26.17*).

CPR 1998, Rule 26.16 (Table 2) sets out the four complexity bands for the intermediate track. There is no specific mention of which complexity bands apply to clinical negligence cases within the intermediate track. This creates ambiguity and scope for argument. Accordingly, it is advantageous to have at least a working knowledge of all of them. Since clinical negligence claims are not specifically mentioned here it is prudent to be prepared to make submissions that your case should be assigned to band 4.

This band does include cases which have 'serious issues of fact or law' and this seems to be the most relevant to the average clinical negligence case. However, what are these serious issues of fact or law in your case if breach and causation have been admitted? Is band 4 necessarily going to be the case for all quantum-only clinical negligence cases valued between £25,000 and £100,000?

Since band 4 is suitable for cases with 'serious issues of fact or law', does this exclude cases from FRC which still have both (i.e. serious factual and legal issues) following service of the defence? One of the possible entry points to FRC set out above was whether *full* admissions are necessary. *'Serious issues of fact and law'* could also allow the unanticipated or accidental ingress of a case into FRC which has some disputed allegations on breach of duty or causation of damage. The well-weathered maxim of 'every case turns on its facts' gets a fresh makeover.

For example, if the remaining contested allegations add little to the value of the case, should the case nonetheless be fairly allocated to the intermediate track? Alternatively, there may be a complicated chain of causation of consequential losses after the initial, avoidable injury. This could well meet this test, especially where the need for multiple witnesses and/or experts and/to commonly contested heads of loss are involved. But will it on *your* case before *this* district or deputy district judge? We anticipate encountering a rehashed version of the well-known costs budgeting/point of dispute that *this* clinical negligence case is not complex at all when weighed against all of the other clinical negligence cases in this track and band. It also remains to be seen how judges deal with cases where there is a variation of the traditional 'causation defence'; where breach and initial causation of damage is admitted but the part of causation of damage which explains the majority of the claimant's injury remains denied. Does this fall within the scope of the admissions these rules cover? If they do not, it is a multi-track case. If they do, then it risks being allocated to intermediate track and assigned to a complexity band.

Allocation & Assignment: Relevant Factors

The factors relevant to accurately forecasting the likelihood of such possibilities lies in the new rules themselves and in considering what habits, strategies and tactics are likely to create some benefit or advantage to one side or the court in managing its workload and lowering costs in civil cases. The former is considered in this chapter and the latter in subsequent chapters.

The allocation rules for the intermediate track do provide us with some guidance on these issues. *CPR 1998, Rule 26.12(1)* requires the court to 'have regard' to certain criteria. It is notable that it this rule does not require more than this; for example, it does not say that they 'must' be applied – it just requires that they be considered as part of the allocation decision. At this point, it is worth remembering that allocation is a case management decision and so include a hefty amount of discretion and are notoriously difficult to successfully appeal. However, the potential for persuading the judge that other factors should be given more weight does exist and applies equally to both sides.

CPR 1998, Rules 26.13(1) & *(2)* set out these factors:

- **The case's financial value excluding:**
    - **Any undisputed amount.** Accordingly, it is possible that the defendant could reduce the value of a claim by making

a payment on account. Requesting payments on account of damages where liability has been admitted could therefore bring a case which has a full value of over £100,000 within FRC.

- **Interest.** This is less likely to cause problems because interest is at the discretion of the trial judge and defendants so not admit an entitlement to it. If this behaviour changes, it would not count towards reducing the value of the case.

- **Costs.** Although the amount of costs paid on account following admissions of liability would not be counted towards the value of the case, this is not the end of the matter. Will we simply see payments on account of costs cease for intermediate track cases? There was already a strong argument from defendants pre-FRC that it was more proportionate to settle the case outright than for them to make a payment on account of costs. With the new rules, it is possible that pursuing admissions become counter-productive to claimants, and this is considered later in this book.

- **Contributory negligence.** This is rarely a sustainable allegation in clinical negligence cases. However, if it is pleaded then this provision likely means that the financial value of the contributory negligence is not deducted from the value of the main claim to calculate the financial value. As will be seen below, this does not necessarily make the counterclaim irrelevant.

- **The amount of allowable fixed costs**. These amounts are considered below.

- **The remedy sought**. In most clinical negligence cases, the remedy will be damages. It is possible that there may be some with additional remedies and so specific planning will be needed if you wish to persuade the court that this affects either track allocation or complexity band assignment.

- **The likely complexity of the facts, law or evidence.** Ideally, this will be known in advance of allocation and assignment with the supporting evidence for your position being known. It is unclear whether the reference to 'likely' in this rule precludes evidence going to the complexity of the facts, law or evidence preceding the allocation/assignment. In one sense, it would make sense to exclude matters which have no bearing on what needs to be done to conclude the case. Such a view lends support to the potential for the defendant cutting the Gordian knot of a complex but modestly valued case by admitting liability pre-allocation in the hope that it can persuade the court to allocate the case to the intermediate track moving forward and so greatly reduce your costs risk.

- **The number of parties or likely parties.** No minimum number is given in this rule and so it may be that this will only be relevant where there are specific isolated and unusual features of the number of parties which will increase the costs. Any overlap with the other factors in this rule may well be evidence relevant to those rather than this one. Group litigation by itself does not preclude FRC applying (*CPR 1998, Rule 26.13(3)*).

- **The value & complexity of either the counterclaim or other claims.** This factor needs to be read in conjunction with the exclusion of the value of the counterclaim from the financial value of the claim. As such, it is unclear exactly how this will apply in practice beyond saying that the financial value of the counterclaim might be higher than the main claim or, added together, the combined value of both might exceed £100,000. However, detailed allegations of contributory negligence may add to the complexity of the case making it unsuitable for the intermediate track. Likewise, this provision appears to apply to additional claims (*CPR 1998, Part 20*) and so, for example, if not all of the potential defendants were identified or pursued by the claimant, adding them under *CPR 1998, Part 20* may take the case out of the intermediate track.

- **The amount of oral evidence which may be required.** We already know that the intermediate track is unsuitable if you need more than 2 experts in different disciplines per side. We anticipate that context will be everything here. Potentially relevant matters are likely to relate to how the causation of consequential losses and the quantum valuation are to be proved. Proving loss of earnings for an employed claimant with a period of 1-2 years' of loss might well require 1 or 2 witnesses (including the claimant). However, proving this for a self-employed or small business owner may require several lay witnesses and a forensic accountant. It may be that a considerable number of witnesses are required to support a contested head of loss. Do their statements need to be long or short? We anticipate that defendants will continue to argue that such evidence is unnecessary whilst claimants may decide that 'additional' lay witnesses are required to (a) increase the value above £100,000 if possible; or (b) maximise the value of the case within the intermediate track if not. The major counterbalance to this may be the amount of FRC and the losses that can be incurred if incurred costs exceed the FRC figure.

- **The importance of the claim to persons who are not parties to the proceedings.** There is no further detail provided and it is, of course, open to a judge to consider any of these factors and to decide to give little or no weight to one or more of them. Who, conceivably, would have an interest in whether the case is more appropriate for the intermediate or multi-track? If we exclude generic or wide cohorts (such as funders, insurers, the parties' lawyers, the judge or the general public), it is possible that the track or complexity band could impact on parties to a linked action; close family members reliant on the claimant's ability to recover fully to support or care for them; the ability of witnesses to attend trial; or the provision of treatment by the impugned clinician. What we can anticipate is that clear evidence will need to be adduced to persuade the judge.

- **The views expressed by the parties.** As noted above, the court does not have to agree with the parties' agreement on allocation. It would be prudent to be prepared to justify your reasoning.

- **The circumstances of the parties.** How this is relevant to the allocation or the circumstances in which it would supervene the value of the case is not set out in the rules. Logically, it seems unlikely that run of the mill issues would not be sufficient to remove an otherwise suitable case from the intermediate track. However, in circumstances where real injustice can be demonstrated (and supported with evidence), it is conceivable that the court can be persuaded that the multi-track is the appropriate track. The extent to which exceptions are permitted in the context of the overall objectives of these reforms is considered further below.

Now that we know more about how cases are allocated, we can look at how much successful lawyers get paid.

How Much Costs Do You Get?

The central pieces of information to know in order to successfully manage a clinical negligence FRC case load are:

1. How much do I get paid; and

2. How much work can I do?

Once you know the answers to these, you can plan your strategy. So why are we not including 'how do I get out of FRC?' as a central question? The reason is because this is not a long-term strategy for success. On average, being able to run a case profitably within the FRC straitjacket is likely to prove more successful than always trying find ways out of it.

CPR 1998, Rule 45.50 Table 14 sets out the amount of FRC for the intermediate track. These show the amount of FRC for each of the four complexity bands and for each stage. They show the total amount of costs payable if your case settles within that stage rather than the amount of costs *per stage*. Accordingly, we have adopted the following approach:

1. Calculate the amount of fixed costs per stage;
2. Calculate the amount of hours per stage; and
3. Allocate your limited time to the tasks you need to complete within each stage.

In the table below, we have used the January 2024 National 1 hourly rate for a Grade C fee earner (£190) for ease of calculation from the SCCO's summary assessment guide for illustrative purposes. Depending on where you are, and on your grade, this may mean you can spend more or less time than shown. If you or your client is based within specified parts of London, then there is a London weighting (please see below).

Putting this together, we get:

FRC for Intermediate Track, CB4

Stage	FRC Amount (per stage)	~% of Total Costs	~Hours (per stage)
S1: Pre-Issue to Service of the Defence	£11,300 – £17,300	31%-30%	59.5 – 88
S3: Defence to CMC/Directions Order	£5,200 – £9,700	14%-17%	27 – 51

S4: CMC/Directions order to Inspection	£3,500 – £5,000	10%-9%	18 – 26
S5: Inspection – Expert Evidence	£4,500 – £6,000	12%-11%	24 – 31.5
S6: Expert Evidence – PTR/14 days pre-trial	£4,000	11%-7%	21
S8: PTR – Trial Date	£6,000 – £10,000	16%-17%	31.5 – 52.5
S9: Trial Support	£700 – £4,200	2%-7%	3.5 – 22
S13: Mediation/ADR for 1 meeting only	£1,200	3%-2%	6

Accordingly, it is clear that the highest-paying stage is from the start to the service of the defence. This incentivises the claimant to attempt to settle pre-action or, if not, by the time of the CMC. After this, the proportion of FRC drops such that the amount of work done to serve expert reports and hold joint meetings is limited per expert. The same applies up to the PTR so this indicates that trial preparation is intended to be done in a short 2-week period before the trial. Furthermore, if the guideline hourly rates increase without corresponding increases in the FRC amounts, then less time can be profitably spent on each case.

If the case settles at any point within a stage, then you get paid the same amount. As such, these amounts provide little incentive for the defendant to settle before the defence is served. This pattern is repeated for each stage; it is more profitable for the claimant's solicitors to settle at the start of each stage and, the more work it takes, the higher the risk of exceeding the amount of fixed costs and making a loss. The defendant may or may not try to make this happen in order to force a lower settlement. If a litigant does not care about the amount it recovers (perhaps a super-rich claimant or a defendant getting paid in any event), then these pressure points have even less force. Such incentives as do exist are considered further in Chapter 11.

The amount drops FRC by ~50% for the work needed for the CMC (including allocation). Perhaps concerningly, there are further drops in the amounts for FRC for finalising and exchanging the factual and expert evidence before an increase again for trial. A modest amount of £1,400 per day is paid for supporting counsel at trial.

Counsel can look forward to receiving £2,300 for preparing the post-issue advice or the particulars of claim or defence (stage 2, not included above) and £2,900 for advising pre-trial following receipt of the defence (stage 7, not included above). Advocacy fees at trial are £5,900 for day 1 and £1,450 refresher for each half day thereafter. A flat rate of £580 is recoverable for the handing down of a reserved judgement (stages 10-12, not included above).

CPR 1998, Rule 45.60 also allows reasonably incurred disbursements to be recovered where they are not already included. Thus, it is *possible*, that additional work by counsel could be recovered on top if their fixed fee. On the one hand, this appears to undermine the purpose of fixing their fees. On the other, clinical negligence is a complex area of litigation and this complexity could create factual scenarios which objectively justify this. If you decide to instruct counsel to do work in addition to the clearly permitted FRC tasks, then it would be prudent to plan out how you will recover the additional costs and have the risk of non-recovery agreed and signed off by your manager in advance. The *CPR Committee's November 2023 Minutes (para. 24)* states that counsel is entitled to their full trial fee is the case settles the day before trial but 75% if it settles within 5 days of trial. Accordingly, we can reasonably anticipate that counsel will do their trial preparation and advise on final settlement within these periods. It is possible that savvy defendants will make time-bomb offers to expire before this and so planning for this should be incorporated into our strategy planning to minimise the risk of this.

As can be seen, pre-service conferences are not envisaged nor are more than one conference. If a defence to counterclaim is needed (this is very rare in clinical negligence), then stage 2 allows a further £1,200 can be recovered under stage 2. In-house specialists can recover these fees if counsel is not used.

In addition, the following fees are allowed but could go to either counsel or the solicitors:

1. S12: Attendance at court for the handing down of a reserved judgement and consequential matters. £580 is allowed for all complexity bands. Since counsel is likely to be needed, this fee is likely to go to them.

2. S15: Attendance at an infant approval hearing. £1,200 is allowed for all complexity bands. Since counsel is likely to be needed, this fee is likely to go to them and would include the advice for the court. Consequential matters (such as preparing the forms, dealing with queries or dealing with the Court Funds Office) are not included and so would need to come out of the other FRCs.

FRC for Intermediate Track, CB3

Stage	**FRC Amount (per stage)**	**~% of Total Costs**	**~Hours (per stage)**
S1: Pre-Issue to Service of the Defence	£7,900 – £12,400	30%-28%	41.5 – 65
S3: Defence to CMC/Directions Order	£4,200 – £8,700	16%-20%	22 – 45.75
S4: CMC/Directions order to Inspection	£2,400 – £3,900	9%-9%	12.5 – 21

S5: Inspection – Expert Evidence	£1,500 – £3,000	6%-7%	8 – 16
S6: Expert Evidence – PTR/14 days pre-trial	£4,000	16%-9%	21
S8: PTR – Trial Date	£4,000 – £7,000	16%-16%	21 – 36.75
S9: Trial Support	£600 – £3,600	2%-8%	3 – 19
S13: Mediation/ADR for 1 meeting only	£1,200	5%-3%	6.25

Within this complexity band, the 'behaviour pattern' largely mirrors that for CB4. However, you can do 70% of the work to remain profitable in stage 1.

FRC for Intermediate Track, CB2

Stage	FRC Amount (per stage)	~% of Total Costs	Hours (per stage)
S1: Pre-Issue to Service of the Defence	£6,500 – £11,000	25%-25%	34 – 57.75
S3: Defence to CMC/Directions Order	£4,200 – £8,700	16%-20%	22 – 45.75

S4: CMC/Directions order to Inspection	£2,200 – £3,700	8%-8%	11.5 – 19.5
S5: Inspection – Expert Evidence	£1,500 – £3,000	6%-7%	7.75 – 15.75
S6: Expert Evidence – PTR/14 days pre-trial	£4,000	15%-9%	21
S8: PTR – Trial Date	£6,000 – £10,000	23%-23%	31.5 – 52.5
S9: Trial Support	£435 – £2,610	2%-6%	2.25 – 13.75
S13: Mediation/ADR for 1 meeting	£1,200	5%-3%	6.25

Likewise, within this complexity band, the 'behaviour pattern' largely mirrors that for CB4. However, you can do 57-63% of the work to remain profitable in stage 1.

FRC for Intermediate Track, CB1

Stage	**FRC Amount (per stage)**	**~% of Total Costs**	**Hours (per stage)**
S1: Pre-Issue to Service of the Defence	£2,350 – £4,600	20%-19%	12.25 – 24.25

S3: Defence to CMC/Directions Order	£4,150 – £8,750	35%-36%	21.75 – 46
S4: CMC/Directions order to Inspection	£1,100 – £3,100	9%-13%	5.75 – 16
S5: Inspection – Expert Evidence	£800	7%-3%	4.25
S6: Expert Evidence – PTR/14 days pre-trial	£1,450 – £3,700	12%-15%	7,5 – 19.5
S8: PTR – Trial Date	£700	6%-3%	3.5
S9: Trial Support	£290 – £1,710	2%-7%	1.5 – 9
S13: Mediation/ADR for 1 meeting only	£1,200	10%-5%	6.25

For this complexity band, the 'behaviour pattern' shifts from stage 1 to stage 3. There is more incentive to settle before the CMC than there is pre-action due to the amount of FRC.

The likelihood of any given clinical negligence case being suitable for these complexity bands becomes clearer once we look at how each is defined. This information is found in *CPR 1998, Rule 26.16 Table 2.*

- **Complexity band 1:** *Any* claim where the trial is likely to last under one day and there is only one issue in dispute. Whilst the examples given in *Table 2* all involve factual disputes, it is not impossible that a clinical negligence case involving an elderly client or a fatal claim for bereavement damages and funeral expenses could qualify. Unlikely, but not impossible given the many different permutations which can arise.

- **Complexity band 2:** *Any* less complex claim where there is more than one issue in dispute. The example given shows that both liability and quantum can be in dispute. As liability expert evidence is usually not required, there may be more overlap here than usual between PI and clinical negligence cases.

- **Complexity band 3**: *Any* more complicated claim which is unsuitable for band 2. Since the examples given are within the more specialist areas of PI, this gives more comfort for believing that clinical negligence cases will be in band 4. However, bear in mind that the remaining quantum issues in clinical negligence may not *necessarily* be more complicated in a contested complicated PI case.

- **Complexity band 4**: *Any* claim which is normally allocated to the intermediate track but which is unsuitable for the other bands. The example given is of a PI case with serious issues of fact or law. Since these are not defined, can it safely be assumed that all quantum-only clinical negligence cases will be assigned to this complexity band in the absence of clear guidance?

As long as the trial judge is likely to be assisted by hearing oral expert evidence, then band 1 seems inappropriate. The more that disputed issues of causation of consequential losses remain in play, heads of loss are denied as being irrecoverable in law; and/or disagreements exist over the valuation of general damages or heads of special damages, we anticipate that band 4 will be reasonable. However, the rules do not *require* that all clinical negligence cases be allocated to it.

Application Costs

In addition to limiting recoverable costs of the main action, cases falling within this regime have limited recoverable application costs. These are set out in *CPR 1998, Rule 45.8 Table 1*. For cases falling within the intermediate track, the pre-action and pre-trial application costs are fixed at £333 plus court fees. Using the approach outlined above, this is approximately 1 hour 45 minutes work for the preparation, negotiation, attendance and follow up. This includes pre-action disclosure and so it may be necessary to have submissions on the likely track ready although be aware that QOCS protection does tend to make it harder to win these and so there is a reasonable argument that it is better to issue proceedings and await standard disclosure.

You recover £750 for applications for summary judgement and interim payments (about 4 hours work).

Part 36 Changes

We cover this in Chapter 11.

Part 45 Costs Changes

There are two section of *CPR 1998, Part 45* that are relevant to clinical negligence (assuming that cases will not be allocated to the fast track):

- *Section I* (*Rules 45.1-45.15*); and
- *Section VII* (*Rules 45.49-45.51*)

The first point to note is that *CPR 1998, Rule 45.6* states that *Section VII* does not apply to protected parties. Accordingly, claims involving protected parties must be allocated to the multi-track. Bear in mind that *CPR 1998, Rules 21(b)* and *(d)* distinguish between 'children' and 'protected parties' so a child who is not also a protected party may have their case allocated to the intermediate track.

In terms of the other general provisions, the court retains its discretion as to whether one party is entitled to costs, when they are to be paid and whether they should be limited to a proportion of their entitlement (under *CPR 1998, Rules 45.1(2) and 44.2(6)(a)*). There is no discretion as to the amount of costs; *CPR 1998, Rule 45.1(3)* states that the amount of costs must be the fixed costs amount for *Rule 45, Section VII* unless that rule allows them to be different. Where there is more than one claimant, *CPR 1998, Rule 45.5* requires that they much have different causes of action for multiple sets of FRC to be claimed. Otherwise, the amount is the single one.

The amount of FRC is the amount allowed at the date of issue of the claim form rather than the date of any later amendment to the rules (*CPR 1998, Rule 45.1(8)*). The rule does not say what happens if the case settles pre-action and this is likely because allocation has not occurred at this point. There is no express rule requiring FRC to be applied if the case settled pre-action. The extent to which a defendant is likely to persuade a cost judge to award FRC (or an amount close to this) on a provisional assessment is likely to depend as to whether it formally admitted liability before settlement. As such, insisting on admission may not be in the claimant's best interests (depending on what retainer they have agreed to) and it may prove commercially sensible for defendants to make settlement offers including suitable admissions to support such a costs argument.

CPR 1998, Rule 45.2 confirms that VAT is added to the amount of the FRC rather than being subtracted from it.

Where either the conducting solicitor works and the client lives, carries on business or works within certain areas of London, the amount of FRC allowed in *CPR 1998, Rule 45.50 Table 14* is increased by 12.5% (*CPR 1998, Rule 45.3*). These areas are as set out in *CPR 1998, Part 45 PD, para.2.6*:

> *"...consists of (within London) the area served by the County Court hearing centres at Barnet, Brentford, Central London, Clerkenwell and Shoreditch, Edmonton, Ilford, Mayors and City of London, Romford, Wandsworth and Willesden and (outside London) the County Court hearing centres at Bromley, Croydon, Dartford, Gravesend and Uxbridge."*

Since Central London County Court is likely to be the assigned court centre for intermediate track clinical negligence cases, it seems probable that London-based firms will be able to claim this enhancement for their London-based clients. In *Otto & Others v Inner Mongolia Happy Lamb Catering Management Ltd & Others [2023] EWHC 3151 (Ch), HHJ Matthews* indicated that it was sufficient for a firm to have its base in the area claimed for because this is where the overheads were being incurred. It is possible, however, the at the rules committee will at some point recommend an amendment to *Form N260*, requiring the location of remote working to be stated if the fee earner does not regularly attend the office they are attached to.

Litigants in person can claim a reduced rate of 2/3rds of the FRC for the period in which they were acting (*CPR 1998, Rule 45.4*). Accordingly, the much-reduced hourly rate they can claim in the multi-track does not apply and this also means that a lawyer taking over a case from a litigant in person will receive less than if they had acted from the start.

Defendants' costs (in cases where QOCS protection has been lost) are also subject to the same FRC as claimants under *CPR 1998, Rule 45.6.* The amount used to calculate their entitlement is the value of the claim given in the claim form (rather than any offer amount or counter-schedule). The effects of set-off are within *CPR 1998, Part 36* and so are considered in Chapter 9.

Although FRC are fixed, *CPR 1998, Rule 45.9* does allow parties to apply for more than the usual amount. If the court agrees that there are *exceptional circumstances.* The judge hearing the application (which is likely to be contested) can summarily assess the costs or order a detailed assessment. As will be seen in Chapter 5, very little is accepted as being 'exceptional'. Under *CPR 1998, Rule 45.11*, if you fail to get 20% more than the permitted FRC amount, then the court will penalise you by awarding either the amount of FRC or the assessment amount (whichever is smaller, *CPR 1998, Rule 45.12*). You will also not get the application costs and may have to pay this amount to the defendant. So, if you assume that this rule allows you to circumvent FRC, you are likely to find that it does not.

Vulnerable clients and witnesses, by their very nature, require their solicitors to do more work. *CPR 1998, Rule 45.10*, at least *prima facie*, allows recovery for this additional work. However, there must be evidence of how the client's or witnesses' vulnerability required the additional work. Thus, if this evidence is ambiguous and could be attributed to another cause, the court may decide not to award an additional amount. If they do, the judge can either summarily assess it or order a detailed assessment. *CPR 1998, Rules 45.11* & *45.12* apply here as well so we anticipate that fee earners will need to keep very good evidence of how the vulnerability is increasing costs as the case progresses.

The position is similar if you believe that your opponent has increased costs by acting unreasonably. As we discuss in Chapter 5, there is arguably an incentive for doing so. *CPR 1998, Rule 45.13* does impose a sizeable penalty on litigants who have been found to have acted unreasonably. If the court considers that the receiving party has acted unreasonably, the other party can apply for an order reducing the FRC amount by 50%. Conversely, if the paying party has acted unreasonably, the court can order that they pay an additional 50%. *Part 36* consequences and disbursements are not affected. The sticking point is the definition of 'unreasonable behaviour'. This is defined as being behaviour for which there is no reasonable explanation. This strikes us as being circular.

By contrast, the test for indemnity costs is not circular; 'unreasonableness' is judged against failing to accept a settlement offer which was later proved to be reasonable against the information available at the time the offer was made. This is an objective measure by which the conduct can be fairly judged. Wasted costs are defined by the *Senior Courts Act 1981, s51(6)* as being costs arising from the improper, unreasonable or negligent act or omission of a representative. *CPR 1998, Rule 46.8* and *PD46 para. 5* then sets out a clear set of procedural steps which must be taken to obtain the order. If we are to apply the ordinary dictionary definition, then the *Oxford English Dictionary (online edition)* provides two definitions for 'unreasonable': *"not guided by or based on good sense"* and *"beyond the limits of acceptability or fairness"*. In any event, the bar appears to have been set very high for conduct which increases your costs amounting to being 'unreasonable'.

Where one party successfully applies for either reallocation or re-assignment, then the FRC of the new track apply to all stages retrospectively (*CPR 1998, Rules 45.14(1) & (2)*). The costs of this application are also fixed, coming within *CPR 1998 Rule 45.8, Table 1* (*CPR 1998, Rule 45.14(3)*).

Should a conflict arise between the amount of fixed costs and the costs consequences of a *Part 36* offer, then *CPR 1998, Rule 45.15* provides that the costs consequences under *CPR 1998 Rules 36.23* & *36.24* take precedence).

The practical effects of *CPR 1998, Part 45, Section VII* has been set out above. However, it is useful to briefly summarise the underlying provisions. For as long as the case is not allocated to the multi-track, the *only* costs that can be recovered are the *Table 14* fixed costs and the *CPR 1998, Part 45, Section IX* disbursements (*CPR 1998, Rule 45.50(1)*). *CPR 1998, Rule 45.60* defines a recoverable disbursement as one which is reasonably incurred and which does not cover work already falling within *CPR 1998, Rule 45.50 Table 14*. That said, this rule also says that the court "*...may allow...*" such disbursements not that it 'must allow' them. Accordingly, we anticipate that there is scope for argument from the paying party that the court does not have to allow the full amount in the particular circumstances of this case. This is considered further in Chapter 5.

CPR 1998, Rule 45.50(2) states that the time for deciding when a particular stage has started or ended (and so which stage costs are payable) is the date first set by the court (and not a later date agreed by the parties). For example, if the parties successfully apply by consent to adjourn the CMC, then stage 3 would appear to have ended before the CMC happens. If the case is settled between these two dates (perhaps by acceptance of a *Part 36* offer), then stage 4 costs would appear to be payable. This rule does not expressly say whether a date set by the rules or substantive law also must be the 'original date'. As such, if the parties agree to extend the time for service of the defence, does stage 1 end 14 days after the service of the particulars of claim in any event? This rule may be deliberately intended to create consequences for agreeing extensions of time so it should not be safely assumed that this possibility is counter intuitive.

For the purposes of calculating the amount of FRC payable in *CPR 1998 Rule 45.50 Table 14, CPR 1998, Rule 45.50(2)(iv)* defines 'damages' as being either the agreed damages or the amount awarded at trial. The formula used in *Table 14* differs for each stage but is essentially '£x + £y% of damages'. Accordingly, agreeing even seemingly modest damages reductions will impact on the amount of FRC a claimant receives. This is not so for defendants because their entitlement is based on the value signed off by the claimant in the claim form (*CPR 1998, Rule 45.6, supra*).

Perhaps importantly, *CPR 1998, Rule 45.50* contains a reminder that *CPR 1998, Rule 44.2* gives the court wide discretion as to whether to award all of the costs a party believes it is entitled to. There is quite a wide range of possibilities here which could be used by either party to change the standard costs entitlement. Very broadly, the court's discretion is wide enough to potentially make applications for *de facto* reallocation or re-assignment after the case has settled or for pre-action costs to be allocated to the multi-track arguable if the criteria under *CPR 1998 Rule 44.2* are met.

Whereas the solicitor's costs in *CPR 1998, Rule 45.50 Table 14* are cumulative (so you get the single amount shown if your case settles in that stage), the amounts for counsel (or in-house specialist) are added together if they do all of that work (*CPR 1998, Rules 45.50(2) (c) & (d)*). Interestingly, *CPR 1998, Rule 45.50(4)* as drafted arguably requires that the statements of case and pre-exchange or -trial written advice (you do not recover for both) must be dealt with by the intended trial advocate if counsel is used. It may be that the drafting was intended to distinguish between a specialist legal advisor and trial advocate in respect of drafting the statements of case as opposed to pre-trial advice and trial advocacy. If so, this is not the only interpretation of this rule, and it may be commercially viable for a paying party to challenge paying the fixed costs where counsel has been changed. Whilst we recommend not changing counsel to maintain consistency of approach throughout the case, this is frequently done in our experience. Setting this to one side, *CPR 1998 Rule 45.50(4)(d)* requires that the use of a specialist/counsel must also be 'justified'. We anticipate costs arguments, however unjustified, that the statement of case or advice was not justified in a quantum-only case worth between £25,000 and £100,000.

Although *CPR 1998, Rule 45.51* does set out additional provisions for trials of preliminary issues, it is not immediately obvious when this would occur in quantum-only cases worth between £25,000 and £100,000. The key point is that the receiving party is entitled to one set of FRC calculated at the stage the case has reached (plus any 'specialist advisor/counsel' fees). If the case then proceeds to trial and the same party wins, they then get an additional payment covering the 'additional' work but using *CPR 1998, Rule 45.50 Table 14* (calculated using *CPR 1998, Rule 45.51(2)*). If the other side wins, then they get paid FRC as per *Table 14* (*ibid.*). This rule distinguishes between an 'additional' amount if the same party wins with the 'normal' amount if different parties win the preliminary and substantive trials but does not stipulate whether there is a set-off. Presumably there would need to be in practice and so the preliminary issue costs could be wiped out creating a pyrrhic victory. Another point to note from this rule is that you can only receive one payment of the fixed ADR costs.

These rules do not make provision for where a trial is adjourned part-heard; the court has to postpone the trial date just before it starts (if a judge is unavailable); or one party successfully applies for an adjournment. In these circumstances, no additional FRC are payable unless these can properly be said to amount to 'exceptional circumstances' which we explore further in Chapter 5.

Are Inquest Costs Included?

Following the publication of the *CPR Committee's November 2023 Minutes (para. 21)*, as matters presently stand, the cost of representing the family of the Deceased are excluded from the FRC regime. Accordingly, where there is clinical negligence case arising from an

Inquest, the costs of representation should not eat into the amount you will receive.

This amendment followed the MoJ's *'FRC: Consultation on Issues Relating to the New Regime (July 2023)', paras. 19-21* and recognises the potential unfairness of including inquest costs within the FRC regime to bereaved families. In practice, we are likely to still see arguments raised that the incurred costs were not reasonable and proportionate. However, we can plan for this and these costs should be now recovered in addition to the FRC amounts for the clinical negligence case (and be subject to assessment).

Effect of Breach of Contract Allegations

These are not separately mentioned within the rules. Insofar as a breach of contract claim is made within a clinical negligence case (normally against a private clinician), then the factual matrix is usually the same for the contractual and tortious allegations. One note of caution, however, is that our experience that obtaining the contract and related evidence can often require additional work. As such, there is a risk that this work will eat into the amount of recoverable costs and so make these cases proportionately less profitable than those against NHS defendants.

Another point to note that it is sometimes necessary to restore the company which owns the clinic to the Company Register. There is no separate amount of FRC for this within the intermediate track. The *July 2023 MoJ Consultation (paras. 22-24)* makes a provisional recommendation that a similar provision should be included as will exist for noise induced hearing loss claims. Under *CPR 1998, Rules 45.56 & 45.61(2)*, £1,280 is allowed (plus disbursements). This approximates to 7 hours work using the methodology above. The *CPR Committee's November 2023 Minutes (para. 23)* recommended that these costs be brought within the FRC regime via a new rule (*CPR 1998, Rule 45.15A).* The actual costs are not yet available at the time of finalising this book.

Effect of Human Rights Act Allegations

CPR 1998, Rule 26.9(10) only excludes from the intermediate track *Human Rights Act 1998* cases which relate to the police. As such, there is no separate amount of FRC awarded for such cases.

Conclusions

In this chapter, we have summarised the new rules and their effect on the amount of recoverable costs we can expect to receive for cases falling within the intermediate track. There is a risk, intentional or otherwise, that assuming that these rules will be interpreted in the way which best suits us will be ill-founded with the effects that this work becomes even less profitable.

Our intention in setting out an illustrative number of hours for each stage within the intermediate track is to help a conscientious fee earner consider how all of the tasks done in a multi-track case can be done in an intermediate track one whilst remaining profitable.

The commercial incentive to haggle over these FRC amounts is there and it is at least possible that some will seek to persuade a district, or deputy district, judge that the particular case before them is so straightforward that it should be in a lower complexity band or track. You can now see the costs consequences more easily than otherwise.

Similarly, knowing that you will receive a set amount of costs no matter what work you do, may engender the view that compromise is good. Collaboration and settlement is considered in more detail in Chapter 11. For now, you can see from this chapter the effects on costs of simply 'splitting the difference' between the parties' respective settlement offers and of failing to reach a negotiated settlement at ADR.

CHAPTER THREE

CASES OF £25,000 OR LESS VALUE

Introduction

In this chapter we are going to discuss cases worth up to £25,000 and the new rules that are proposed to come into force. We shall also summarise where these rules originated from and how much of that has been taken into account.

The new rules related to low value clinical negligence claims will come into force, if ready, in April 2024. Until then, cases that are worth up to £25,000 would be caught under FRC only if considered to be suitable for the existing fast or intermediate tracks.

However, once the new rules are finalised, most clinical negligence claims where the value is below £25,000 will be caught under pre-action FRC irrespective of the track they could be allocated to post-issue. The fact that it could be any of your current cases makes the situation even more urgent.

As a result, we shall also touch base on the main things to consider when going forward, and how to address any cases that might be caught under FRC.

How Things Started

Before the *Civil Procedure (Amendment No. 2) Rules 2023* were published, there was an ongoing consultation process looking at how to introduce FRC into clinical negligence cases worth up to £25,000. The results of this consultation were published in September 2023. They are likely to come into force in April 2024 (or October 2024 as the new rules have not been finalised as at the date of this book was finished).

In this chapter, we will look at what has been taken into account when making the proposals in order to understand what concerns and approaches were considered relevant to fairly introduce FRC into clinical negligence. This is also helps to understand the *Civil Procedure (Amendment No. 2) Rules 2023* in their wider context.

These proposals for cases are closely related to the *Civil Justice Council's FRC in Lower Value Clinical Negligence Claims Report (October 2022).* These arose out of Sir Rupert Jackson's *Supplemental Report on Fixed Recoverable Costs (31st July 2017)* (*'the Report'*) but have diverged from it. Therefore, in order to better understand the rules, we shall briefly look at Sir Ruper Jackson's Report first.

Sir Rupert Jackson's Report

Sir Rupert's recommendations played a pivotal role in shaping the *Civil Procedure (Amendment No. 2) Rules 2023.* He emphasized that fixed recoverable costs in clinical negligence cases should be accompanied by procedural changes, a stance diverging from the 2023 rules, which lack such provisions. Sir Rupert also recognized the inherent complexity of clinical negligence cases compared to civil litigation cases of similar value, underlining the importance of this distinction.

Whilst the Report suggested that clinical negligence cases were not ready for fixed recoverable costs, Sir Rupert recommended adapting the Department of Health's 2017 report for lower-value clinical negligence cases and considering the inclusion of certain other cases in the framework, aligning with the ongoing clinical negligence consultation. Despite the Report's acceptance of some claimants' lawyers' arguments and the potential for cost savings in cases under £25,000, it did not offer guidance on achieving collaboration between claimants and defendants. This oversight, shared by the 2022 Department of Health consultation and the *Civil Procedure (Amendment No. 2) Rules 2023*, raises concerns about striking a balance between cost reduction and ensuring access to justice and fair compensation.

The Goal

In *Chapter 1, para. 1.2,* Sir Rupert expressed the view that the holy grail of reform is to arrive at a system where the *"actual costs of each party are a modest fraction of the sum in issue, and the winner recovers those modest costs from the loser."* This bears a certain similarity to opening costs offers made by defendants' costs draftsmen. At *para. 1.9,* he said that *"[c]ontrolling the costs of litigation and providing clarity at each party's fina*ncial *commitment are vital elements in achieving access to justice."*

Clinical Negligence

The Report, Chapter 8 (which deals specifically with clinical negligence cases), sets out both sides' arguments. Sir Rupert took the view that the 36% of cases that are worth more than £25,000 can continue to be safely costs managed by the existing rules on proportionality and budgeting. The *Civil Procedure (Amendment No. 2) Rules 2023* changes this.

Chapter 8, paragraph 5, Sir Rupert set out his proposed way forward including:

- FRC must be linked to procedural reform for it to succeed (*para. 5.1*). However, no further comment is made about how this might be achieved.

- A joint working party be created to promote access to justice by concentrating on cases worth less than £25,000 (*para. 5.4*). As these make up the bulk of clinical negligence cases, creating a stand-alone scheme will promote access to justice and act as a possible precursor to cases *"of somewhat higher value."*

- A minority of higher value cases might be suitable for the intermediate fixed recoverable costs track for cases worth up to

£100,000 (*para. 5.5*). Sir Rupert suggested that these are cases where liability is admitted early (leaving only straight-forward quantum issues to be determined). It appears that the *Civil Procedure (Amendment No. 2) Rules 2023* are based on this proposal. However, it was also stated that the vast majority of clinical negligence cases over £25,000 would proceed as they currently do, however, albeit potentially influenced by changes to incurred costs.

These recommendations complemented the DoH's proposals for cases worth under £25,000 (*para. 5.6*). The procedural rule and protocol changes set out in that consultation paper did not constitute the sort of bespoke process Sir Rupert recommended in *the Report*. To briefly recap the process set out in DoH's consultation paper has largely remained unchanged through to the September 2023 proposals.

Sir Rupert's recommendation for a workable FRC scheme for clinical negligence fell a long way short of what the defendants' representatives were lobbying for. However, if the figures quoted in the report genuinely represent the mix of clinical negligence case seen in practice, around 64% of clinical negligence cases faced being subject to fixed recoverable costs at some level. The remaining 36% cases were to remain subject to budgeting and proportionality rules and, therefore, subject to robust challenges. The *Civil Procedure (Amendment No. 2) Rules 2023* eats into this 36% of cases (by imposing to cases worth up to £100,000) in addition to the September 2023 proposals.

Background Information Used

At the end of this *Chapter 2*, Sir Rupert reproduced his organogram flow chart from *The Reform of Civil Litigation (2012), p222* illustrating the five strategic objectives the original reforms. FRC are therefore linked to every part of the overall reform picture via proportionality and by controlling costs in advance. Costs management (i.e. budgeting) is an alternative means of achieving this aim. Limiting the cost of expert evidence is a sister-branch also affecting advanced costs control. As such, costs clarity and precision is not directly related to advanced costs control.

At *para. 3.4*, Sir Rupert quoted from *para. 6.29* of *Briggs' LJ Civil Courts Structure Review, Final Report* to say that clinical negligence cases are "*... an area where the playing field is at first sight sharply tilted against the individual claimant, facing a sophisticated insurance company as the real ... Defendant."* Costs budgeting, QOCS and increased general damages have powerfully promoted access to justice.

At *para. 3.3*, Sir Rupert recognised that the reforms to date had already had a significant impact on reducing costs.

At *para. 3.6* of *Chapter 2*, Sir Rupert stated that he always intended that some lower value multi-track claims would pass from budgeted costs management to FRC as the final stage of his reforms. Accordingly, the final position ought to have been that FRC should only eventually apply to clinical negligence cases above £25-£100k where liability has been admitted early and quantum is straightforward. 'Early' here does not mean in the defence or even pre-allocation (see Chapter 2 of this book) but in the letter of response.

By limiting recoverable costs, litigants are more likely to instruct firms whose actual costs are closest to the FRC. So, this is a key point to remember if you want to change your retainer as your competitors may not do (see further Chapter 7). *Para. 1.2* set out the holy grail (*supra*). At *para. 1.3*, Sir Rupert set out 3 approaches to achieving this: (a) making procedural amendments to reduce actual costs as far as is possible; (b) to control the amount of recoverable costs in advance; & (c) to restrict recoverable costs to that which is proportionate under *CPR Rule 44.3(5)*. Accordingly, this can be interpreted as the amount of FRC being the presumed proportionate recovery amount. If so, it provides a basis for a defendant seeking to persuade a costs judge that a similar amount should be recovered even if FRC do not apply. Of course, the value of the claim is not the only consideration (see Chapter 2) and those other factors may be more important.

Sir Rupert Jackson's Supplementary Report attempted to strike a fair balance between limiting the costs of clinical negligence litigation and maintaining access to justice. In return for fixed recoverable costs only applying to cases worth less than £25,000, it was considered reasonable to accept that they should apply to cases which are not necessarily 'simple'. If these recommendations are eventually accepted and rule changes properly protect the individual claimant, then FRC may constructively promote access to justice at a reasonable cost.

We should not lose sight of the fact that negligence is inadvertent but can often have very significant consequences going beyond the amount of compensation awarded. The individual claimant does not ask to be injured and the prospect of meeting the legal tests without proper legal advice is beyond most people. Clinicians have an equal right to receive proper legal advice in defending themselves. The key to reducing costs lies in the early, accurate agreement on the central disputed issues so that these can be focussed on and resolved as quickly as is possible without selling either party short.

Following this report, the road forked. The reform proposals followed cases under £25,000, whilst cases between £25,000-£100,000 were left alone.

CJC's Report (Oct 2019)

Sadly, the subsequent consultations did not achieve a fair balance; instead giving primacy to costs savings and in seeking to get an early agreement on the issues by requiring the claimant to serve all of their evidence with the letter of claim.

The CJC's 2019 report attempted to find a joint solution to how to apply FRC to clinical negligence cases but ended up only compromising. The main elements contained in the September 2023 proposals are present but did not go as far:

- Not all cases worth under £25,000 were to be included.

- Two sets of FRC figures were included (one from each side).

- The underlying belief was that most cases would conclude (one way or another) without court proceedings being needed. Concerningly, patient safety and learning lessons from past mistakes were both excluded.

- No progress at all was made on either the levels of ATE premiums or experts' fees within the FRC regime.

- The purpose of changing the pre-action process was said to be to drive cultural change (*p37*). However, complex or sensitive cases were to be excluded (because FRC are an unsuitable regime).

One of the statistics used to justify them was that 25% of cases currently (in 2019) settled without any expert evidence (*p23*). This still seems to be an astonishing statistic and wholly outside of our experience in practice.

There were serious question marks over the adequacy of the proposed safeguards for claimants (set out at *pp27-28*).

It could not be agreed whether cases involving an inquest (where neglect findings had been made); or dental, cosmetic & care home claims should be included.

The claimants' representatives wanted all fatal cases excluded; all cases involving protected parties; and secondary victim cases. In contrast, the defendants' representatives felt that fatal cases were suitable and were only prepared to agree to excluding neonatal death cases. They felt that protected parties could reasonably be included with an additional FRC amount and would not agree to excluding secondary victim psychiatric claims.

No agreement was reached as to what procedural changes would be required (or what the appropriate FRC) would be for cases if court proceedings were required (*para. 4.04, p38*). Another statistic which was apparently accepted was that 75% of cases settle pre-proceedings.

The underlying assumptions were that cases worth under £25,000 are straightforward on liability and quantum issues and should therefore resolve pre-action.

Problem areas also remained. No agreement was reached as to whether counsel's fees should be included within these figures or be disbursements. There were no proposals to sanction failures by the defendant to comply with the timescales despite the sequential exchange of evidence. Patient safety and learning lessons from clinical mistakes were also excluded.

It was suggested that clear instructions, standard headings, properly sorted records and solicitors not producing chronologies would reduce costs (*p 66*). Nothing was proposed which would ensure that the defendant would send its experts the claimant's letter of claim (as opposed to asking them separate questions). Sequential exchange of reports was promoted on the basis that it saves costs. It is unclear why the defendant's position was favoured or what the safeguards were for what represents a radical departure from fair practice. Experts' fees could not be agreed. Rather than criticise experts' charging rates, the report refers to inefficient use of experts' time by instructing solicitors. ATE premiums were also left for others to resolve.

The CJC working group considered that these proposals did not adversely impact on patient safety or learning opportunities (*pp68-75)*. Further, sequential exchange of expert evidence was believed to promote these aims and it outright rejected AvMA's contention that FRC impacts access to justice. However, it offered no explanation for any of these conclusions and appeared to accept that learning lessons will occur by virtue of defendants being responsible bodies.

Ministry of Justice Response (September 2021)

Page 3 gave the impression that the Response did not apply to clinical negligence cases but that some reform would occur:

> *"We have carefully considered the way forward in the light of responses to the consultation and developments since, including the Government's desire to extend the use of fixed recoverable costs in other cases not covered here, such as clinical negligence claims..."*

Similarly, *p11, para. 1.4* stated: *"Separately, DHSC are setting the way forward on extending FRC in clinical negligence cases..."*

Page 11, Para. 3.1i stated that there would be no intermediate track at all and that any introduction of FRC would be limited to those 'simpler' cases identified by Sir Rupert:

> *"The Government agreed with the principle of extending FRC to all the cases recommended by Sir Rupert for his proposed intermediate track. However, we do not consider it necessary to introduce a new track, with the costs and complexity that that would involve. Instead, we consulted on assigning these intermediate cases to an expanded fast track (meaning that certain simpler 'intermediate' cases, as identified by Sir Rupert, will also be allocated to a fast track regime, where appropriate). This should bring greater consistency and simplicity."*

Page 44, Para. 13.15iii repeated Sir Rupert's recommendation that clinical negligence cases above £25,000 would only be suitable for FRC if there was an *early* admission of breach and causation.

Page 72, para. 12.5 expressly excluded clinical negligence cases with *para. 12.4* confirming that they would only be introduced when the DoH had finalised its bespoke scheme for cases worth under £25,000

DoH Consultation (January 2022)

The aim of the consultation is summarised at *p6* as being:

> *"We believe that the cost savings we expect as a result of implementation of our proposals would represent an important contribution towards addressing the overall rise in clinical negligence costs.*
>
> *The aim of our streamlined FRC scheme is to promote and enable quicker, more proportionate and more cost-effective resolution of lower value clinical negligence claims so that people who have experienced harm can receive compensation more quickly and the delays, distress and avoidable legal costs associated with these claims are reduced."*

This again indicates that an underlying assumption is that lower costs recovery will lead to quicker settlements. Logically, this requires that less work will be required to obtain the same results as claimant clinical negligence obtained pre-FRC. If such evidence exists, it has not been publicly scrutinised or peer reviewed. Setting that to one side, we can see that access to justice and fair compensation were not stated to be one of the goals of these proposals. Using FRC to counter the rising costs of claims is a recurring theme throughout this consultation. For example, at *p12*, it says: *"Legal costs, particularly the costs incurred by claimant lawyers, have risen in their own right over the last decade and a half, and though costs have levelled out more recently, they remain at a historically high level."* At *p14*: *"As shown, claimant legal costs for lower value claims are historically high overall and disproportionately high in relation to defendant legal costs"*. This was a very one-sided view which is generally not accepted by claimant lawyers.

The consultation essentially recycled the October 2019 report but the results were not published until September 2023 (again without any prior notice). At *p7* promising: *"[t]he government will carefully consider responses to this consultation and provide a full response. Analysis of the responses will help the government in its consideration of next steps, should the scheme be implemented."* As will be seen below, the response essentially ignored the claimant lobby.

This consultation did, however, accept AvMA's submissions that cases involving stillbirths and neonatal deaths should be excluded from the FRC regime. These cases, on average involve more expert evidence and are proportionately of greater importance to claimants. As such, they are inherently ill-suited to the imposition of FRC. Cases where more than two liability experts and/or 'genuine' multiple defendants were to be excluded – so adding in all the partners at a GP practice would not count.

September 2023 Consultation Response

These proposals are recommended to be adopted in April 2024 but require the Rules Committee to prepare the draft rules. The intention was that these will be ready by December 2023 but they were not published. If the rules do not come into force in April 2024, the next usual implementation date is October 2024. There is a chance that these proposals will not be implemented either at all or without further amendments. We assume below that they will be implemented in substantially the same form as these proposals (as amended by the CPR Committee's recommendations) because of the way the various consultations to date have proceeded. Accordingly, we recommend practitioners prepare for this. One caveat with this is that differences in the wording of the procedural rules may have consequences we have not foreseen here.

This consultation response essentially recommends that the *January 2022 Consultation* be adopted with only modest concessions being made to accommodate claimants' representatives' views. The *Ministerial Foreword (pp3-4)* and *The Case for Change (pp8-9)* makes it clear that the overriding policy justification is to save costs. *Pages 9-10* assert that these proposals are consistent with Sir Rupert Jackson's recommendations without objectively justifying this statement. It should also be noted that the number of respondents was remarkably small (~90).

The *Introduction (p5)* introduces a new pre-action protocol for these claims (called the 'PAP for Lower Value Clinical Disputes'). There is then a clear delineation of different claims bands:

- **'Small Claims' are those with a settlement or judgement value between £1 and £1,500.** These are 'normally' allocated to the small claims track and this applies pre-action. This supports the view set out in Chapter 2 that clinical negligence claims can be (rarely) allocated to the small claims track. Claims involving a *Human Rights Act* claim will be in the low value band (*p21*).

- **'Low Value' or 'Lower Damages Claims' are those where the awarded or agreed damages are for personal injuries are between £1,501 and £25,000.** These will be subject to either the light or standard tracks in the pre-action period. The term 'track' may be changed when the new rules are published.

- **'Medium Value' claims are those worth between £25,001 and £100,000** now covered by the intermediate track.

Pages 15-16 make it clear that the intention is to strongly promote pre-issue settlement by introducing enforced change:

> *"The aim of the LVCD Protocol is to facilitate resolution, by requiring parties to exchange expert evidence in the pre-action phase and to participate in resolution stages. The LVCD Protocol will describe the behaviour the court expects of the parties prior to the start of proceedings."*

This essentially works on the assumption that a 'cards on the table' approach will force settlement. The difficulty is that the proposals maintain the proposal that the claimant must serve all of its evidence. Simultaneous exchange would be far fairer and would remain consistent with the pre-action timetable.

a. Section 5.5: The FRC Amounts

The consultation response recommends adopting the midpoint between the claimants' and defendants' figures. As such, claimants stand to receive less than they believed was reasonably necessary and proportionate.

Standard Track

Standard Track Stage	Claimants' FRC Amount (per stage)	~% of Total Costs	~Hours (per stage) (£190/hour)
Start to Stocktake	£6,200.30-£13,250	83%-91%	32.5-69.75
Stocktake to End of Protocol	+£1,250	17%-9%	6.50
Post-ENE to Trial	N/a	N/a	N/a

Light Track

Light Track Stage	Claimants' FRC Amount (per stage)	~% of Total Costs	~Hours (per stage) (£190/hour)
1: Start to 21 days after LofR is due[1]	£2,020.18-£6,250	57%-75%	10.5-32.75
2a: to Stocktake	+£1037.53-£1,625	29%-19%	5.5-8.5

2b: Stocktake to ENE	+£500	14%-6%	2.5

[1] Note that this means that the light track stage 1 costs end after the case exits from this track (see below).

Where the claimant is a child or a protected party (but not otherwise vulnerable), *Table 3 (p53)* recommends an additional £1,800 be recoverable. This equates to an additional ~9.5 hours work (using the approach above).

The outline of the new scheme (which is subject to the new rules being published), should be viewed in light of these FRC amounts.

b. Section 5.1: The Pre-Action Protocol

The pre-action process is stated to be mandatory with both the processes and requirements needing to be followed (*p22*). *"It will be for claimants at the outset of the process to assess claims and ensure they follow the correct process."* Bear in mind that it is the settlement or judgement amount which qualifies a case for FRC under these proposals so, if your initial risk assessment gets the value or litigation risk wrong, you will stand to have run an unprofitable file.

The *PAP* itself begins with the letter of claim. However, the requirements of what must be served with the letter of claim effectively means that this starts from when the case is accepted. It concludes when one of these events occur: pre-action abandonment; pre-action settlement; either both parties or the defendant decides that neutral evaluation following the mandatory stocktake is pointless; or 28 days have passed after the neutral evaluation. Note that this does not include the situation where the defendant wants neutral evaluation but the claimant does not. This could occur where the defendant is pushing for 'resolution' by abandonment but the claimant believes they have a strong case. In such cases, it appears that neutral evaluation is required. It also does not stipulate what happens after the protocol period ends but there is a gap before limitation ends.

This potentially will allow the claimant to reassess their case and take the risk of incurring the costs of conducting further investigations. If so, then this may need to be factored into the decision about the level of detail that is prudent to include in the evidence served with the letter of claim.

Page 23 makes it clear that the claimant will need to justify a decision not to follow the low value *PAP* in both the letter of claim and particulars of claim (and follow the *PAP for the Resolution of Clinical Disputes*). This is limited to whether a valid exclusion applies rather than to another reason. The requirement that this be set out in the particulars of claim means that a statement of truth will be required implying that the consequences of signing a false statement apply. If the case is issued, then it will be allocated to one of the 4 'normal' tracks under *CPR 1998, Part 26*. Accordingly, and depending on the outcome of the *Summer 2023 Consultation on the Intermediate Track*, it may be that it will be clearer whether a case worth under £25,000 must be allocated to the multi-track.

Otherwise, the only proposed exit points from this new *PAP* is where the defendant confirms in writing within 21 days of the letter of claim being served that the case is time-barred or where it fails to provide a letter of response within 6 months (*ibid.*) Thus, whilst the claimant decides if a new case should be entered into the new PAP (with the expectation that it will be unless a valid exclusion applies), the defendant controls if it exits it (but in very limited circumstances). Nothing is said here about agreeing to extend the time for the letter of response (c.f. *s5.8 Sanctions*, below). Whilst there is no overt incentive for claimants to agree such extensions, there may be circumstances where it is unreasonable to refuse a request. Since a dispute over this is likely to eat into the FRC amount, the claimant will need to be confident over their decision. If the claim does exit, the *PAP for the Resolution of Clinical Disputes* then applies.

FRC apply to all of the work done up until the scheme is deemed to have concluded (*p24*). However, it does not say what happens where the scheme was not followed but the case later settled below £25,000. It may be safest to assume that it applies for the entire pre-action period.

c. Section 5.2: The Light & Standard Tracks

Unlike the intermediate track, there is no requirement that breach and causation be admitted. If it is within 8 weeks of the letter of claim being sent then the light track is considered to be the appropriate track (*p27*). This essentially means that the defendant is in a position to accept the claimant's supportive evidence and gets instructions from all of its interested stakeholders within this period. This is much longer than giving the defendant 21 days to admit liability if a supportive duty of candour investigation report has been obtained. This may still have its use because, if an early invitation to admit liability is refused, it provides the claimant with a good indication that the standard track will apply. Concerningly, it is stated that disputes over causation of consequential losses should be dealt with as part of the second part of the light track.

> *"Under the proposals it is always for claimants to determine whether a claim is suitable for the light track and for defendants to determine whether, by an admission of breach of duty, and an admission that the breach caused loss, including injury, the claim should proceed on the light track, or potentially transfer to the standard track. Only claims with an admission of liability of this kind will proceed on the light track process in the new protocol."* (p31)

Although the light track is intended to cover cases where breach and causation are unlikely to be disputed the list of suggested cases (*p32*) which are potentially suitable is not necessarily limited in this way:

- The parties have agreed in writing that expert evidence is unnecessary;

- The defendant has made a binding admission on breach under the Welsh Redress Scheme (remember that fixed costs already apply under that scheme and the claimant has 6 months to consider an offer of up to £25,000. It is not immediately obvious why anyone would choose to then use the light track in great numbers);

- Where a Serious Incident Report identifies a breach of duty causing an avoidable injury;

- Never events;

- *Res ipsa loquitor* (which is extremely rare in clinical negligence cases);

- Following an Inquest (it does not say that a finding of neglect is required).

If the admission is received within 8 weeks, then interim costs are payable for stage 1 of the light track. Where the defendant does not admit liability within 8 weeks from the letter of claim, the case automatically transfers into the standard track (*p32*). Conversely, where the defendant admits breach and causation within 8 weeks of receiving a standard track letter of claim, the case transfers to the 2nd stage of the light track (*ibid*).

Instead of agreeing 'limitation suspensions', the proposals recommend that either an agreement to 'extend limitation' should be reached or proceedings should be issued and a stay agreed. The first part of this makes little real sense because the limitation date cannot be extended because it is statutory in nature. This is why limitation amnesties are required. A successor agreement to the SCIL/NHSR Covid-19 Amnesty discussion remains to be agreed but would be relevant here if your firm is a signatory to it. The draft version (as at December 2023) bears certain similarities to the standard track process.

Another concern is that the rules on accrued interest under *Part 36* will be amended to avoid unfairness to defendants who follow the new process (*p33*). As will be seen below, the claimant must make a *Part 36* offer with the letter of claim, this appears to indicate that there will be no real consequences of the relevant period being 21 days. Again, the new rules will need to be scrutinised when they are published.

d. Section 5.3: The Processes

Page 36 shows that these have been proposed despite the majority of respondents disagreeing with them. All of the defendant respondents agreed with them. It is understandable why the consultation is seen in some quarters as having been farcical.

Most cases which appear to be of modest value (you need to be very good to reliably and consistently accurately predict that a case estimated at, say, £35,000 eventually settles for this), need to be considered for inclusion in the standard track. The recommended process is:

- The claimant investigates their case and decides which track is suitable (light, standard or multi). If they believe that either the light or standard tracks apply, the letter of claim must include (*pp40-1*)
    - Essentially, it should be in a similar format to the existing one in the *PAP for Resolution of Clinical Disputes*:
        - A 'brief summary' of the key facts and dated (including treatment from other health providers (presumably to assist the NHS to recover treatment costs);
        - A 'concise summary' of the allegations on breach and causation (including the causal link between them);
        - A 'description' of the adverse outcome and C&P;
        - Details of the value and losses. Note that *p40* does not contain the requirement that the supporting documentary evidence is required to be served (as was included in the consultation itself);
        - Sufficient information to allow a CRU certificate to be obtained;

        - Funding information (including whether it was entered into before or after April 2013 indicating that there are still concerns that low value children's claims from over 10 years ago have not been notified);
        - The disciplines of the experts instructed; and,
        - Additionally for Welsh claims, confirmation of whether the Welsh Redress Scheme has been followed.

    This is relatively uncontroversial in the sense that this information should already be provided and template letters should already be available to most practitioners.

    - Collated, sorted and paginated medical records. The index should be provided along with copies of the core records
    - Breach and causation expert evidence (limited to 3 different expert disciplines). However, note that *p41* does *not* include this limit;
    - Witness statements (signed with a statement of truth; which are complaint with *CPR 1998 Part 32 & PD 32* and limited to 2 witnesses);
    - Any separate C&P expert report (again, no limit is stipulated at *p41*);
    - A settlement offer (there is no specific mention of a *Part 36* offer being mandatory).

- The defendant is required to respond as follows:

    - Admit breach and causation within 8 weeks. If they do, the case goes onto the light track;

- o Send a letter of response within 6 months (not 4);
- o If it does not do so within 6 months, then the case reverts to the *PAP for Resolution of Clinical Disputes* (this does not necessarily mean that FRC will not ultimately still apply).
- o There is nothing in the response to say that the defendant must serve like-for-like documents or make a counteroffer. *Annex B, Diagram 2 (p87)* says only that the defendant must send a letter responding to the letter of claim and either accept or reject the offer.

Since the light track process is only where it appears that liability has already been admitted, the process should be more straightforward. The proposals are:

- Whilst the consultation response is not completely clear, the inference is that letters of claim in the light track do not require expert evidence to have been obtained. The contents of the letter of claim is essentially the same as for the standard track with the addition that an explanation of why the case is suitable for the light track. It would seem prudent to include the document which the claimant believes admits breach and causation although this has not been included in the proposals. The evidence bundle is likewise similar except that the expert evidence does not need to be disclosed (if it has been obtained). If expert evidence has been obtained, all that it is needed is to confirm the disciplines in the letter of claim (*pp42-43*).
- Once the letter of claim has been sent, as above, the defendant has 8 weeks to confirm whether breach and causation is to be admitted. Where the defendant either disputes this or does not respond within 8 weeks, the claim restarts in the standard track and the penalty is that the defendant pays 5% on top of the light track stage 1 FRC. It appears that the consultation point requiring the

claimant to restart within the standard track within 8 weeks of it exiting from the light track has not been adopted. If this is going to be in the new rules, it is likely that the claimant would need rely on the ability to extend deadlines due to experts' delays to meet this in many cases.

Accordingly, this may delay the case because the claimant would need to investigate the case to the point where it can comply with requirements of the standard track letter of claim. The defendant would then have 6 months under the standard track to consider the claim; the protocol period will not have ended.

- Where the case remains in the light track, this is essentially to cover quantification of the claim. A mandatory *inter partes* stocktake is required within 4 weeks at which the discussion is to include whether expert evidence is required. If so, it appears that the expert should be instructed jointly within 2 weeks. It is important to remember that joint instructions require the letter of instruction to be agreed and for the claimant to understand the risks of obtaining jointly instructed expert evidence.

- There is not much time allotted for the expert reports and, again, this is likely to be an area where the parties will need to consider agreeing an extension. Any delay is likely to eat into the amount of FRC but the proposals appear to ignore that different medical disciplines have vastly different reporting times. The proposals are that the report should be available within 8 weeks where no C&P appointment is required and 12 weeks where it is.

Experience indicates that a paper-based C&P report is far less persuasive and comprehensive than one based upon interviewing and examining the claimant. If this is put into the new rules, caution is required. Similarly, there is scope for dispute over the questions being asked. Even though the limited value range of £1,501-£25,000 should really limit the scope for disagreement, the level of FRC partly depends on the amount of damages awarded or agreed. Both sides have a commercial incentive to maximise or minimise the case's value and this is nothing new. However, it is magnified under FRC and the need to agree on the terms of the joint instruction risk acting as a barrier to completing this step.

- There is then a long-stop date preventing the expert report being significantly extended. A second 'further evidence' stocktake must be held 12 weeks (if no C&P appointment was required) or 16 weeks (if it was). Put another way, this is 4 weeks after the date the report is due. Accordingly, if the expert's waiting list goes beyond this and no alternative can be found, there seems to be little alternative to extend this date even if the rules seem to prevent this. The purpose of this 2nd stocktake is to settle the case (*p41*).

- If this does not occur, then a non-binding neutral evaluation is required within 4 weeks of the 'further evidence' stocktake. This is essentially a paper-based review before a neutral barrister. The decision must be made available within a further 4 weeks. Following this, there is a 28-day period during which the parties are encouraged to exchange settlement offers (*p42*).

Section 5.4: Evidentiary Requirements & Template Letters

There is a clear disparity between the consequences of not complying with these proposals (*p47*):

> *"There may be costs consequences for claimants where the quality of evidence bundles presented to defendants is poor and impedes their ability to respond. Defendants must ensure they respond within the 6-month period regardless of the standard of evidence."*

Bearing in mind that defendants have an entitlement to offset their costs if their *Part 36* offers are not beaten (*CPR 1998, Rule 44.14*), it might have been anticipated that this proposal would be more even handled. However, it appears that there is no chance of defendants facing costs consequences.

With this in mind, the test for the evidence the claimant presents is ambiguous. It must be *"sufficiently detailed and of sufficient quality for the other party to understand the issues and respond to points raised"* (*p47*). This is essentially subjective and it can be readily anticipated that defendants could assert that it is sub-standard as a means of justifying its own delays. This approach has been seen for years under the *PAP for Resolving Clinical Disputes* and in requests to 'clarify' *Part 36* offers. As such, it would be prudent for claimants to have a clear record of the checks made and steps taken to ensure that this 'quality standard' has been met. An attendance note which does this and can be safely disclosed if needed (without waiving privilege on other matters) should be set up as a precedent template.

Page 47 raises the possibility that new template letters of claim will be introduced for both tracks. There is a rather generic comment as regards expert reports: *"Expert report model elements should also be used as a guide for standard track claims and, where applicable, for light track claims."* Without wanting to prejudge this, the risk of using template sections for expert reports is that the opinions expressed become mechanical and lack the requisite degree of independence. The ultimate goal always has to be how the opinion will look at trial and the claimant's experts are being forced by these proposals to effectively finalise their evidence without seeing the defendant's case. As a minimum, experts should make it clear in their reports that their *CPR 1998 Part 35* duty to the court requires them to be permitted to revisit their opinions in light of any additional information that comes to light. It is surprising that experts' joint meetings have not been incorporated into either pre-action track.

e. Section 5.6: Neutral Evaluation

Page 57 essentially shows that this is effectively an advice on prospects and quantum from Counsel. Practitioners will be familiar with this, the difference is that the evaluator is advising as a neutral rather than on the settlement range.

Interestingly, the evaluator does not have to be a barrister:

> *"Choice of evaluators is not restricted only to barristers, but open to suitably experienced legal professionals. Experience, expertise and impartiality requirements will be set out in guidance alongside expectations of the role and the evaluation itself, as well as circumstances in which it would be permitted for evaluators to move beyond the paper only process and seek clarification from the parties on expert evidence."*

It is not immediately obvious why you would want this to be done by someone who is not a clinical negligence specialist. In a FRC scheme, especially one which has been imposed and mostly ignores the claimants' submissions, it is essential that the neutral evaluation is efficiently done without requiring the parties to provide assistance. However, the recommendation is that the evaluator must be jointly instructed and the defendant is responsible for paying the fee.

Somewhat surprisingly, the evaluator's fees are rather generous vis-à-vis the legal costs:

Evaluators' Fees

Scope of Work	Evaluator's Fee	~% of Total Claimant's Costs[1]	~Equivalent Hours (per stage)
Liability & Quantum	£2,500	40%-19%	13
Liability Only	£1,500	24%-11%	8
Quantum Only	£750	12%-6%	4

[1] This is a percentage of the standard track stage 1 costs.

The reason for illustrating the fees in this manner is to show the equivalent amount of work the evaluator will be paid for vis-à-vis the conducting fee earner. 13 hours to provide a liability and quantum advice seems high given that these cases are supposed to be straightforward. Unlike claimant's solicitors, the evaluator does not have to account to their client for any 'profit' if they do less then this. In reality, of course, the evaluator's hourly rate is unlikely to be £190/hour. That is not the point, because FRC ignores solicitors' hourly rates. The point is that these proposals do not impose the same costs constraints on the evaluator than they do on the claimant's solicitor despite adding a new stage to the litigation pre-issue process.

f. Section 5.7: Excluded Claims

Here, at least, the claimants' representations were listened to. *Page 62* lists the following types of case which are not subjected to either scheme:

- Still births and neonatal deaths (including secondary victim claims for parents). However, fatal claims generally, other secondary victim claims (which are now much less likely following *Paul v Royal Wolverhampton NHST & Other*

Appeals [2024] UKSC 1) and other complex cases are not so excluded.

- Where more than 3 expert disciplines are required to deal with breach and causation. This is an increase on the January 2022 consultation proposals (which required only one expert per discipline for breach and causation).

- Where there are multiple defendants as long as the allegations against them are materially different. Please note that there is no definition of what amounts to material differences. One the one hand, allegations against the partners in a GP surgery are likely to be the same. However, how will allegations against a private surgeon and the hospital that they work at be seen (negligent treatment is different to a non-delegable duty and vicarious liability but are they materially so?)? It is reasonable to anticipate that this is fertile ground for disagreement.

- Limitation is raised by the defendant as a defence to the claim. On this point, in some cases, it may well be commercially advantageous to the defendant to not raise limitation and use the FRC rules to reduce the claimant's profitability to the point where the case becomes inviable to proceed. Making an application under the *Limitation Act 1980, s33* for the court to exercise its discretion is not straightforward and examples of where this is done for cases worth under £25,000 are likely to be fairly rare.

- Litigants in person will not be required to work within the FRC regime. However, it should be remembered that they are only entitled to a much lower hourly rate than lawyers in any event.

Page 62 allows the court to revisit the claimant's decision to rely on an exclusion and (particularly in respect of the number of expert disciplines), there is certainly scope for defendants making applications for it to do so:

> *"However, if the court is not satisfied that a claim qualifies for a specified exclusion and the claim has a value at settlement or following judgment in the value range of the LDFRC scheme, then that claim would be subject to fixed costs for the pre-issue period."*

g. Section 5.8: Sanctions

On the face of it, claimants should be aware that these appear to be weighted in favour of defendants:

- Evidence Quality (*p68*): Failing to provide evidence of sufficient quality (see above) may be seen as unreasonable conduct attracting a 50% reduction to the amount of FRC.

- Failure to Respond (*p68*). In contrast, if the defendant fails to provide a letter of response on time in the standard track, the case reverts to the *PAP for the Resolution of Clinical Disputes*. Although the case would exit FRC at this point, the rules state that it is the settlement amount which determines whether these tracks apply and the case could still be allocated to the intermediate (or even fast) track after proceedings are commenced.

  Furthermore, there are likely to be disputes where the defendant has requested an extension and the claimant has refused this on the basis that these proposals do not permit it. If the reason is that expert evidence cannot be obtained in time, then an extension may be objectively reasonable. Finally, the claimant will have already limited its costs in complying with the *PAP* so the defendant has already benefited from this.

For the light track, the penalty is that the case transfers to the standard track and the defendant must pay an additional 5% for the stage 1 light track costs. This amounts to £100-£312.50 (once the value of the claim is known) so is likely to be the minimum amount of £87.50 (5% of £1,750) at the point in time when the payment falls due. This does not appear to be a significant penalty.

- Other deadlines (*p68*). Where one party cannot meet a deadline and the parties cannot agree to extend it, the sanction depends on which party defaults. If it is the claimant, they will be penalised by a 50% reduction in the amount of FRC. If it is the defendant, they will pay 50% more.

  In the context of the FRC amounts and schemes, these appear to be quite draconian. It is reasonable to anticipate that there will be an incentive to try to prove fault on the part of the other party to justify non-payment and a reduced incentive to agree justifiable requests. That said, delays reduce profitability and so this may prove to be beneficial overall.

- Failing to use neutral evaluation (*p69*). If the claimant unreasonably refuses to engage with this, they risk losing 50% of their FRC. In contrast, the defendant only stands to face the issue of proceedings and the same considerations as set out above appear to apply if the case settles for less than £25,000 or is allocated to the intermediate (or fast) tracks.

- Failure to accept the evaluation (*p69*). If the claimant disagrees with the evaluator's opinion, then they must beat the amount of damages by >20% at trial. So, if the recommendation is that the value is £15,000, then the claimant must obtain at least £18,001 at trial. If they do not, then they lose 50% of the FRC.

The proposals do not say whether this also applies to settlements. If it does not, then this may leave from for manoeuvre by the claimant. However, where is the incentive for the defendant to agree unless it wants to avoid the issue of proceedings? On top of that, there is nothing to stop the defendant making a *Part 36* offer at (or slightly higher than) the amount the evaluator has recommended safe in the knowledge that it cannot offset its costs if the claimant cannot beat this. If it does apply to settlements, then why would a defendant agree to this unless there is a real risk that the case could enter the multi-track?

There is certainly an argument to see this as providing a significant (and forced) incentive to settle cases. This should be included in any risk assessment from the outset of the case and as the case proceeds.

h. **Section 5.9: Implementation Date.**

The key point here is that the recommendation is that cases which start before the implementation date will not fall within the regime as long as proper notification was provided before the commencement date. The response gives a letter of claim as an example and so this would be prudent to do as long as there is sufficient evidentiary support to justify this. (*p71*).

Letters of claim which do not enjoy such support or which are served close to the implementation date may well be challenged in the same way as CFAs signed shortly before the Jackson reforms commenced on 6th April 2013 were.

If not already done, a decision to serve a letter of claim should be taken by January 2024 if the implementation date is 6th April 2024 (perhaps later if implementation is delayed).

How the Proposals Fall Short

The following 10 points would assist in managing the risks posed by these proposals (and to attain the goals Sir Rupert set out):

1. In any single department, the cost of the successful cases need to outweigh the costs of the unsuccessful ones. If we take an average acceptance rate of 10-15% on new cases and accept that some cases will be rejected either after receipt of the medical records or preliminary reports, then the remaining 36% of cases over £25,000 value need to comfortably exceed the costs of a far higher proportion of cases than the DoH figures suggested. This needs to be factored into any fixed recoverable costs matrix which is produced.

2. It follows from this that practitioners on both sides must have a rigorous risk assessment process in place which is repeated at key points in the case. Whilst this will differ between firms and between each side of the litigation, identifying the key pressure points in the case and reassessing the prospects of success at those points goes a long way to avoiding incurring disproportionate or otherwise irrecoverable costs.

3. The substantive and evidential rules are not being relaxed. Even if adequate procedural rule amendments are made, disclosing expert evidence unilaterally without protecting that party if further evidence comes to light, is inherently unfair. Access to justice and equality of arms ought not relate only to costs.

4. Admissions made under the duty of candour ought to result in early admissions of breach and causation. Too often, they do not with wholly avoidable costs being incurred reinvestigating these issues. Such conduct ought to result in a case being taken outside of any fixed recoverable costs matrix on these issues. More work is needed on building up the trust between each sides' lawyers such that they accept that their opponent has the evidence they say they have.

5. If the case is genuinely one worth under £25,000, then the valuation exercise will often be relatively straight-forward given the availability of the JC Guidelines and reported cases. Both sides ought to be able to identify the appropriate range of settlement based on the evidence to hand. Where there are genuine prognosis issues, these ought to be identified and a plan put in place to deal with them in order to promote settlement. The cases which fall outside of a simplified process need to be identified and allowed to remain in the multi-track.

6. Any fixed recoverable costs scheme needs to include sufficient costs leeway to investigate issues further if additional evidence comes to light. It is not always practical to identify all possible interpretations of the evidence at the letter of claim stage because the defendant's position is not yet known (especially where it has indicated that it does not accept the duty of candour or similar findings). If further evidence comes to light, or a relatively minor issue later attains major significance, then reasonable costs ought to be allowed to deal with it so that the trial court is ultimately assisted.

7. The impugned clinicians' witness statements ought to be taken and disclosed far earlier than is currently done where the defendant seeks to rely on the exact wording of the medical records and/or on that clinician's standard practice. Too often, this evidence is not disclosed until the usual pre-trial direction date. To reciprocate, claimants ought to be more amenable to disclosing their witness evidence where the central liability issues are fact sensitive. Mutual, simultaneous exchange would be a useful step in the pre-issue negotiation period for suitable cases.

8. Experts' fees need to be properly accounted for. A supplementary consultation was also launched in September 2023 to consider the disbursement levels in cases worth <£25,000. Those proposed in the DoH's 2017 scheme were far too low and did not take into account that experts in some fields charge far more than in other areas. Any scheme ought to permit acceptable fees for individual

or groups of disciplines at the usual market rates. Consideration ought to be given to allowing additional costs for each expert discipline which is reasonably required to address the issues in dispute thereby promoting the early, accurate identification of those issues.

9. Better discipline from both sides will be required around experts' joint meetings. Lengthy and/or complex agendas or one side simply trying to insist on its own agenda being used assist no one and should be avoided even at present. Under a fixed recoverable costs system, neither side is likely to recover those costs. They should be allowed to occur pre-action.

10. Both sides will need to avoid getting mired in unnecessary barriers to settlement. In the absence of the substantive law of negligence being simplified, differences of opinion on whether part of a case is likely to succeed at trial will almost certainly persist. Unless both sides are prepared to settle a case on a commercial basis (i.e. the time and expense of running the remaining disputed issues to trial), many cases will continue to appear to be uneconomical or disproportionate. Claimants would need to accept that they get less than they want and defendants need to be prepared to offer compensation on cases they think they will successfully defend.

Practical Steps

As matters presently stand, all included cases which settle for £25,000 or less after the rules come into force are likely to be subject to FRC. Accordingly, it is prudent to consider advising your client on the following matters now:

1. **Review your caseloads.** How many cases are likely to fall within this FRC regime? How confident are you in your quantum evaluations? What is the risk that the settlement value will be less than £25,000?

2. **Should a letter of claim (or other 'notification' of the claim be sent to the defendant before the assumed implementation date (currently 6th April 2024)?** Valid notifications avoid the case falling into the FRC regime. Whilst there is no official guidance as to what amounts to a valid notification, the proposal's explanatory note specifically refers to letters of claim. Thus, a letter of claim complying with the *PAP for the Resolution of Clinical Disputes* is likely to be sufficient. However, letters of claim which are written without the benefit of sufficient evidentiary support may not constitute this. Similarly, anything short of a compliant letter of claim may prove insufficient leading to FRC being held to apply. If you have a genuine reason for not sending a letter of claim, document your advice to your client on file and have it signed off by your supervisor.

3. **Assess how many cases you are likely to have post-implementation that are likely to fall within this FRC regime.** Everything else being equal, they are likely to be similar to what you have now. If so, how will you make your billing target? If you need more cases to do so (this seems likely), is your department geared up to obtaining these through its existing marketing plan? If you believe you will have fewer cases (perhaps your firm will stop accepting these cases), how are you going to get higher value work?

4. **How are you going to accurately decide if a new case falls into the FRC regime or not?** The proposals require the claimant to make this decision and penalises incorrect choices. If you elect for the light or small track but the case turns out to be multi-track, your incurred costs will be lower and you may have missed some crucial piece of evidence or prematurely disclosed expert or factual evidence. Conversely, if you decide that the multi-track is suitable but the case settles for less than £25,000, you risk that file being unprofitable. The answer lies in ensuring that

you have clearly documented your decision-making process and advice on your file. However, this takes additional time which needs to be worked into the amount of FRC you know you will recover.

5. **How are you going to comply with the standard track requirements to disclose your factual and expert evidence on liability and quantum up front?** Evidence which does not fully cover all of the issues is less likely to be accepted by the defendant. If the rules do not require the defendant to make like-for-like disclosure with its letter of response, then claimants' solicitors will not be able to advise their clients as to the strength of the defendant's position. We will only know whether or not they agree with our carefully prepared case. Applying our experience of the pre-FRC rules, we cannot safely assume that the issues will have been properly considered. Logically, defendants only need to state that they disagree with a particular case for the claimant to face significant risk. If NHSR continues to refuse to make commercial offers, then claimants can assume that the defendant has supportive expert evidence but this is an unsafe assumption with no strong evidential basis. One method of reducing this risk would be to ask in an open letter for disclosure of the defendant's like-for-like evidence and the obvious time to do so would be in the letter of claim.

6. **Should your client comply with the standard track requirements?** This is likely to be a vexed question requiring careful consideration. The proposals limit the length of the lay and expert evidence but experience tells us that one size does not fit all situations. They also penalise 'unreasonable behaviour' with a 50% costs penalty and this decision will be taken by the court following an application. Thus, there are significant (and deliberate) costs penalties aimed at ensuring compliance.

This potentially conflicts with our duty to provide independent legal advice. An early decision on whether each expert can discharge their duty to the court in providing their full and independent opinion on all relevant matters within their sphere of expertise whilst complying with the new artificial limits is preferable. Whether it is practical within the FRC straitjacket is a challenge. This must be repeated for each expert and lay witness.

Once the evidence is obtained, a separate decision is required as to whether it is safe to disclose it openly. If you do, then any faults or gaps in the evidence or experts' reasoning is likely to be exposed and difficult to correct later. Accordingly, there is a tranche of situations where not disclosing this evidence is likely to improve the chances of winning the case. These will include situations where there is an incomplete factual matrix (for whatever reason).

Again, carefully documenting your reasoning and advice is likely to be key to avoiding a later finding of unreasonable conduct, as is setting your position to the defendant. Whilst its response should not be discounted out of hand, neither should it be uncritically accepted at face value. As can be seen, this is likely to increase the costs you are incurring leaving less for other aspects of the pre-action process. One possible solution would be to disclose the evidence with the letter of claim but under cover of the Part 36 offer letter on a protected basis (or perhaps even on a wholly 'without prejudice' basis). The proposals do not prevent this as currently worded.

7. **Is it worth making a protective *Part 36* offer at all?** This is likely to be another vexed question. The clear assumption is that cases under £25,000 should settle pre-issue. In a sense, that is reasonable; after all the settlement range is £1,500-£25,000 and a deal should be achievable. However, for as long as NHSR refuses to permit commercial deals, it

is a naïve hope. The reality is that FRC provides a commercial incentive to fight over every pound. Accordingly, we should ask ourselves whether it is in our clients' best interests to make a single realistic offer and never budge from it; to make a high offer and negotiate down; or to make an issue-based offer (or other non-monetary offer). The latter is not precluded by the wording of the proposals. Although 100% offers (and, perhaps, 90%+ offers) are not seen as valid for the purposes of gaining the *Part 36* additional benefits, they are not precluded by the standalone procedural code of *CPR 1998 Part 36*. The proposals do not stipulate that a Part 36 offer is required but do say that the 21-day relevant period is required, and so other settlement offers Thus, in the right circumstances, it may be reasonable to make a settlement offer outside of *Part 36* in the best interests of your client on the particular facts of their case. Again, carefully documenting your decision-making process and advice on file is likely to be crucial.

8. **Who do you want to make these decisions?** You, counsel, costs draftsmen or the court? This may seem trite, but you may be content to leave key decisions to others. If you have prepared the case as best you can within the FRC straitjacket, is it practical to have protracted correspondence with your opponent or experts? Following the processes in the light and standard tracks religiously (and enforcing the time limits) may prove to be the more effective and profitable course of action. Maintaining the decision-making control may prove to be less so. Conversely, every time you leave the decisions to the court, you are taking a 50/50 risk. If you rely on costs draftsmen to deal with FRC arguments then, no matter how excellent they are, they were not involved in the key case progression steps you took and so can only try to use the minutiae of costs law to correct errors retrospectively. Similarly, the proposal's intentions appear to be to exclude counsel from the pre-

issue process. Using them proactively and prospectively therefore risks paying them out of your FRC amount. Using them retrospectively risks them being unable to rectify unforeseen consequences either at all or cost-effectively.

9. **What are your suppliers charging?** Although the response to the separate September/October 2023 disbursements consultation are not yet known, there is little confidence that the status quo will be maintained. As such, medical records pagination, tracing agents and the other organisations claimants' solicitors use all face the spectre of either losing work or adapting to an environment where they get paid less. Market forces may well operate to enforce such change but it is also prudent to have up front conversations with them in advance of needing their services to avoid (or at least minimise) the risk of their fees making your file unprofitable. When doing so, it is advisable to plan for the eventuality that the court may ultimately disagree with you if you believe that their fees should fall within the 'reasonably incurred' cohort of disbursements. It is also prudent to avoid overly exposing your clients to this risk irrespective of any departmental decision outside of your direct control.

10. **How are you planning to win cases profitably pre-action?** We have set out an example of how much time you can spend on FRC cases to remain profitable above. However, to ensure you can do this, you need to have a clear understanding of the steps you need to take to risk assess new enquiries and onboard clients; investigate each case; obtain compliant evidence; respond to unexpected events and requests; deal with objections (reasonable or otherwise); effectively manage the mandatory stocktakes and neutral evaluations; and constructively negotiate monetary settlements (not non-monetary 'resolutions'). This essentially requires you to understand how your mini

processes for each step will work in practice and how you will adapt to changing circumstances. Knowing the overall time you can spend on each case helps to break down the time you can spend on each step and remain profitable. If you 'overspend' in one step, you can pivot to spend less time on another step during the case as long as you remain focussed on (a) how the case will look at trial; and (b) using this to highlight the risk to the defendant to maximise the prospects of getting a fair pre-issue settlement (either from it or the neutral evaluation).

Initial Investigations (Evidence Gathering)

One of the key aspects of successfully managing a FRC caseload within these proposals is likely to be gathering sufficient evidence to persuade the defendant to admit liability in its letter of response. Failing that, the backup objective is to persuade the neutral evaluator (who may or may not have a clinical negligence background. If both of these goals fail, then the further backup objective is to be able to properly plead the particulars claim to win the case at trial without having to undertake significant reappraisals of the case in the pre-trial period. This latter objective is very much a third choice if the new rules cement the punitive proposal that the claimant has to beat the neutral evaluators decision by 20%. This is likely to be less of an issue where liability remains disputed.

1. **Understand the central allegations.** This is crucial to managing the initial investigations profitably and persuasively. The underlying assumption of the FRC proposals is that sub-£25,000 cases settle. The risk is that they will 'resolve' by being abandoned. Having a bullet point summary of what is being alleged on breach, causation and consequential losses from the outset is essential for framing the initial investigations.

2. **Analysing the medical records.** The proposals require that the sorted and paginated 'core' records should be disclosed and experience shows us that defendants are likely to require all of the records. The proposals also assume that chronologies are luxury items which can safely be dispensed with. Knowing the central allegations allows you to review the unpaginated and unsorted records cost effectively in order to identify the core records. These are the records which support or undermine the existing central allegations. This better informs the decision whether to incur the cost of external pagination (which may not be fully recoverable). Some records do come in 'pre-sorted' or even paginated and so this may help. However, such efforts are very unlikely to have been done with reference to the central allegations and so cannot be safely taken at face value. Using part of the limited time under FRC to separate out these core records is therefore likely to be time well spent. The remaining records should be retained in case the defendant request them before standard disclosure occurs and they can pay for any additional sorting and pagination. The proposals do not prevent such costs shifting.

3. **Witness statements.** Justifying your decision as to how many witnesses you need is crucial for both winning the case and proving that the multi-track is the correct track for the case. Understanding the central allegations assists in deciding which witnesses were actually present at the index events and can provide relevant evidence. This includes clinicians who the defendant may not call. Being required to front load the case to the extent required by the proposals means that claimant solicitors should make a positive decision whether to at least attempt to take a statement from clinicians involved in their client's treatment (even impugned clinicians). Evidence of these attempts to do so should be retained to assist later in proceedings if the case does not settle (for example, to give you the option of taking supplementary statements from them after exchange).

Taking unstructured witness statements is a quick method of using up the amount of FRC and using template headings in conjunction with the central allegations minimises this risk. Since we are yet to see the proposed template witness statement, the version currently within the CPR 1998 is likely to be similar to the eventual template.

4. **Selecting & instructing suitable experts.** This is another key decision for the same reasons given for witnesses. It is important to remember that this decision is likely to be subject to considerable scrutiny where the number of experts take the case into the multi-track and so you need to prepare to justify it to a non-specialist procedural judge even where the defendant agrees. More prosaically, the selection of experts needs to be based on their ability to provide internally logical, well-reasoned, persuasive and watertight opinions. There is still a need to review their specific expertise and to be satisfied that it matches the central allegations.

5. **Instructing and reviewing expert evidence.** As a minimum, the expert reports need to objectively assess the central allegations in order to be persuasive. Ideally, they need to predict and discuss the potential reasons the defendant may have for maintaining that the applicable legal standards on breach and causation have been met as well as properly considering the effect of comorbidities and previous medical history. In the current climate, it is also likely that experts will also need to consider the impact of generic factual matters related to the ability of the impugned clinicians to provide treatment to the requisite standard (in light of the pressures on the NHS). In order to try to plan for this, options include requesting this factual evidence with the medical records and instructing your experts to set out what evidence they would need from the defendant to address these issues.

6. **Quantum evidence.** Understanding the central allegations on causation of consequential losses assists in focussing the investigation as to what documents are required. These are likely to be documents which are relevant to the individual heads of loss alleged to have been suffered by the claimant. Documents in the possession of third parties are likely to be potential money pits especially where they are not released without a court order (as with police reports). The more that the claimant can provide themselves, the better. As with the medical records, reviewing these ocumentts in light of the central allegations is the most cost-effective method.

Ongoing Risk Assessments

Given the limited amount of time that can be spent under the proposed FRC regime, it might be supposed that undertaking ongoing risk assessments is counterproductive in maintaining profitability.

From one perspective, this might be correct. Once the case has been accepted, then there is little incentive to build WIP and further risk assessments may not appear to be progressive. On the other hand, incurring costs on unmeritorious cases or incorrectly assuming that the case is a multi-track case, reduces to profitability of that case and undermines your financial performance overall.

Accordingly, ongoing risk assessments at these stages are likely to be a constructive use of the available FRC amounts:

1. The initial decision to accept the case considering the viability of the central allegations;

2. Testing the central allegations against the medical records and witness statements;

3. Testing the central allegations against the expert evidence;

4. Testing the central allegations against the expert evidence;

5. Testing the central allegations against the letter of response;

6. Testing the central allegations against the counter-offer; and

7. Testing the central allegations against the neutral evaluation.

These individual risk assessments do not need to be lengthy, they do need to accurately assess the risks as they stand at that stage, however. If proceedings are required, then the risks need reassessing at regular intervals as case management stages are reached. Each risk assessment needs to account for the amount of costs incurred and the amount of FRC remaining for that stage.

Not all cases that were reasonable to accept under the previous rules will remain so, A useful rule of thumb is to consider whether the amount of unrecovered costs is likely to exceed the amount of FRC, success fee and any agreed payment to cover this shortfall. If it is not, then the case is probably one which should not be accepted.

Different lawyers and firms will have different risk appetites and so it would be imprudent to suggest that some sub-disciplines of clinical negligence will be inherently disproportionate to accept. However, those areas which require additional amounts of client care; have complex factual matrices; are 'document heavy'; or which have uncertain treatment standards are likely to be less well-suited to FRC and so there are increased risks of access to justice being reduced in these areas.

Evaluating Quantum

For the most part, claimant lawyers are not used to accurately valuing cases before sending the letter of claim because (a) the evidence is usually incomplete; and (b) ATE insurance products do not cover the cost of expert C&P evidence before liability has been resolved pre-action.

However, the proposed FRC regime seeks to make this mandatory. The following guidance may assist:

1. Accurately assessing quantum as exceeding £25,000 (including litigation risks) before you incur significant costs justifiably takes the case out of the FRC regime.

2. Relevant factors include the severity of the initial injury; the severity of the ongoing symptoms; whether the length of the recovery is more than 2-3 years; the extent of loss of earnings and/or gratuitous care; the actual and observable impact on the claimant's day-to-day life; and the existence of clearly identifiable heads of loss (and their relative recoverability at law).

3. The availability of supporting documentary evidence and whether the cost of obtaining and analysing it is proportionate to the value of that head of loss. For example, the documents required for a self-employed worker are harder to analyse than for an employee and the approach to be taken needs careful planning.

4. The existence of clear guidance in the JC Guidelines and of close case comparators. The greater the ambiguity, the harder it will be to secure the best possible settlement.

5. The extent to which the alleged impact on the claimant is consistent with the average person's response to that injury. Whilst everyone is different and pain is subjective, consequences which appear to be unusual increase the risk that allegations of fundamental dishonesty will be made later in the case.

Whilst investigating quantum thoroughly is prudent and may take the case out of this FRC regime, there is a greater commercial incentive for defendants to challenge the assumptions and evidence submitted. Since the proposals apply to settlement value, it is prudent to reduce your exposure to having cases potentially within the £25,000 limit if possible but to be able to negotiate a settlement promptly if the risk seems likely to materialise. Accepting cases with prospective values of say £30,000, £50,000 or £100,000 does serve to minimise the initial risk but does not exclude it and reduces the amount of incoming cases.

Conclusion

The *Civil Procedure (Amendment No. 2) Rules 2023* have taken the concept of FRC and the structure of its costs stages from Sir Rupert Jackson's *Report* but without including the safeguards.

While it is still unclear whether (and in what precise form) these rules will actually come into force, we surely should start working towards them as if they are going to affect us. This is a crucial point because there is a significant risk that, suddenly, all of our cases that are going to settle for less than £25,000 and where the letter of claim has not been sent prior to April 2024 (or other implementation date) will be affected.

While it is our advice that you should draft suitable letters of claim for existing cases, it is also crucial to filter all new cases that come in to establish whether it is profitable to run the claim or not and to have a solid strategy in place to win these cases profitably.

The points to consider that have been discussed above and ultimately while it will be the choice of the firm itself, access to justice will inevitably be affected in a more than unfair way.

While it is still unclear whether these rules will actually come into force, we surely should start working towards them as if they are going to affect us. This is crucial point because suddenly, all of our cases that are going to settle for less than £25,000 and where the letter of claim has not been sent prior to April 2024 will be affected.

While it is our advice that you should start working towards drafting those letters of claim, it is also crucial to filter all new cases that come in to establish whether it is profitable to run the claim or not.

Ultimately, while it will be the choice of the firm itself, access to justice will inevitably be affected in an unfair way from the claimants' perspective.

CHAPTER FOUR

CASES OF OVER £100,000 VALUE

Introduction

In previous chapters, we have already looked at the cases that are worth up to £100,000 and how we should deal with them. However, what if the case value is still unknown, and/or what if it seems that the case value is just slightly above £100,000 – is there a risk that it can still be caught by FRC?

Unfortunately, the answer is 'yes'. However, the reality is much more complicated than can be described by a simple *'yes'* or *'no'* answer, and hence why we will be discussing what might happen with the cases that are 'borderline' in this chapter below.

Where do I start?

A good starting point is to value your claim as early as possible. Yes, it is almost contradictory to what we have discussed already because we did express empathy with trying to value your cases early, as this can never result in any precision. However, what we have learnt too is that, in order to be able to deal with FRC, we will have to put some sort of figure – whether we want this or not. Accordingly, it better to be as good a shot as one can.

Once you know what the value is (a rough estimate is fine), you can then see if, in case all of the conditions are met, the case would fall outside of the multi-track. In this instance, we are talking about the cases where the settlement value is lower than £100,000 even though it was believed to be worth more during the case.

What to do next?

Once you have estimated how much your case is worth, you need to decide how certain this is. Depending on how confident you are that the case is worth much more than £100,000, you will need to proceed investigating it using either multi-track or FRC principles. You will later need to confirm what the value actually is.

We all know from practice that the case value can change based on, for example, an expert's report that is not as supportive as you might have thought or on your client not providing information that you thought they might have. Weak links in the chain of causation are another significant risk factor.

Therefore, until you have all the evidence and are sure about your case value, you will not be able to *'relax and enjoy'* dealing with the case knowing that it will not be caught under the FRC. Overconfidence is a trap door leading to disappointment.

If nothing else, remember that trial judges tend to take a broad-brush approach to valuing cases and such deductions can often have dramatic percentage deductions to quantum. A £135,000 case can suddenly become an £80,000 case.

Cases worth over £500,000

If you think at the very start that your case is worth more than £500,000, the chances that the case will fall under FRC are very low. Even on a broad-brush approach, you would need to see a deduction of 80% or more. Unfortunately, there is still a chance in these cases that some evidence comes in that might reduce the case value significantly. Examples include fundamental dishonesty allegations, weak links in the initial chain of causation or multiple challenges to the heads of loss.

In that case you should consider whether, for example, if the expert's report is only partly supportive, that there is a chance you will still run the claim in the same 'multi-track' way. If there is a claim to be run even if a part of the evidence is supportive, then the risk increases of the case being caught under FRC later on.

However, overall, the risk in this instance where the case value is estimated to exceed £500,000 is relatively low and you should be able to run the case as if it falls outside of FRC. This is particularly so if you have had a chance to reevaluate your case after all of the evidence has been reviewed etc.

Cases worth less than £500,000 (but more than £100,000)

If you think that the case is going to be worth less than £500,000, then the risk that it might as well settle for as close to or even lower than £100,000 is much more likely than you might think.

Considering all the points raised above that relate to e.g. your expert evidence not being as supportive, etc. there is always a risk that your case value might settle for much less than what you have originally thought.

If you have come to the conclusion about the case being worth more than £100,000 after you have obtained your expert reports and/or evaluated the rest of the evidence, then you might be in a much better position to actually set the boundaries and expectations as to how this could go. Otherwise, you will want to be careful still and expect that the case value might still drop. There is a high risk of these cases being good targets for applications to reallocate or reassign where the evidence changes or issues are narrowed.

Defendant's Case Valuation

We are aware that experience shows that it is rather difficult to say how much the defendant might value the case for early on. This is not a conversation you are likely to have with the defendant or their solicitors – unless it suits them. Even where we have asked them proactively for their final or borderline figure, there is no requirement or incentive for them to do so before the evidence is complete. It is unlikely that they would tell us the real position under FRC rules which do not compel them to do so (see Chapters 2 & 3).

As solicitors, we cannot start 'spying' on our opponents. However, it will be important to estimate what the defendant might say on valuation more than ever in the new FRC regime. This is because, if you think that they are likely to disagree with your case valuation (and argue against it later) then is it not reasonable to ask yourself whether, perhaps, that this should be taken into account?

You might be aware of such things from their responses, from practice as to what things they tend to argue about and are not willing to compensate for, from their first offers etc. The earlier we can anticipate what they might think, the better. Accordingly, using part of the available costs allowance (whether FRC or 'multi-track') to ask the right questions in order to build up useful evidence is a pragmatic use of your time.

This is because, if you want to settle the case sooner than later, having the best information should result in you advising your client more confidently to accept the defendant's offer or make one closer to your proposed figures. If you end up settling for less than £100,000, and the case is caught under FRC, you have a much better chance of maintaining profitability.

This again would be the scenario where liability has been admitted in full, which means that there would have been an admission on the injuries suffered. If this admission covers at least the one that related to the arguments made within the causation issues, then the rest could be disputed. If what is left arguably falls outside of the multi-track, FRC could apply retrospectively if you have not planned to head this off.

If the case settles for much lower than what you anticipated and/or what the case is worth on its full value, then it is more likely to have a disputed issue with liability and so would fall outside of the interim track even if the case value is below £100,000. If these cases must indeed be allocated to the multi-track, then FRC does not apply (but see Chapter 2).

Therefore, while it is important to take into account of any counter arguments that you can think of when valuing the case, the weight give to what the defendant might think may not always be too high overall. It is good to collect all of the necessary facts and then see whether there would be some fundamental issues. However, even if the defendant has admitted liability then you still remain less in control (under the FRC regimes) and so should trust what you think the case value is based on the evidence you have and the applicable litigation risks to retain as much control as you can.

Defendant's Position

Liability Admitted and you have some indication regarding their case valuation

If the defendant has admitted liability and you know that they are likely to argue that the case is worth less than £100,000, the chances of the case being caught under FRC is higher. This is because there is a risk that either the claimant will choose to accept their offer (that will be lower than £100,000) or you making an offer that is lower than £100,000 to settle the case. This is of course not necessarily going to be the case, but the defendant might push for this to happen, because they will be aware that if they do settle for anything below £100,000, the case will be dealt with under FRC.

If you think they consider the case to be worth above £100,000, then the chances are lower for the case to be caught under FRC (subject to what we have said above).

Liability Admitted but have no indication regarding their case valuation

If the defendant admitted liability but you do not know their position on case value, then you will have to trust your own case valuation.

If the case is valued to be worth more than £100,000, then the chances are lower that the claim will be caught under FRC. However, there is still a risk that if the case value is borderline or just over £100,000 that the defendant will push for this to settle below £100,000 for the case to automatically then fall under FRC. Therefore, the chances are still relatively high.

Liability denied

If liability is denied, (e.g. either both breach of duty and causation, or either one is being denied), then the chances of the case being caught under the FRC are low despite the value you think the defendant has valued the claim at. There is a risk that the ambiguity in the rules mean that more limited admissions may also be sufficient to trigger the intermediate track, however (see Chapter 2).

Liability status is unknown but you have some indication regarding their case valuation

If the defendant has not yet admitted liability and/or has not formally denied it, then you are at risk that liability could be admitted, and so if you also have an indication that the case is valued to be below £100,000 by the defendant, then the risk is higher for the case to be caught under FRC. The Summer 2023 consultation response may confirm that a full admissions must be made in the letter of response for cases to qualify for the intermediate track but delays in receiving the letter of response remain likely. It may prove plausible to argue that failing to serve a letter of response within 4 months is a relevant matter supporting allocation to the multi-track.

If you know that the defendant thinks the case is worth above £100,000, then despite liability status, the risk of the case being caught under FRC remains low (at least at the CMC/allocation hearing).

If you know that they are likely to argue that the case is worth less than £100,000, the chances of the case being caught under FRC is high. This is because there is a risk that either the claimant will choose to accept their offer that will be lower than £100,000 or of you making an offer that is lower than £100,000 to settle the case. This is of course not necessarily going to be the case, but the defendant might push for this to happen, because they will be aware that if they do settle for anything below £100,000, the case will be dealt with under FRC.

If you think they consider the case to be worth above £100,000, then the chances are lower for the case to be caught under FRC.

Liability status is unknown and you have no indication regarding their case valuation

If the defendant has not yet admitted liability and/or has not formally denied it, then you are at risk that liability could be admitted, and you have no indication as to what they might think about the case value, then the risk of the case being caught under FRC is high and will remain high until you know their liability status and/or any indication of the case value that they might put to this case.

The table below summarises the risks of the case being caught by FRC rules depending on the defendant's position.

Defendant's Position			
Liability Status ↓ **Indications re Case Value→**	**Yes, below £100,000**	**Yes, above £100,000**	**No indication**
Admitted	Chances of the case being caught under FRC is **high.**	Chances of the case being caught under FRC is **low.**	Chances of the case being caught under FRC is **high.**

Denied	Chances of the case being caught under FRC is **low.**	Chances of the case being caught under FRC is **low.**	Chances of the case being caught under FRC is **low.**
Unknown	Chances of the case being caught under FRC is **high.**	Chances of the case being caught under FRC is **low.**	Chances of the case being caught under FRC is **high.**

Should I ask?

While this has not been something we normally do and/or ask, you might be wondering if it is worth asking the defendant the same question they always ask us – please provide evidence regarding case value.

The thing is that the defendant will be at disadvantage here because until we do provide them with the evidence we have and the schedules we prepare etc. they can have only a very rough idea as to how much the case could be worth.

However, what might change is to ask them of their case valuations in admitted cases where causation issues are clear. You might attempt to seek an agreement regarding pain, suffering and loss of amenity (PSLA) related to causation issues and have any other discussions related to ongoing problems and/or special damages for later. At least at that point you could have some indication that may, or may not, help you when going forward. As far as is possible, it is better to know this in advance, rather than shortly before the CMC/Allocation hearing.

As a big majority of a case valuation is usually special damages, it might be difficult to get the answers you want by agreeing on PSLA. However, if the injuries are severe then this might really help. This could be even the case where the PSLA is 'only' £70-80k, but if it is agreed with the defendant that this is to be your bottom line, then you are in a stronger position to prove (in case there is a bigger claim related to e.g, treatment costs, etc.) that the case is unlikely to fall under FRC.

At the end of the day it is all about collecting relevant information and trying to see if any of that can help you when deciding whether you should work as if the case is being dealt with under the FRC, or not.

Making a difference

When valuing clinical negligence claims with a potential value of over £100,000, claimants' solicitors should focus on those areas which are likely to persuasively tip the balance at trial. These issues include:

1. **Severity of Injuries:**

    - Emphasize the severity of the injuries suffered by the claimant, particularly if they result in long-term or permanent disability, impairment, or pain and suffering.

2. **Breach and Causation:**

    - Establish clear evidence of each breach and the probable causal link between them and the avoidable injuries sustained and losses incurred.

3. **Medical Expert Opinions:**

    - Ensure that the expert opinions fully consider all aspects of the claim, including assessments of the extent and impact of the injuries. Ask them to consider whether reports from experts in other medical and non-medical disciplines will assist them.

4. **Long-Term Care Costs:**

    - Calculate and document the future costs of medical treatment, rehabilitation, and ongoing care that the claimant will require. Consider whether a care expert is required.

5. **Loss of Earnings:**

    - Assess the claimant's past and future loss of earnings, taking into account any career limitations and lost promotions resulting from the injuries.

6. **Specialist Equipment and Accommodations:**

    - Include costs for necessary specialised equipment, home modifications, or accommodation required due to the injuries. Consider whether expert evidence from physiotherapists, occupational therapists or similar disciplines is required.

7. **Pain and Suffering:**

    - Highlight the evidence of the physical and emotional pain and suffering endured by the claimant, as this is a significant component of compensation. Relate this as closely to known case comparators and the JC Guidelines as possible.

8. **Loss of Enjoyment of Life:**

    - Articulate how the injuries have affected the claimant's quality of life, including their ability to enjoy hobbies, social activities, and relationships.

9. **Psychological and Emotional Distress:**

    - Document any psychological or emotional distress, such as anxiety, depression, or post-traumatic stress disorder, and seek compensation for it.

10. **Rehabilitation and Therapy Costs:**

    - Detail the expenses associated with rehabilitation, therapy, counselling, and any other interventions aimed at improving the claimant's condition. Consider whether a rehabilitation expert is required.

11. **Future Medical Expenses:**

    - Project and substantiate future medical expenses, including surgeries, medications, and ongoing treatments.

12. **Expert Witnesses:**

    - Allocate time to carefully cross-referencing the expert reports to ensure that all of the issues regarding the extent of their injuries (and the necessary care and other consequences arising from them) have been fully explained.

13. **Precedent Cases:**

    - Research and reference similar cases with high-value settlements or awards to strengthen the argument for adequate compensation. Refer to established legal precedents and relevant case law that support the valuation and potential compensation levels for similar cases.

14. **Detailed Schedules:**

    - Prepare comprehensive quantum reports that outline all heads of loss and their associated costs. You can expect the counter-schedule to seek to minimise the value of the claim so prepare to head those arguments off.

15. **Miscellaneous Costs:**

    - Carefully consider the costs of items and expenses which have been missed from the other heads of damage and ensure these are factored into the overall claim value.

16. **Early Negotiations:**

    - Engage in settlement negotiations with the defendant or their insurer at an early stage, leveraging the strength of the case to achieve a favourable outcome.

By focusing on these critical issues, you enhance your chances of building a compelling case and effectively value clinical negligence claims with a potential value exceeding £100,000, aiming to secure fair and just compensation for your clients. By doing so, it will be easier to see off potential allegations that the case value has been inflated to avoid FRC applying.

Conclusion

Some strategy points to take away is that it is going to be important to not only value the cases at the start, but to constantly re-evaluate them if new evidence is going to come in. We consider more in Chapter 9.

It is worth introducing new templates for letters to the defendants not only informing them about the case by way of early notification letter but also letting them know of the estimated case value and how it changes. In addition, it might be worth also asking them what is their position both liability and case value and what is likely to be disputed booking at the initial information provided by us.

All of this information is designed to help you to determine whether the case falls outside of the FRC where the claims are borderline i.e. worth roughly less than £150,000. The new rules allow either party to apply to the court for reallocation and reassignment where the position changes. (see Chapters 2 & 3). In such cases, you could find yourself subject to

FRC even where you have justifiably incurred costs under the usual multi-track processes.

CHAPTER FIVE

LESSONS FROM PI FRC

Introduction

Although FRC is new to clinical negligence lawyers, PI lawyers have been grappling with it for years. Given the overlap between these two areas, many of the potential solutions and tactics which the nascent fixed costs practitioner might be considering have already been tested before the courts.

Learning from others is our greatest resource, using their knowledge and lessons in order to use the same methods yourself whilst avoiding the same mistakes tips the odds in your favour. To quote *Sun Tzu* (*'The Art of War'*), *"[w]hen envying another's success, find out exactly what they have done to achieve it. Thereby you will discover the necessary qualities and ability required for success."*

As a result, in this chapter we shall discuss the struggles that PI lawyers have been dealing with over the years and what we could take away from that. This would be relevant to all future clinical negligence claims that could be caught by FRC (both for the cases worth below £25,000 and those that could be considered suitable for intermediate track).

Similarities & Differences

In seeking guidance from existing case law, it is important to remember that we are not necessarily comparing like with like. The PI FRC rules have gone through several iterations and there are several different processes which relate to different types of PI. Lower value clinical negligence claims will have their own regime but even with the October 2023 rules, clinical negligence remains apart from general PI.

Intermediate track FRC probably only relate to clinical negligence cases where 'early', 'full' admissions of breach and causation have been made. Even with this smaller cohort of affected cases, not all within the financial range qualify and there are still exceptions within the rules. But therein lies one of the most important lessons we can learn from PI; *viz.* whether the exceptions are merely mirages which, like a will-o-the-wisp, tempt the unwary into the nearest caliginous bog.

The broader issue to be wary of is the propensity of paying parties to seek to avoid paying more than the minimum the law requires them to. This is certainly not a new issue and no one should be criticised for seeking to limit their client's costs exposure. However, there has been an extraordinary amount of satellite litigation focussing on this. The problem that this creates for claimants is that the increased chances of unrecovered costs, uncertainty and delayed payments make FRC seem even more of a bad deal. This tends to speed up the 'race to the bottom' where cutting corners in order to keep within the FRC amounts appears sensible. However, clinical negligence is proportionately more complex than comparable PI cases. It may be thought that greater complexity will suffice to justify moving outside of FRC. Given the types of cases that are deemed suitable for FRC, this may well be a very unsafe assumption to make. How exactly are the remaining issues likely to be different from a comparable PI case in the £25,000-£100,000 range?

Swings & Roundabouts

Added to this is the surprising concept of measuring the case the court is hearing against a notional basket of other clinical negligence cases. This notional basket is just that; it is entirely mythical and infinite. It has never been formally defined nor its limits delineated. Yet, in order to support your client's position when challenging aspects of FRC, you probably need to understand how your particular case compares to the 'average' case in order to persuade the judge to exercise their discretion in your client's favour.

Sharp v Leeds City Council [2017] EWCA Civ 33 provides the authority in this area. The context was set out by *Briggs LJ* at *para. 1*:

> *"While the difference of a little less than £1,000 may appear modest as the casus belli for successive vigorously contested appeals, the issue gives rise to important practical consequences in terms of the costs/benefit of making PAD applications in small personal injuries claims of this kind, so that it is entirely understandable that this question has been pursued by way of a second appeal in order to obtain an authoritative determination of the point."*

We can infer from this that FRC does nothing to prevent a litigant with deep pockets from pursuing a point well beyond what would be considered reasonable or proportionate for that individual case (especially where it stands to gain a longer-term benefit from obtaining a legal precedent). This is in stark contrast with the individual clinical negligence claimant who has no such wider interest.

PAD applications are far more common in PI cases than clinical negligence ones (where the claimant's medical records are routinely disclosed). Accordingly, as clinical negligence lawyers, we may be forgiven for not understanding the wider implications. As is common in PI cases of this type, the disclosure only occurred after the PAD application was issued but before the hearing. The need for the application arose because the defendant had breached its pre-action disclosure obligations under the applicable protocol. The general question at issue was whether claimants' costs fell inside or outside of the FRC regime. If they fell within it, no costs were recoverable (because they had not been included within the allowable FRC costs) but if they fell without then costs would be summarily assessed. It was also possible that costs recovery could be permitted relying on 'exceptional circumstances' if FRC applied.

Briggs LJ held that FRC *"plainly applies"* to PAD applications (*para. 30*). From the point of entry into the FRC process *"... the...recovery of the costs...at all subsequent stages is intended to be limited to the fixed rates of recoverable costs, subject only to a very small category of clearly stated exceptions"* (*para. 31*). The relevant rules clearly set out what was recoverable and that these were *"the only costs allowed"* (*para. 32*).

Exposing recalcitrant defendants to a variable level of recoverable costs was not the answer. The answer is to either decide whether 'exceptional circumstances' exist or to await the Rules Committee to increase the FRC amounts (*para. 39*). However, the usefulness of the 'exceptional circumstances' test was immediately reduced: *"[i]t may well be that the frequency with which defendants fail to comply with their Protocol disclosure may make it difficult to pass the exceptional circumstances hurdle...although I would not regard deliberate disregard of those obligations as unexceptional just because it was frequently encountered"* (*para. 40*). No guidance was provided as to when this conduct would be seen as exceptional.

Furthermore (*para. 41*, our emphasis):

> *"By contrast, to throw open PAD applications generally to the recovery of assessed costs would in my view be to risk giving rise to an undesirable form of satellite litigation in which there would be likely incentives for the incurring of disproportionate expense, which is precisely what the fixed costs regime,* ***viewed as a whole****, is designed to avoid.* ***The fixed costs regime inevitably contains swings and roundabouts****, and lawyers who assist claimants by participating in it are accustomed to taking the rough with the smooth, in pursuing legal business which is profitable overall."*

A reasonable inference here is that the wording of the rules created an entirely hidden trap for claimants. Ordinarily, breaches of the rules are punishable in costs because they undermine the proportionate resolution of cases. The FRC rules did not say otherwise. The amounts of costs that were being awarded were modest and were no deterrent to defaults occurring repeatedly. They amounted to a 'slap on the wrist'. However, the FRC rules did not expressly include PAD costs as recoverable and, coupled with the desire to reduce costs, this proved fatal. Moreover, the only penalty for default was removed in order to facilitate this outcome.

From a clinical negligence perspective, the most worrying aspect is perhaps that the ubiquitous nature of the default effectively prevented the conduct being 'exceptional'. Regularly ignoring mandatory pre-action protocol was not to be penalised by permitting costs in excess of the FRC amount (which simply ignored the issue). Where poor conduct is the norm, it is not the exception. Primacy is given to reducing costs. Let that sink in.

The rules and established practice can lead you to believe that an exception will help you deal with poor conduct. You only have to spend money on the application costs to get it. However, too late you find that the rules mean something entirely different and you have lost out. You have fallen into the caliginous bog.

If failing to follow the rules is not exceptional, what about other behaviours which increase your costs? Whether you are persuaded that this drama will play out in your particular case is largely immaterial. What is important is recognising the *risk* that it will. Each loss reduces the profitability of your firm's FRC work and each firm can only sustain unprofitable work for so long. The courts, however, only see each loss very differently; just one more addition to the notional and infinite basket of cases FRC says exists to make the regime fair overall. There is no real reason to see 'swings and roundabouts' as being limited to PAD applications.

'Satellite Litigation'

Here, we are using this term in a general sense to cover applications which fall outside of what is needed to win the case. The purpose is usually ancillary to the central issues and the effect (perhaps unintentionally) is to drain the profit margin on these cases. As such, satellite litigation is 'undesirable' (especially to the claimant). The courts do not always use consistent definitions and this can make some case reports seem confusing.

On the face of it, disputing the amount to be paid seems counter-intuitive. If the amount of FRC is 'fixed', how can there be a dispute?

This issue tends to arise where the parties disagree over what the rules allow to be recoverable. We saw this in one respect in *Sharp (supra)* in relation to the costs of PAD applications.

What happens when the parties cannot agree on this? More relevantly, how does the claimant resolve the issue without losing money? In *Nema v Kirkland [2019] EWHC B15 (Costs), Master Leonard* considered whether commencing assessment proceedings was reasonable. The alternative method was to have issued an application. The amount in dispute was £564 in disbursements (*para. 25*). From the claimant's perspective, this made the difference between claiming an additional £1,500 + VAT against £250 + VAT (in addition to the recoverable disbursements) (*para. 35*). It is illustrative of the technical nature of these arguments that both sides submissions were based on detailed analysis of the fixed costs rules and the interaction with *CPR 1998 Part 36* and that the claimant's submissions were supported by three Court of Appeal decisions.

Despite being unpersuaded by either side's submissions on how 'non-fixed' disbursements should be categorised (*para. 48*), *Master Leonard* nonetheless concluded that the claimant's interpretation of the rules amounted to a disproportionate approach *"...adding as it does a significant layer of potential additional cost, in this case to a dispute over £564"* (*para. 55*). In addition, *"...the Claimant's interpretation of the rules could render CPR 36.20 largely redundant. It could also lead to inconsistency"* (*para. 58*). As such, the notice of commencement was struck out, most likely leading to the profit margin from this case being either eroded or extinguished entirely.

There were several considerations held to be determinative here when considering the viability of a proposed solution: its relative proportionality; its ancillary effects; and its congruency. These can be seen as coalescing into a single maxim; *viz.* that the court is likely to accept the most parsimonious solution. This is relevant to whether or not incurring disbursements (such as additional counsel's fees outside of those expressly permitted) are recoverable.

In terms of our ability to plan for this, it is also noteworthy that *Master Howarth* (and the defendant) drew support from the earlier costs case of *Mughal v Samuel Higgs & EUI Ltd (SCCO, unreported 6 October 2017)* where the notice of commencement had been struck out. Since such cases are not published, the practice points that can be drawn from them not readily available to us.

Both *Nema* and *Mughal* were cited in *Doyle v M&D Foundations & Building Services Ltd [2022] EWCA Civ 927*. Settlement had been reached by a consent order (as opposed to accepting a *Part 36* offer). The order contained a provision for costs to be subject to detailed assessment. The defendant submitted that "*...it was inherently improbable that [it] would have agreed to pay standard basis costs when the fixed costs regime was likely to be much more favourable to the paying party*" (*para. 43*). Nonetheless, the Court of Appeal disagreed.

Objectively. there was no inherent ambiguity in the ordinary meaning of the phrase used and it was imputed that experienced solicitors should be aware of both the meaning of legal terminology and that fixed costs can be disapplied by agreement (i.e. you can 'contract out' of FRC) (*paras. 49-51*). Since the case did not conclude under *CPR 1998 Part 36*, "*...the parties intentions are not to be understood in that highly restrictive context.*" The apparently similar *Adelekun v Ho [2019] EWCA Civ 1988* (now see *Adelekun v Ho [2021] UKSC 43*) could therefore be distinguished (thereby avoiding incongruency). Accordingly, there was "*[n]o such fetter on the application of the natural and ordinary meaning of the agreed wording as to costs arises in the present case, where the parties reached a free-standing settlement agreement. That agreement included a simple and well-understood provision that the appellant would pay the costs subject to detailed assessment*" (all at *para. 56*). Thus, the 'least parsimonious' approach was achieved by not imputing additional meaning into a common phrase where there was no evidence of mistake. Since they had contracted out of fixed costs, the 'proportionality' of the solution within the FRC regime was effectively irrelevant.

Accordingly, it should not prove surprising if a defendant objects to a consent order using this phrase. It may also object to a consent order at all in light of the *CPR 1998 Part 36* provisions and it is possible that an avoidable argument could arise if you have a consent order which conflicts with *Part 36*.

In *Soares v Wilson (2022, unreported)*, the claimant accepted a settlement offer which said fixed costs would be paid but required a *Part 36* offer (which cannot include costs). It was not entitled to seek costs in excess of the FRC amount and, here, the *Part 36* offer merely ratified the earlier settlement offer. This is consistent with *Doyle, Ho, Nema & Mughal* (all *supra*) in that *CPR 1998 Part 36* creates its own, restrictive microcosm which does not allow 'contracting out' of FRC. The *CPR Committee's October 2023 Minutes* indicate that *CPR 1998, Rule 45.13* may be amended to expressly permit this and its *November 2023 Minutes* formally made this recommendation,

McGreevy v Kiramba [2022] EWHC 2561 (SCCO), contains a set of facts which seem to be more relevant to what could well be encountered in clinical negligence cases which settle before allocation.

Liability was admitted pre-action and settlement occurred after service of the particulars of claim and the provisional allocation but before final allocation. The defendant initially made a *Part 36* offer of £50,000 before serving its defence. After filing its directions questionnaire (confirming that the case was suitable for the multi-track), it made two offers on the same day: a *Part 36* offer of £75,000 and a 'time-bomb' Calderbank offer of £100,000 but with fixed costs only (although it called it a *Part 36* offer). The claimant countered with purported acceptance of the Calderbank offer plus legal costs shortly before it expired. The defendant then made a further *Part 36* offer for £100,000. This was accepted on the basis that costs would be recovered on the standard basis. The defendant responded saying that it had made it clear that the £100,000 was contingent on FRC applying (*paras. 12 & 15-20*) and that it had not therefore 'contracted out' fixed costs. Accordingly, there was no agreement as there had been in *Doyle (supra)*.

The claimant disagreed but also sought recovery of its costs on the standard basis using the procedure for claiming an amount exceeding fixed costs pursuant to *CPR 1998, Rule 45.29J* (i.e. 'exceptional circumstances') because both parties had confirmed that the case was suitable for the multi-track in their directions questions

Master Leonard held that the parties had 'contracted in' to FRC when the claimant accepted the Calderbank offer. The claimant could have used different wording but did not (*para. 30*). The use of "without prejudice' save as to costs' did not protect them (*para. 31*). Whether or not the later *Part 36* offer formalised this agreement (as an alternative to a consent order) was unnecessary to determine (*para. 33*). Accordingly, the claimant had also agreed to accept the amounts of fixed costs set out in the rules (*para. 36*). *Master Leonard*'s comments on the relevance of allocation are concerning: "*... given that this case was likely to be allocated to the multi-track there was every incentive for the Defendant to make a pre-allocation offer which might persuade the Claimant to settle on the basis that only fixed costs would be recoverable" (para. 39).*

The position as regards whether 'exceptional circumstances' applied is more nuanced from our perspective. On the one hand, "*...the only real ground given for exceptionality is that before allocation this case was considered, by all concerned, as suitable for the multi-track. To treat that in itself as a sufficient reason for a finding of exceptionality would be inconsistent with the express provisions of CPR 45.29B and would fall into the error identified in Qadar v Esure [Services Ltd [2016] EWCA Civ 1109 of disapplying the fixed costs regime before allocation" (para. 63).*

On the other hand, this is not directly applicable to clinical negligence cases because these do not start within a FRC regime. The case needs to 'qualify' for FRC and is not formally within the regime until allocation. This is the opposite scenario to *McGreevy*. However, this case cannot be safely ignored entirely because fixed costs can be 'contracted into'. Conversely, it (at least *prima facie*) appears to suggest that it is wrong to contend that FRC applies because a case would probably be allocated to the intermediate track.

It appears that parties can still agree to 'contract out' of FRC under *The Civil Procedure (Amendment No 2) Rules 2023. CPR 1998, Rule 44.1* now simply states: *"'fixed costs' means costs, the amounts to which are to be fixed by these Rules."* *Doyle* was decided under *CPR 1998, Part 44* rather than the fixed costs rules under *CPR 1998, Part 45* (*para. 52*). However, it is highly questionable as to why any properly advised defendant would do so. The *CPR Committee's November 2023 Minutes (para. 20)* made it clear that its intention is that the parties can contract out of FRC. As such, it is prudent for practitioners to be aware of the relevant case law.

Procedural Battlegrounds

It is apparent that the substantive, evidential and procedural law has not been simplified as Sir Rupert Jackson suggested. PI litigation is replete with instances of points being taken on issues which should be agreed if costs reduction via collaboration was the central aim of both sides of the profession. Clinical negligence may face a similar vista notwithstanding the increase in collaboration seen in recent years.

The reason for this is that FRC creates a commercial incentive not to collaborate on an equal footing. Once breach and causation has been admitted, the defendant knows that it will be paying a fixed amount of legal costs. It controls when to do this up to the point of allocation. Whilst it still has some measure of uncertainty over disbursements and the ATE premium, it knows that amount the claimant's solicitor can recover. It also knows that 'exceptional circumstances' are hard to prove and that it can now offset its costs against the claimant's costs if the claim fails to beat its *Part 36* offer. Neutrally, these measures are intended to promote earlier settlement. A (possibly) unintended consequence, however, is that putting the claimant's solicitors to extra work if it does not agree with the defendant's position makes each case less profitable for them. If the claimant has used up their fixed costs before the case settles, they are then working at a loss.

There is therefore the chance (or risk, depending on your perspective) that the case settles for less than it would have done. Greater complexity is inversely proportional to reduced profitability. Using the costs formula in *CPR 1998, Rule 45.50 Table 14 (Complexity Band 4)*, for every £1,000 above £25,000 that the case settles for, the claimant's solicitor recovers £140-£220 depending on the stage that has been reached when settlement occurs (assuming that FRC do not apply before allocation in stage 3). Adopting the hourly rates approach from Chapter 2, this is the equivalent of 44-69 minutes work (or 8-12 units) per £1,000. Extrapolating this, from the point of allocation to the intermediate track, they know that FRC applies and there are ~57-88 hours of work to be saved by settling promptly somewhere between £25,000 and £100,000. Whilst this may seem an artificial approach to adopt, it does show where the tipping point between profit and loss lies.

However, to a certain extent, this assumes that both sides want the same outcome – to collaborate to achieve a mutually beneficial result. The Prisoner's Dilemma (a thought experiment from game theory) indicates that this is an unsafe assumption. In any given case, one side may see an advantage in not cooperating with their opponent. Unless a cartel (or oligopolistic) mentality somehow prevails where both sides regularly cooperate to settle cases at the point which maximises their (or, more properly, their clients') mutual benefit, there is no particular reason to believe that seeking to a 'win' for your client at the expense of your opponent will not be the normal behaviour. This creates fertile ground for a procedural battleground in an adversarial system. Why is it in your client's best interests to collaborate if the compromise means the claimant gets less compensation or the defendant pays more costs? How do you prove to them that you have represented them to the best of your ability?

This can be illustrated further by considering the commonly encountered process blocks in clinical negligence litigation. These can be categorised as those caused by:

- Clients
- Defendants
- Courts
- Experts

- Third Parties
- Fee-earner
- Firm

All of these have the potential to increase costs and delay settlement. 'Swings and roundabouts' likely precludes obtaining more costs than the FRC allows for all but those blockages caused by the defendant. Even here, poor conduct it is not guaranteed to be sufficient to amount to 'exceptional circumstances'.

1. Disagreements over when FRC apply.

CPR 1998, Rule 45.49 states *"[t]his Section* [i.e. Section VII] *sets out the costs which are to be allowed in any claim which would normally be or is allocated to the intermediate track."* Likewise, *CPR 1998, Rule 45.50(1)* states that, until the case is allocated to the multi-track, the only costs which are allowed are fixed costs *"...in any claim which would normally be or is allocated to the intermediate track."*

As we saw in Chapter 2, clinical negligence cases must 'qualify' for inclusion in the intermediate track and this decision occurs at the allocation hearing (CMC). In contrast, *McGreevy (supra)* illustrates that FRC can apply before this (albeit in a regime where the case starts within FRC). If one considers that these rules are not just for clinical negligence cases, then the scope for potential disagreement or new case law broadens.

Strictly in respect of clinical negligence cases, the rules impose a number of criteria. Prima facie, all of these should be met before a case can be properly said to be 'likely' to be allocated to the intermediate track. Notwithstanding this, it is easy to imagine situations where the case settles pre-action and the parties disagree over whether the case was 'likely' to have been allocated to the intermediate track. We have seen similar arguments pre-October 2023 and there is no reason to presume this will change. If the defendant is willing to agree a suitably worded consent order providing for costs to be subject to detailed assessment if not agreed, then it is likely to have 'contracted out' of FRC. If, however, the case settles by way of a *Part 36* offer, then the claimant may well have 'contracted in' to fixed costs. If no agreement is possible either way, a court application is likely to be necessary with all of the additional risk and delay that this entails. On balance, this benefits defendants more than claimants.

The solution here is likely to be to ensure you have gathered evidence as to the likelihood of all of the qualifying criteria being met as you deal with the case pre-action.

2. Disagreements over whether suitable admissions have been made.

This has always existed to some extent. Pre-October 2023, it was most commonly encountered when partial admissions were made or in some instances of seeking default or summary judgements. The issue is magnified with FRC because it can make the difference between the defendant paying FRC or not.

Reverting to first principles, liability consists of a breach of duty of care which has caused an otherwise avoidable injury. Accordingly, there will be a tranche of cases where there is one alleged breach and a clear chain of causation. An example might be a scaphoid fracture where a failure to x-ray has led to a long delay in diagnosis and reduced hand function via avascular necrosis. It ought to be fairly clear whether the letter of response admits the single breach of duty and the avoidable injury.

However, what if there were several alleged breaches of duty or a more intricate chain of causation? The A&E nurse failed to properly examine the claimant; a sprain was diagnosed; he returned a few days later in any event and was x-rayed but the wrong angles were done; overall no advice to return within 10-14 days if the pain did not improve; and the claimant never thought to help himself by seeking medical attention until he was still encountering problems 2 years later. The overall value is unchanged from the first scenario but there is greater scope for some admissions on breach and causation being made. The defendant could assert that it has done enough to trigger FRC whilst the claimant contends that the rules require a full admission to do so.

Even at this fairly modest level of added complexity, the rules become strained. Since they are not just for clinical negligence, they understandably do not define what extent of admission is required. Relying on first principles might result in FRC applying where a single admission on breach which causes a modest avoidable injury being sufficient (but leaving the majority of the claim in issue). This would be likely to leave the claimant unable to prove the balance of the claim within the FRC amounts.

One possible solution to this would be to clearly set out the causal effects of each alleged breach in the letter of claim. By doing so, it makes it easier to see the consequences of any admissions. Alternatively, there is likely to be a temptation to reduce the allegations in the letter of claim to the minimum necessary. Whilst simplicity does have its advantages, it also carries with it the risk that there is no back up plan if what initially appeared to be the strongest allegations are undermined by additional evidence. Claimants will not always know (or be able to accurately infer) the impugned clinicians' evidence when the letter of claim is prepared.

3. Disagreements over causation of consequential losses

There is also the temptation to assume that the links in the chain of causation after the avoidable injury will fall into place. This is all the more so when cases within the £25,000 to £100,000 damages range are considered 'simple' by senior lawyers (who often have not run one for many years).

Added complexity arises from a variety of possible sources. Pre-existing medical conditions or co-morbidities can significantly effect the nature and extent of the claimant's avoidable injury as well as their prognosis. Life expectancy evidence is often disputed. The reasons for a claimant's lost earnings are usually not agreed without examination of the claimant's personnel, occupational health and employment records. Self-employed claimants are even more time-consuming, especially where sales and company records require analysis. The extent to which a claimant is unable to care for themselves, do household chores or DIY or provide their previous levels of support to their family can all be contentious even with supportive evidence.

The traditional approach of dealing with this after the admissions of liability have been obtained (as is usually required for the legal expenses insurance to cover the disbursements) risks delaying the case and so increasing the costs being incurred. Pre-October 2023, it was relatively commonplace to receive letters of response requesting quantum details notwithstanding this. There is no reason to presume that this will change. Front loading the evidence on these issues and the early preparation of a full schedule of special damages or loss before the letter of response is one possible solution. However, where expert evidence on C&P is required, this becomes more difficult. It may well prove to be the case that the claimant's prognosis is unclear or reports are required in other disciplines. Where it does not, there is likely to be increased pressure on claimants to serve their supporting evidence in order to obtain a settlement and, where we do, we can expect this evidence to be carefully scrutinised by the defendant.

4. Disagreements over quantum/quantum law

Similarly, there is no particular reason to believe that the pre-October 2023 practice of challenging the case comparators used to support a valuation of general damages will change. The range of objections can range from simply objecting outright to the cases used to sophisticated counterarguments. Since there is no obligation to raise objections all together, there is the scope for objections being raised piecemeal. Whatever the pros and cons of doing this, the consequence will be to eat into the amount of FRC.

'Controversial' heads of loss which were already frequently objected to by defendants pre-October 2023 are likely to remain so. This is likely to require explicit advice to claimants as to whether they are likely to recover them (partially or at all) later in the case. If the supporting evidence is front-loaded, this leaves less of the FRC available for other aspects of the case. If the evidence-gathering is left until later, then there are risks that any served evidence is inconsistent with the later evidence and that the remaining amount of FRC is insufficient to properly deal with this. Everything else being equal, this may well lead to some heads of loss either being abandoned or not being claimed at all. Each time this happens, this makes defendants more confident in resisting these heads of loss.

5. Disagreements over allocation and assignment.

As well as disagreements over the starting point for FRC, the new rules allow for disagreements over whether a case should be intermediate or multi-track and (even where the intermediate track has been agreed), over which complexity band is appropriate.

Given the pre-October 2023 arguments seen over costs budgeting, there is little reason to believe that rigorous disputes over the relative complexity of a qualifying case will not be encountered. Differing perspectives on the relative complexity of a case can be entirely valid or can be due to one side ignoring some or all of the available evidence. Perhaps counterintuitively, the more that corners are cut in progressing a potential FRC case, the greater the chance that a key piece of evidence will be missed. Accordingly, it is safest to assume that such challenges will be encountered regularly. This means we should plan to head these off during the longer pre-action period rather than trying do so in the shorter pre-allocation period.

Moreover, there is nothing to prevent both allocation and assignment being in issue. We can reasonably anticipate that this will occur where the claimant values the case at over £100,000 whilst the defendant does not. Alternatively, it can arise where the parties disagree over whether the other qualifying criteria for the intermediate track have been met. In such cases, care must be taken to avoid focussing all of your efforts on allocation only to find that you end up not only in the intermediate track but also in complexity bands 1-3. Using some of the FRC amount to gather evidence to support your likely position is again a sensible solution but again diverts resources from other parts of the case. Ignoring it risks making the case unprofitable if the amount of FRC is insufficient to get the settlement you believed was achievable.

On balance, relating the allocation and assignment issues to the remaining central issues (following service of the defence) is likely to provide the best solution to this problem. Doing so allows you to justify your view on whether the qualifying criteria for the intermediate track have been met whilst simultaneously providing a backup position on complexity if the allocation argument is lost. Strategically, this can be seen as the difference between a fighting withdrawal and a rout.

6. Disagreements over the directions

A pessimistic but reasonable view is that such disputes were ubiquitous pre-October 2023 even with standard directions being used. Whilst *CPR 1998, Rule 28.13* does state that the parties *"...must endeavour to agree appropriate directions..."* in the intermediate track, the rules provide no teeth to enforce this. Besides, this only requires the party to try to agree the directions, not that they must be agreed within a practical timeframe or costs limit within the FRC 'straitjacket'. Similarly, *CPR 1998, Rule 28.14(1)* broadly covers the same issues as are covered by the standard multi-track directions order without proposing suggested or mandating set directions.

Adapting the multi-track standard directions is sensible but leaves the scope of disagreement. Is this an overly gloomy perspective given that cases falling into the intermediate track must be suitable for more limited amounts of evidence. Afterall, *CPR 1998 Rules 28.14(2) & (3)* allow:

- Standard disclosure (unless the court orders otherwise);
- The maximum length of all witness statements and summaries is 30 pages (unless the court orders otherwise);
- The maximum length of each expert report is 20 pages (unless the court orders otherwise). This excludes necessary photographs, plans, academic or technical articles (see below);

- One expert per party as of right;
- Two experts per party where this is proportionate and reasonably required; and
- A trial length of 1-3 days

Within this, there is ample scope for disagreement. The greater dispute is likely to be over what amounts to an appropriate timetable. The rules do not say that a trial has to occur within a set timeframe, and we know that the courts have significant backlogs. The defendant has no incentive to agree to short timetables whereas the claimant does. That said, the lack of need for a CCMC may provide sufficient incentive to agree to suitable directions orders. If so, there is no guarantee that the court will not want to satisfy itself that the order is sufficiently robust for the intermediate track.

7. Disagreements over disclosure

Bearing in mind that intermediate track clinical negligence cases ought not to involve breach and causation issues, the focus of standard disclosure ought to be on those documents required to prove the valuation of the consequential losses.

The extent to which updated medical records are required to achieve this could well prove contentious bringing as it does the risk that they may be irrelevant, or worse, raise new issues. This is not confined to medical records, and the extent to which a particular item of loss will be agreed in the absence of unambiguous supporting evidence remains likely to be dealt with on a case-by-case basis.

The risk of not having persuasive supporting documents runs deeper than having to agree to a lower settlement. If the documents are incongruent with the witness evidence or expert evidence, then this may open the door to fundamental dishonesty. Dealing with this issue well into proceedings runs a significant risk of driving a wedge between the claimant and their legal team as well as evaporating the amount of available FRC.

Since the defendant rarely discloses documentary evidence in respect of consequential losses or quantum issues, it can afford to raise objections with relative impunity and stand to gain reductions to the overall settlement value and reduce the profitability of the case to the claimant's solicitor.

8. Disagreements over witness evidence

Similarly, this is likely to affect the claimant more than the defendant. The limit on the length of witness statements and number of lay witnesses permitted in the intermediate track coupled with the need for the claimant to prove every link in the chain of causation creates additional risk.

As such, there is a significant incentive for you to accurately calculate what evidence is required well before allocation occurs. If this is more than is permitted in the intermediate track, then that is a strong indication that the case is suitable for the multi-track.

9. Disagreements over expert evidence

The most obvious area of dispute is likely to be over the number of experts each side contends for. Once liability is admitted, defendants are likely to push for the minimum number of experts. They do not have to prove their case and so it is incumbent on the claimant's solicitor to make a persuasive case for why additional experts are reasonable and proportionate.

Additionally, the wording of the rules leaves scope for dispute over the length of the reports. They do not include matters such as the expert's cv, summary of the instructions, pasting in extracts from the medical records or background information on the medical terminology or relevant conditions. All of these could well count towards the page limit and the expert may genuinely believe that these are required to discharge their duty to the court. Not only could this reduce the room for properly covering the remaining disputed issues, but it may justify an application for permission to rely on the report or to exclude that expert's evidence.

The CPR Committee's November 2023 Minutes (para. 18), seeks to address these concerns by introducing new sub-paragraphs:

- *CPR 1998, Rule 28.14(3)(c)(i)* will require that the nature of the instructions, the conclusions and the expert's reasoning are included in the 20-page limit.

- *CPR 1998, Rule 28.14(3)(c)(ii)* will exclude the expert's cv and supporting materials from the 20-page limit.

Accordingly, and assuming these amendments do materialise, it is prudent for practitioners to include them in their instruction letter template and in their checklist template for reviewing the expert's report. Whilst reports are unlikely to be 20 pages long, it is important to ensure that the 20 pages which explain the experts' opinion remain properly reasoned (see *C v North Cumbria University Hospitals NHS Trust [2014] EWHC 61 (QB)*)

Preparing and agreeing the agendas for the experts' joint meetings is usually time-consuming If counsel is not going to be paid for drafting the agendas then the solicitor will need to do so. The devil is often in the detail. Some experts prefer not to use agendas but the resulting joint statements can lack the necessary structure to help the trial judge.

Prevention is better than cure and so heading this off is sensible (despite this diverting some of the available FRC amount from other parts of the case).

10. Disagreements over pre-trial issues

In the cut and thrust of an adversarial system, the possibility of last-minute issues arising can never be safely excluded. More prosaically, perennial disagreements over the trial bundle are likely to remain. For every issue that remains in the run up to trial, the amount of work required increases. Again, prevention is better than cure.

Conclusion

The primary lesson to take from the existing PI FRC decisions is that seemingly disproportionate points have been consistently taken by defendants. The reason for this appears to be that defendant insurers see a commercial advantage over the larger number of cases they deal with. The courts have permitted this by most holding that, over the entire range of cases, there is no unfairness in a given case and the most parsimonious interpretation of the rules furthers the overriding objective.

We cannot yet know what decisions clinical negligence insurers make. Where FRC applies to a given case, it is reasonable to assume that proper legal advice will include consideration of limiting a defendant's costs exposure. Accordingly, where claimants have not taken effective action to protect themselves, they are likely to run the risk of finding their profit margins reduced or extinguished.

CHAPTER SIX

CASE VALUE: HOW MUCH WILL THE CASE BE WORTH?

Case Value

Case value, as we will talk about both in this chapter and others, is going to be one of the most important issues to consider early when dealing with your cases now. This is because it will help you and others to determine whether your case is likely to be caught under FRC.

As a result, we consider it important to remind you what things to take into account when valuing your cases and why it is important to get it right.

In addition, we want to ensure that if we are going to be dealing with cases under FRC, that we are able to put a preliminary value on the case quickly without too much unrecoverable work. While that comes with practice and knowledge, some practical tips will be shared in this chapter.

Valuing Claims

Valuing a case accurately is definitely one of the most important tasks that clinical negligence lawyers need to do. A lot of other things depend on the case value, and if the case is not properly valued, it can create problems later on. There is a significant commercial advantage in getting this right.

The provisional case value is not the defining factor, because as we will see, the ultimate 'marker' will be how much the case has settled for. However, if the case is properly valued initially, then this should provide a fairly accurate framework for effective case management.

Therefore, in this chapter we will discuss some issues that we might face when valuing cases and will remind you what things to take into account in order to ensure that case valuations have been properly completed.

Undervalued claims

If the case is undervalued, it means that the client has potentially received less than he/she should have. This could happen if, for example, the case has not been properly investigated, or if the client was convinced to accept a much lower offer despite there being no risk factors supporting such an advice.

In those circumstances, if the client realises that his claim has been undervalued, and/or if the client is unhappy about the advice given and thinks that their claim was worth more, they might start their own investigations as to whether the claim was undervalued. You may have a claim being brought up by professional negligence solicitors investigating this further, spending time dealing with complaints and risking reputational damage.

While these things may happen rarely, it is still important to ensure that no case is unnecessarily undervalued. It always helps if you conduct proper investigations into a claim, take accurate instructions from your client about their symptoms and then provide accurate advice. Consistently getting higher settlements than other firms gives you a significant advantage in a competitive market.

Sometimes it might be just and reasonable to settle the claim for slightly less than it is worth, and/or what the client might want to recover. However, any such actions should be clearly thought through in light of the available evidence and an approval from the client sought and recorded.

Overvalued claims

If the claim is overvalued, while your client might be very happy about that, there could be some professional issues that both the client and you/the firm might face as a result. Therefore, again it is important to be accurate in your valuations and always have a reason behind any number that you consider pursuing as your case value.

If the case is overvalued and you are trying to settle your claim, the client might later face some cost consequences in case the claim is settled for less (if heard at trial). It could also create an issue in situations where proceedings need to be issued and you later on realise that the court fee was way overpaid due to the case value being much lower; this is something that ultimately might end up being irrecoverable and the costs of any difference borne by the firm. Where the losses claimed appear to be excessive when compared to the nature of the initial injury, the chances of allegations of fundamental dishonesty being raised increase.

With the new rules coming into force, if the case is potentially overvalued, it could also create problems if it turns out that the case might now be caught by FRC. This could result in a loss of time and costs spent running the file and the costs of the same could be borne by the firm or the client.

The table below summarises the level of the risk for the cases to be caught under FRC if they are either overvalued or undervalued.

Risks with FRC	
Overvalued Claims	**Undervalued Claims**
There is a risk that if the claim is overvalued and the case is actually worth less than £100,000 that it might be caught under FRC.	There is no risk that if the claim is undervalued that there might be any surprise for the claim to be caught under FRC.

In order to avoid this, always consider your 'borderline' value, i.e., what you think would be the minimal value of the claim if your evidence is not very strong and you are faced with the risks of litigation.	Undervaluing your claim might take you away from an opportunity to have dealt with the case outside of the FRC mindset. It is also important to be confident in the evidence that you have and ensure that you do collect all necessary information and/or approach those experts to add value to the claim.

Value your cases right

The standard practice to date has been to value our cases when all the evidence has come in. However, this might no longer be the only attempt that we will have to make.

While it is difficult to put a figure on the claim at the start of the case, with FRC coming into play, it is more important than ever to value your case as accurately as one might want to at the start of the claim.

Therefore, in order to help with the process, we shall share some of our personal experience and what the guidelines have to say about that to help anyone to get their heads around what cases could be worth.

Who is my client?

In order to be able to start valuing your case, it is important to determine who your client is. If the case concerns a deceased client, then it might be easier to value the claim. In that case we will need to consider whether there are any dependents, and/or if there is anyone who might be eligible for a bereavement award. If none are applicable, then your case is unlikely to be worth more than £10,000.

However, if your client is someone who still lives then different things will need to be taken into account, which might or may not help to clarify things for you.

The table below shows what main things you might want to consider under each category depending on who your client is.

WHO IS MY CLIENT							
Representatives of the Deceased			**Alive**				
Dependents	Bereavement Award	Length of the pain and suffering	Life Expectancy	Age	Length of the pain and suffering	Multiple injuries	Effects on the quality of life

1. Fatal Claims

When dealing with cases concerning a person who passed away, there are a few things that one might want to consider when thinking about the case value. Also, to highlight, any children stillborn would not be considered legal people according to law as they were born dead and, as a result, any stillbirth cases would be considered under the category of a live person as the client would always be a mother bringing a claim on her behalf.

a. Bereavement Award

It is a good starting point to determine whether there is anyone eligible for a bereavement award. This award would usually go to a family member. The bereavement award is currently at £15,120 for anyone who had passed on or after 1 May 2020. Therefore, that automatically adds over £15,000 (or slightly less if the death occurred before 1 May 2020) to your claim, and therefore, is a big factor to consider when deciding what the case could be worth.

In a short summary, the criteria are as follows:

Compensation Rates for Bereavement Awards

- £3,500 to £7,500 – for anyone who died on or after 1 April 1991
- £10,000 – for anyone who died on or after1 April 2002
- £11,200 – for anyone who died on or after1 January 2008
- £11,800 – for anyone who died on or after1 January 2012
- £12,980 – for anyone who died on or after1 April 2013
- £15,120 – for anyone who died on or after 1 May 2020

Who is Entitled to a Bereavement Award?

- Surviving spouse
- Surviving civil partner
- Parents (if the child was under 18)
- Unmarried couples *(living together as husband and wife/same sex couple for at least two years prior to death).*

b. Dependency Claim

Another important factor to consider is whether there can be a dependency claim. These claims would arise in cases where there were people in the deceased's life dependent on their finances and/or the services (such as care and assistance) they could offer.

Due to the nature or requirements for the deceased to be classified as someone on whom other people can depend, this would normally involve an adult rather than someone under the age of 18 that passed away. It is possible to push this to 21 or more on the right facts.

People who might be eligible to claim for dependency would fall under the following categories.

- Spouses, civil partner or former spouses or civil partners of the deceased
- Couples who had been living together in the same household for at least 2 years before the deceased passed away
- Any parent of the deceased or any person the deceased treated as a parent (such as a step-parent)
- Any child or descendant of the deceased
- Where the deceased was married or in a civil partnership, any person the deceased treated as a child or parent in relation to that marriage or civil partnership (such as a step-child)
- Siblings, aunts or uncles of the deceased

c. Extent of the Injuries Suffered

When it comes to the pain and suffering of the deceased person, as in some cases people unfortunately pass away within a few days or weeks after any negligent treatment, the award for their pain and suffering can be quite small, and usually limited to around £5,000.

However, if the length of the injuries was longer and the award had been suffering from pain and/or some loss of mobility etc. then the award could be higher.

Following that it is crucial to determine the length of the injuries in order to estimate whether the claim will be of limited value for the pain and suffering, or whether we will be able to claim a bit more.

2. Living Claimants

a. Life Expectancy

Your client's life expectancy could be a very important factor to determine whether the case is likely to exceed a certain FRC threshold.

We know from practice that cases where the clients are anticipated to live for years with their pain and suffering are usually worth more than those where the claimant either recovers from the injuries suffered or passes away.

In cases where the claimant recovers fully from their injuries, life expectancy might not be that important. However, if there are ongoing disabilities and/or if it is a cancer patient, life expectancy can play an important role in case value.

Therefore, if it seems that the claimant might pass away within e.g. a few years' time, it would be reasonable to be cautious about the case value as the case might be worth less than for the same reason. Expert evidence on this issue is likely to be required and, if so, it is far better to obtain it before allocation than be required to obtain it afterwards.

b. Age

Your client's age can also be an important factor when determining case value.

Similarly, as with the life expectancy, if your client's injuries are ongoing and most importantly, if the injuries are going to be permanent, the younger your client is the more you might be able to claim for them. This is because unless their life expectancy is impaired, it is assumed that they will be suffering from their injuries for longer and so might be eligible for a higher award.

At the same time, any special damages that you might claim might also add up due to the fact that the time gap between when their disabilities started until when it is anticipated that they might pass away will be much longer.

In addition, if you are dealing with minors, as the law is more protective of children, they might be eligible for slightly a higher award due to the mere fact that they are children.

This is mainly because it is deemed that if the person has to live with the pain for longer should be compensated for the same.

In addition, the cases where the person has to live longer with the pain and/or disability will likely to attract a higher amount for special damages related to anything that they will need as a result of their prolonged or permanent injury/disability.

c. Length of the pain and suffering

If your client's injuries are ongoing and/or permanent, the case is likely to be worth more than a similar case where the claimant might have recovered from the injuries quickly. This is based on the same principle that the more the claimant is going to suffer from, the higher the award for their compensation is going to be.

Sometimes it is hard to determine whether the injuries suffered are permanent, especially at the start of the case and before any expert evidence is obtained. In that case it might be helpful to do some research as to whether there are any efficient treatment methods for the client's symptoms, If there are none, then there is a higher chance that the client might be left with what is called a 'permanent injury.

In addition, the client's story of events could also help to provide some information as to what their doctors are saying and whether their symptoms are gradually improving or not.

Problem cases are likely to include those where your C&P expert advises that prognosis is uncertain at the time of their examination. In some cases, it is possible to still value the case based on a reasonable estimate of the anticipated prognosis. However, the defendant may try to delay the case in the hope that the worst-case scenario proves to be unfounded and does not happen so they pay less under the applicable FRC regime. Ultimately, if there is sufficient evidence for the trial judge to make the finding you want, then there is less reason to delay the case.

d. Multiple injuries

Occasionally your client might be suffering from multiple injuries. Sometimes they are both physical and psychological. Neurological symptoms can bridge the gap between these. Some of the injuries may be accelerated (but not entirely caused) by the negligence whilst others may be only superficially caused by it. Some may even be outside of the scope of the duty of care entirely, caused by an intervening event or the result of pre-existing or undiagnosed co-morbidities. It is not for no reason that they say "the more the merrier" and it directly applies in clinical negligence cases too when it comes to quantum disputes.

The more injuries we can say any breach of duty has caused, the more we can anticipate to add onto the case value. However, one needs to be careful that sometimes some injuries are expected to cause some overlapping side effects, and therefore, always adding individual lump sums regarding any additional injuries/symptoms might be unreasonable. Conversely, the more injuries there are, the more work is required and the harder it is to complete the valuation work within the FRC straitjacket. The more ambiguous the supporting evidence is, the more chance there is of the settlement value being lower than the maximum value of the case.

In practice, important things to note are unusual side effects, or a psychological injury suffered in addition to any physical injury that could result in a greater amount being added on top.

e. Effects on the quality of life

Another important factor to consider, which can affect both general and special damages, is how much the injury has actually impacted your client.

It might be that your new client has subsequently suffered from a severe injury but, however, their life has not been affected much by it. This could be due to e.g. the client already being affected by other pre-existing medical issues (which means that that is not going to make much difference to their quality of life). Perhaps they are unusually stoic. It could also be that some injuries (even if they sound severe like the loss of sight in one eye), still result in a near-perfectly normal life. In this example, for someone who does not rely on their precision eyesight in their work life can continue to function as normal even if they believe they have suffered a very big trauma. The JC Guidelines and their records usually indicate such situations before you decide to obtain expert evidence.

In this instance, it is important to ask these questions when accepting the case and/or when you have that initial conversation with your client that might help you to determine whether there could be additional elements added onto the case based on how their injuries have been affecting their lives.

What injuries did my client suffer?

The easiest way to start your case valuations is by quickly determining which part of the body has been injured. The Judicial College Guidelines are very helpful at least as a starting point.

The table below is a summary of the injuries caused to different parts of the claimant's body. It is worth noting that this is a rough estimate for a quick estimation of value. It is not a true reflection of the guidelines, but more of a summary of what one can expect to recover in the majority of cases (not extreme cases) and also more less based on some experiences.

Part of the Body	Estimated Amount
Spine/ Paralysis	£200 – 400k
Brain Injury	£100- 400k
Minor Head Injury	£15-30k
Psychological Injury	£20-40k
Eyes/Sight	One eye ~£55k Both eyes ~ £200k
Ears/Deafness	One ear ~ £40k Both ears ~£100k
Smell/ Taste	£20-30k
Chest Injuries	£60-120k
Male Reproductive System	Total loss of function or organs over £100k Less severe injuries £30-50k
Female Reproductive System	Major injury over £100k Less severe injuries £20-40k
Digestive System	£15-35k
Kidneys	Both kidneys over £150k One kidney £30k
Bowels	Long term injuries £50-150k Temporary £15-45k

Bladder	Long term injuries £50-150k Temporary £20-50k
Spleen	£5k
Hernia	£5-15k
Neck	Severe injuries £50-150k Minor injuries £5-20k
Back	Severe injuries £30-100k Minor injuries £5-20k
Shoulder	£10-30k
Pelvis and Hips	£20-50k
Arms	Severe injuries £100k Minor injuries £10-30k
Amputation of Arm(s)	One arm £100-130k Both arms £250k
Elbow	Severe injuries £40-50k Minor injuries £10-25k
Wrist	Severe injuries £50k Minor injuries £5-25k
Hand	Severe injuries to both £150-200k Severe injuries to one £100k Minor injuries £10-30k

Amputation of Leg(s)	One leg £100-130k Both legs £250-280k
Leg	Severe injuries £50-80k Minor injuries £5-20k
Knee	Severe injuries £70-95k Minor injuries £10-30k
Ankle	Severe injuries £30-65k Minor injuries £10-25k
Achilles	Severe injuries £25-35k Minor injuries £5-20k
Amputation of Foot/Feet	Both feet £170-200k One foot £80-100k
Foot	Severe injuries £40-100k Minor injuries £10-20k
Toes	Amputation(s) £30-50k All other injuries £10-20k
Chronic Pain	£30-60k
Facial Injuries	£5-20k
Scarring	£5-15k

Practical steps to take

Drawing all of this together, some practice points for fee earners to consider adopting in order to avoid undervaluing cases within the constraints of the new FRC systems are:

1. **Early Risk Assessment (RA):**

   - Conduct a thorough RA to evaluate the value of the case at the earliest stage. Identify strong and weak points to make informed decisions on quantum.

2. **Focus on Strong Claims:**

   - Concentrate efforts on cases with higher chances of success to avoid spending time and resources on weaker quantum claims. This will not suit everyone's view on promoting access to justice, however.

3. **Efficient Documentation:**

   - Organize and maintain clear, concise, and well-organized case documents to facilitate easy retrieval and minimize administrative time when preparing the formal valuation of cases.

4. **Strategic Negotiation:**

   - Engage in strategic negotiations with opposing parties (and their insurers) to explore settlement options before pursuing full litigation. Fully understanding the risk factors and costs/benefits to your client of becoming entrenched assist with this.

5. **Alternative Dispute Resolution (ADR):**

   - Consider utilising the available ADR methods as soon as your valuation has sufficient evidentiary support. The FRC regimes assume that parties want to resolve cases faster and at a lower cost than traditional litigation.

6. **Legal Technology:**

   - Leverage legal technology tools for document management,

research, and case tracking to streamline processes and reduce administrative overhead. See further Chapter 8.

7. **Cost-Benefit Analysis:**

    - Continuously assess the cost of litigation against the potential recovery to make informed decisions on case progression. FRC allows cases to be reallocated or reassigned to lower tracks and you ought to be prepared to prevent this.

8. **Expert Witnesses:**

    - Utilise expert witnesses judiciously, focusing on specialists who can significantly impact the case outcome, rather than employing multiple experts just to try to avoid FRC.

9. **Effective Case Management:**

    - Implement efficient case management practices to minimize delays and ensure all deadlines are met. Please see Chapter 8 for more information on this.

10. **Client Communication:**

    - Keep clients informed about case progress, costs, and potential outcomes for the range of valuation to manage their expectations effectively and maintain their trust.

Applying these to the gathering of evidence, from the claimant to value clinical negligence cases accurately and cost-effectively, some key questions to consider are:

1. **Medical History:**

    - What was their medical condition or injury before the alleged negligence occurred?

- Can they provide a written, detailed medical history, including prior treatments and medications?

2. **Symptoms and Impact:**

    - What specific symptoms or issues have they experienced since the alleged negligence?
    - How have these symptoms affected their daily life, work, and relationships

3. **Treatment and Medical Records:**

    - Have they sought medical treatment or consultations related to the alleged negligence?
    - Do they have copies of medical records, prescriptions, or receipts from these treatments?

4. **Witnesses:**

    - Are there any witnesses who can attest to the effects of the incident or their condition afterward?
    - Can they provide contact information for potential witnesses?

5. **Documentation and Correspondence:**

    - Do they have any written correspondence, emails, or documents related to the incident or subsequent medical care?
    - Have they kept a journal or notes about your condition and the impact on their life?

6. **Expenses and Financial Impact:**

   - Have they incurred any expenses, such as medical bills, transportation costs, or lost income due to the alleged negligence?

   - Can they provide documentation to support these expenses?

7. **Photographs and Visual Evidence:**

   - Do they have photographs of injuries, the accident scene, or relevant medical conditions?

   - Can they provide any visual evidence that might support their claim?

8. **Rehabilitation and Future Care Needs:**

   - Are they currently undergoing rehabilitation or therapy?

   - Have medical professionals assessed any future care or treatment needs?

9. **Expert Opinions:**

   - Have they consulted with medical experts or specialists who can provide written (factual) evidence on the negligence and its consequences?

   - Can they provide their contact information or reports?

10. **Mental and Emotional Impact:**

    - Have they experienced emotional distress, anxiety, or mental health issues (amounting to a recognised psychiatric injury) as a result of the alleged negligence?

- Can they describe how these emotional factors have affected their life?

11. **Loss of Enjoyment and Lifestyle Changes:**

    - Have they experienced a loss of enjoyment in hobbies or activities due to the incident?
    - How has their lifestyle and daily routines changed because of their condition?

12. **Legal History:**

    - Have they previously brought any claims or lawsuits related to medical issues or injuries?
    - Are there any prior legal settlements or judgments involving their health?

Questions of this type should be incorporated into questionnaires for ease of use. Encourage the claimant to provide as much detail as possible and to maintain open communication throughout the process. Additionally, consider involving more experienced colleagues or consulting with medical experts when necessary to ensure accurate valuation of the case (bearing in mind that they are more likely to be able to assist efficiently if the information you have is directly on point).

By following these practice points, we hope to maximise the value of claimants' cases within the constraints of fixed recoverable costs, ultimately providing quality legal representation while managing costs effectively.

Potential counterarguments

While it is important to remember that the legal profession operates within ethical boundaries and lawyers should always prioritise justice and fairness, defendants' lawyers may use questions such as the following to rigorously evaluate claims and encourage claimant lawyers to substantiate their cases:

1. **Details of Negligence:**

    - Can you provide specific details about the alleged consequential losses and expenses arising from the negligence, including dates, times, and individuals involved?

    - What evidence do you have to support these alleged losses?

2. **Pre-Existing Conditions:**

    - Was the claimant suffering from any pre-existing medical conditions or injuries before the alleged negligence?

    - How do you differentiate the impact of the alleged negligence from the claimant's pre-existing condition?

3. **Alternative Causes:**

    - Have you considered other potential causes or factors that may have contributed to the claimant's injuries or condition?

    - Can you provide evidence ruling out alternative causes (on the balance of probabilities)?

4. **Medical Records and Expert Opinions:**

    - Have you obtained comprehensive medical records and opinions from experts to substantiate your claim?

    - Can you share these records and expert reports with us?

5. **Witness Testimonies:**

    - Have you identified any witnesses who can corroborate the claimant's version of events?

    - Can you provide their contact information and statements (there is no property in a witness)?

6. **Documentation of Damages:**

    - What documentation do you have to support your client's claimed damages, such as medical bills, invoices, or receipts (for private treatment)?

    - Can you verify the authenticity and accuracy of these documents?

7. **Contributory Negligence:**

    - Have you considered whether the claimant's actions or choices may have contributed to the alleged negligence or the severity of their injuries? Note that this does not necessarily need to be proved at trial in order to reduce the profitability of the case.

    - Can you provide information regarding your client's (or even your) own conduct in pursuing a claim which is poorly evidenced?

8. **Consistency of Statements:**

    - Have your client's statements about the incident remained consistent throughout the process?

    - Can you explain any inconsistencies or changes in your client's account? Note that this can be a precursor to an allegation of fundamental dishonesty.

9. **Inadequate Expertise:**

    - Is the expert providing an opinion on your case properly qualified, acting within their specific area of expertise and impartial?

    - Have you considered that the defendant has obtained an opinion from an expert with a different perspective?

10. **Settlement Offers:**

    - Have you received any settlement offers or negotiations from co-defendants or their insurer?

    - Can you provide details of these offers and your response to them?

It is important to approach these questions professionally and with respect for the claimant's rights. Defendant's lawyers should not engage in unethical tactics or attempt to intimidate claimants. Instead, they should seek to ensure that all claims are thoroughly examined and supported by evidence, promoting fairness and justice in the legal process. However, within the FRC regime, this can lead to claimants using up their FRC amounts dealing with these legitimate questions.

Conclusion

We hope that information provided within this chapter will be a helpful guide to what to consider when trying to value your cases and what are the things that matter the most. We understand that it will not be until later in the case that one will be able to accurately decide on the case value, however, the sooner we know what things to take into account, the easier it will be to reach that conclusion later on.

In addition, we want to get into the habit of being able to recognise any cases that could be caught under FRC as early as possible. As a result, we have considered any risks associated with the same in different scenarios, such as if e.g., the case is overvalued at the start, and what is the risk for the case to be caught by FRC later.

We strongly believe that once we get into the habit of thinking about certain things that will help to determine the potential route for the claim, we should be able to adapt to FRC easier too.

CHAPTER SEVEN

CASE FUNDING: ARE THERE ANY RISKS?

Current Position

Clinical negligence cases, unless clients are eligible for legal aid, will be dealt with under 'no win – no fee' agreements. This means that we get no costs unless we win the claim. As long as the client is properly advised, if they receive an award, we will take a certain percentage of their compensation to cover the success fee together with the irrecoverable insurance premium. Pre-FRC, in many cases, they would be done with any other liabilities; they rarely had to worry about the recoverability of our costs (depending on the firm instructed).

However, the million-pound question is whether the situation should change if we are no longer able to recover all the costs that we have incurred as a result of the FRC. This will be the question we will be discussing in this chapter. We shall also discuss whether the insurers should change their position and who will bear the costs of that.

Conditional Fee Agreement (CFA)

The reality is that there is a high risk that a lot of work will be done that will not be recovered. This could be simply because it might be impossible to do the necessary work within the proposed costs limits, and/or the risks of the case falling outside of the multi-track might not have been clear at the start of the case result in some cases being reallocated at later stage.

In those situations where a large amount of costs cannot be recovered, one would definitely want to include a clause in the retainer documents allowing for the difference in costs to be recovered. However, does that mean that the clients will be exposed to this risk on top of the additional liabilities and the risk post-April 2023 QOCS rules (which can also result in claimants paying defendants' fees), and ultimately risk being easily left with nothing with these further deductions?

Therefore, while the temptation is high, it also would be just and reasonable to avoid such clauses and attempt to benefit from the success fee alone, rather than getting the costs back from those to whom you have just secured an award for. This is a competitive market and astute clients may well learn quickly to shop around for the 'best deals'.

What should be emphasised though is the risk of the costs being recovered if the client's own conduct has caused the case to be run differently resulting in additional costs to be incurred disproportionately and/or outside the FRC. There is a difference between seeking to recover costs shortfalls resulting from your own relative inefficient case management to those resulting from the clients' own actions.

Success Fee

One way to ensure that some profits are guaranteed will be to really maximise the recovery of that success fee from the client. Any firms that might be taking anything less than 25% (as a marketing tool) may wish to reconsider this for any new clients.

In addition, if the 25% success fee is not set to be 100% of your basic costs (where the risk justifies this), this might also suddenly become 100% if your firm's risk appetite or basket of cases on which decisions are taken changes in response to FRC.

Is that all justifiable? Arguably yes, especially that now each one of us bear the risk of not only losing the claim but losing the majority of the work/costs incurred running any of those files that could either fall outside the multi-track at the onset or are in the grey area, which will be the majority. Unless you are sure that your case is worth £250,000 or more, you can ultimately end up dealing with something that is suitable for the FRC tracks.

Client's Behaviour

Another thing that some lawyers might be marketing for will be some sort of 'dream client' behaviour plan.

We all know that some clients are more difficult to work with than others, and some are actually quite difficult. This is not necessarily something personal to any of the people that we work for, however, let us be honest and acknowledge the fact that all of our clients had to go through some sort of traumatic event to contact us and a 'normal' behaviour cannot be expected. Moreover, we should acknowledge that we are also to blame; after all we are involved in all of the situations where difficulties arise. The added pressures of working within FRC regimes risk making this worse.

The question therefore is what behaviour, taking into account that under FRC we might not have that much time to address every little detail of our client's concerns and desires, is going to be considered as 'acceptable'? When should we consider warning our clients that, given an excess of certain behaviour, we might need to consider charging them extra to cover the likely shortfall in costs recovery?

While we expect that this will depend on the firm's internal policies, our recommendation is to consider this possibility at the start and acknowledge that there will be difficulties trying to squeeze in all of the required communications (and other work) within FRC cases where the clients have high expectations, are particularly demanding and/or cause additional issues to us. This should be covered in the initial retainer letters and in the 6 monthly costs updates letters as a minimum.

Client behaviour that one might want to consider charging extra for:

a) Dishonest behaviour;

b) Ghosting behaviour and delays in providing instructions;

c) Attention seeking behaviour, i.e. those requiring too much time and attention from you;

d) 'Big talkers', i.e. those requiring an excessive amount of communication or correspondence, and/or are always providing you with too much.

Providing sufficient costs information to allow your client to make an informed choice before the problem arises is crucial here. It is important to remember, however, that the deductions would be made from their compensation and this can mean holding this back if there is a dispute. Clients also need to be informed that they have the right to request an assessment of these excess costs and this may cause significant delays. The court is likely going to expect clear costs information and to see that the 'excess' costs were incurred as a result of specific events rather than being part of a wholesale disregard for FRC or inefficient practices.

ATE Insurance

It is still unknown how insurers are going to react to FRC and whether different premium costs will be implemented. The disbursements consultation in the <£25,000 consultation (which closed on October 2023) indicates that these will be in addition to the published FRC amounts. It has not yet been confirmed whether they will be capped (i.e. as an additional fixed sum) or uncapped (and so subject to reasonableness and proportionality).

As long as the insurers are not at risk of not recovering those insurance premiums, it only makes sense that there will not be any major changes in the policies. There does not seem to be many certain increased risks associated with FRC for them in the intermediate track (where liability should be admitted early). There is an arguable additional risk in the <£25,000 claims because the standard track proposals require that quantum investigations be done in order to send a letter of claim (and so the C&P report fee needs to be incurred before the defendant's position on liability is known).

As insurers have not to date protected us from any shortfall in the recovery of our costs, it is not expected that there will be a change as a result of that either.

In contrast, one might assume that the premiums should go down, because if we are not recovering the costs for our work, should the insurer recover the same amount. This is particularly if it will become popular to charge the claimant with any shortfall. The claimants will be at exposed risk to receive less in damages in those cases, and they will definitely want to see a change with the premiums they pay.

Insurers could actually start favouring cases caught by FRC. A majority of the cases that could be caught by FRC would be the cases that fall within intermediate or standard/light tracks. Whilst the rules indicate that it is unlikely with clinical negligence that the cases would start to suddenly be regularly allocated to fast track, this cannot be excluded entirely. However, if we see an increase of full admissions being made, this would save lots of costs for defendants and these cases might start falling into the FRC tracks – which is perhaps a more realistic scenario. If this behaviour became habitual, then we might see a new round of challenges to the reasonableness of taking out ATE policies at the start of a case. If so, then the solution would need to fairly account for the risks claimants take of incurring experts' fees before the admissions are made.

Early, full admissions on breach and causation mean that the insurers will know that they will get paid no matter the outcome because liability is admitted and so some settlement will be reached either way. The only risk then would be the new rules; if claimants are not careful with analysing defendants' *Part 36* offers then, in any quantum trial, providers would be liable for the amount of defendant's costs equivalent to the amount of compensation paid (with the claimant's solicitor also risking losing their costs). However, again what are the chances of that happening versus the case settling (even if settled before trial)? In that case, the risks outweigh the benefits, and the insurers are likely to benefit the majority of times. Overall. It currently seems likely that premiums will be set on the entire basket of clinical negligence cases (including multi-track ones).

Where insurers might then start making their money back is multi-track claims, as they will know that the claimant might not be charged for any shortfall so they can start asking more from the claimant. Again, whether that is a fair and just move is arguable, however, it might be a better solution for FRC clients than increasing the premiums overall for everyone.

What could be fair is if the recoverable part of the premium increases at least with the cases where the claim is caught under FRC. This is because, defendants benefit from lower expenditure by claimants and their own expenditure would be capped as well (quid pro quo). Thus, these savings mean they should be the ones then charged more for the any increased premium fee even though this would (from their perspective) reduce the desirability of a FRC regime.

Taking into account new rules and all the changes, perhaps their way of keeping the premiums as they are would be a fair compromise after all.

Whilst we are not underwriters, relevant factors affecting ATE premiums may prove to be:

Factors Influencing Whether 'After the Event' Insurance Premiums Are Likely to Increase

1. **Claim Complexity:**

    - Increase: Higher complexity cases in medical sub-specialisms with uncertain outcomes or a history of lower success rates may lead to increased premiums as insurers perceive higher risk.

2. **Claim Value:**

    - Increase: Claims with higher potential damages may result in higher premiums as insurers anticipate larger payouts if the claim is successful to offset lower recovery from FRC cases.

3. **Fixed Recoverable Costs (FRC) Impact:**

    - Increase: If new FRC rules limit the recoverable costs for claimants, insurers may raise premiums to compensate for the reduced cost recovery.

4. **Legal Expenses History:**

    - Increase: Claimants with a history of multiple claims or high legal expenses may face higher premiums as they are seen as higher risk.

5. **Claimant's Legal Representation:**

    - Increase: If the claimant is represented by a law firm with a track record of high-cost litigation, insurers may refuse delegated schemes and charge higher premiums.

6. **Claimant's Track Record:**

    - Increase: If the claimant (or the firm) has a history of unsuccessful claims or frequent withdrawals, insurers may consider them a higher risk and charge more.

7. **Medical Expert Opinions:**

    - Increase: If medical expert opinions suggest a lower likelihood of success, insurers may increase premiums due to the perceived risk. Improvements in machine learning and artificial intelligence could make this easier to assess.

8. **Delay in Reporting Claims:**

    - Increase: Delays in reporting claims can result in higher premiums, as insurers may see these claims as less credible.

9. **Legal Funding:**

    - Increase: If the claimant has secured legal funding through Conditional Fee Agreements (CFAs) or other means, insurers may raise premiums to mitigate potential costs.

10. **Regulatory Changes:**

    - Increase: Changes in regulations or legislation that impact ATE insurance may lead to premium adjustments to account for new risks.

Factors Influencing Whether 'After the Event' Insurance Premiums Are Likely to Decrease

1. **Reduced Legal Costs:**

    - Decrease: If FRC leads to lower legal costs for claimants, insurers may lower premiums to reflect the reduced financial risk of paying defendant's costs.

2. **Improved Claimant Success Rates:**

    - Decrease: If data shows an improvement in claimant success rates, insurers may reduce premiums due to lower perceived risk.

3. **Alternative Dispute Resolution (ADR):**

    - Decrease: If more cases are resolved through ADR methods, insurers may lower premiums as ADR can be more cost-effective.

4. **Safer Medical Practices:**

    - Decrease: Improved medical practices and risk mitigation measures may result in lower premiums as the overall risk decreases. Interestingly, this has not been seen in motor insurance premiums despite FRC having been in place for years.

5. **Claimant's Legal Representation:**
    - Decrease: If the claimant is represented by a law firm with a history of cost-effective litigation, insurers may charge lower premiums. If so, such firms would enjoy a significant competitive advantage over their rivals.
6. **Early Settlements:**
    - Decrease: If more cases are settled early in the litigation process, insurers may offer lower premiums due to reduced legal costs.
7. **Revisions to ATE Insurance Regulations:**
    - Decrease: Regulatory changes that favour insurers or promote competition may lead to lower premiums.

It is important to note that 'After the Event' insurance premium adjustments depend on various factors, and insurers' decisions are influenced by market dynamics and risk assessments. These factors can interact in complex ways, and trends may evolve over time in response to changing circumstances. However, having a working understanding of these issues does add helpful context to the points we have discussed in this book.

Client's Expectations

Once the clients start hearing all the information when we want to sign them up, there will be quite a few questions going through their heads. They will want to ensure that there will be nothing that they will have to pay if they lose their claim and they will want to ensure that they are still left with a maximum amount after they have paid costs to us.

Therefore, how do you explain to your client that it is still worth proceeding with your firm and that you will do not only the best job to maximise their payment, but that you will do the job in the most efficient way that you do not actually end up incurring all the additional costs that they will have to cover for?

To start with, it is good to set your rules and advice right and explain to your client what behaviour from their side might prompt you to incur those additional costs. You can give examples to your client what you expect from them, and that e.g. any chaser letters or any long conversations that are due to your client just not accepting the advice from you could be considered as overtime, so that the client is not surprised that later you tell him that long conversations covering the same things over and over again are above your pay.

With time, you might want to work on some statistics and explain how long it might take you to do certain tasks. And yes, we anticipate it might be okay to propose that some things could take longer, but then again you should explain to your client that that would be the case. You could give your client an option that, in case their claim is later caught by FRC, or if you are sure that it will be, advise them how things are likely to end up and explain that (in order to do a better job), you would spend a few hours extra, and give that option to your client. Ask them whether they want you to thoroughly investigate and draft a very detailed advice or letter to a third party or are they happy with the standard service for which they might not need to pay but equally they might not be guaranteed any success as a result.

You can also have set expectations that would be agreed by your firm in general. Some law firms might be happy to adopt the approach that they can deliver standard advice quickly and they do not need to ask anything additional from their clients, which is fine. However, some firms might try to pitch the opposite, that they do invest time and costs in making their claim presentable etc. but that the claimant might end up paying back more. In order to attract the right client for you, one will need to invest in having the right reputation and marketing in place so that people, before approaching you and your firm, know what to expect from their services.

What we need to remember is that it is still our client's claim and they need to be given an option. There will always be different firms taking different approaches and having their lawyers trained a certain way. However, as long as you give that choice to your client without being afraid of losing them either way, then one cannot only state that you have explained things but when the time comes to get paid, the client will find it harder to argue that there were no options given to them to choose from. It would actually be good to have firms doing things differently in order to create balance and provide options for people to investigate their case the way the clients want them to. At the end of the day, while we can create satisfactory scenarios for each client, none of us can be masters of all and it is best if we acknowledge what you do best and try to continue making money from exactly what you have.

Legal Requirements

The foregoing is congruent with the legal requirements on providing clients with enough information so they can make an informed decision about whether to agree to deductions from their compensation following *Belsner v CAM Legal Services [2022] EWCA Civ 1387*. In essence, as long as the prospective client is clearly informed of what deductions are intended to be made, these will be allowed. However, the disputes should be resolved through the legal ombudsman and not through the courts.

The legal ombudsman has published its updated guidance in November 2023: an-ombudsman-s-view-of-good-costs-service-v3.pdf (legalombudsman.org.uk)

Specifically in respect of FRC, complaints usually arise where the solicitor has deducted more than the client expects. In order to prevent this, the guidance is "... *there might be a significant difference between the costs that are incurred on a time-spent basis and the fixed costs that are recoverable from another party. Clients should be told how fixed costs operate, because they need to appreciate that there is a risk of their costs exceeding the sums that can be recovered, and they need to understand what this means for them."* The amount deducted to cover shortfalls can be limited to an additional percentage of the compensation but the client needs to understand how this is going to work and be calculated in practice.

The fact that the success fee is not recoverable from the defendant must be explained to the client as must any cap on it. The guidance on success fees is: *"If we investigate a complaint where a firm has a policy of charging a substantial success fee in every case, regardless of risk, we are likely to ask the firm to show us that the client has given informed consent to the arrangement. This would include the client being made aware that other lawyers might not adopt the same approach and that lower success fees might be available elsewhere. We understand that both parties should be free to enter into contracts, including making a bad bargain, but we will want to satisfy ourselves, when asked, that the client understood what they were doing and that they made an informed choice to proceed. If we investigate a complaint about this issue, the lawyer is likely to need to justify the arrangement in the context of providing a reasonable standard of service to that client."*

A separate aspect of *Belsner* may also be relevant to how much detail we are required to provide clients with when we bill them for these deductions. This has an element of unintended consequences about it. The Court of Appeal has made it clear that cases which settle pre-action are to be regarded as non-contentious business. This appears to apply as much to all clinical negligence cases as it does to the specific type of RTA case *Belsner* was concerned with. The more pre-issue admissions of breach and causation are made, the more cases would appear to be non-contentious. Moreover, the court did not have to decide whether cases then become 'contentious business' when issued and so this remains uncertain. As we say elsewhere in this book, the more ambiguity there is, the more scope there is for litigation and so the more chance there is that a case becomes unprofitable in a FRC regime.

This is a complex area and a detailed discussion is outside the scope of this book. However, it seems that a practical solution is to send the client a detailed bill which explains how the deductions have been calculated and which is congruent with the explanation provided at the start of the case and with the six-monthly costs updates. Openness and transparency in providing our clients with details of how our charging structures will work has been re-emphasized in several recent non-FRC decisions. In *Diag Human Se & Stava v Volterra Fietta (A Firm) [2022] EWHC 2054 (QB)*, the solicitors were not permitted to claim a success fee which amounted to more than 100% of the base risk. This invalidated the entire retainer (the offending provisions could not be severed leaving some entitlement to costs) meaning they received nothing and had to repay the payments on account from their client. In *Murray v Richard Slade & Co Ltd [2021] EWHC 3383 (QB)*, the very substantial cost of using counsel had not been properly explained to the clients and so was irrecoverable. In *Olukoya v Riverbrook Solicitors Ltd [2023] EWHC 2771 (SCCO)*, the informal resolution from the Legal Ombudsman that the client should pay a small proportion of the rendered bill prevented the solicitors from then seeking full payment from that client. *Kenton v Slee Blackwell plc [2023] EWHC 2613 (SCCO)*; *Turner v Coupland Cavendish Ltd [2023] EWHC 2721 (SCCO)*; and *Richardson & 223 Others v Slater & Gordon UK Ltd [2023] EWHC 2886 (SCCO)* all show that various challenges to profit costs, success fees and the amounts of ATE premiums remain ongoing. These cases all illustrate that, if we decide to charge our clients 'more' under FRC regimes, then we need to be absolutely certain that we have carefully planned to avoid the many pitfalls that await us. This means considering not just the immediate problems but also the second, third and even fourth order consequences. Otherwise, we risk losing even the reduced amounts payable under FRC.

Conclusion

It is likely that a lot of firms might consider implementing new terms and conditions so that they are able to recover the costs from the claimants in the event where their cases are caught under FRC. This then could result in claimants recovering less from their settlements, and/or they might even see a drop of the claims being accepted overall.

However, taking into account that the case might end up being rejected otherwise, or accepted on the basis that more money might be taken, it would only seem reasonable that the latter approach is still going to be better than nothing. Ultimately, no one wants to work for free and the claimant still gets a chance to receive a decent proportion of what they have been awarded.

It is unclear however how the insurers are going to react in these situations. While there are no specifications justifying an increase in premiums, we are yet to see their reaction to this. It could be the case that with all the recoverable costs etc. the parties might decide to proceed without insurance more than they would have otherwise. There are still a lot of risks that the claimants might then face, but it could be an option given to the claimants as well if the premiums are going to rise on top of the legal fees.

CHAPTER EIGHT

EXPERT EVIDENCE & ITS IMPORTANCE FOR EACH TRACK

Importance of Expert Evidence

The importance of expert evidence in each clinical negligence claim is self-explanatory – we need it to run our cases. However, it will also be very important as a deciding factor whether the case can or should be allocated to a certain track.

We have already spoken about the most important factor – case value. Case value will help to form the view of the risks of the case being allocated outside of the multi-track.

However, as we have also learnt by now, case value is not the only deciding factor whether the case automatically falls outside of the multi-track.

If the case is worth between £25,000 and £100,000, the second factor will be the defendant's position on liability. If liability is fully admitted, then there is a high chance that your case will be allocated to the intermediate track. However, there can be an exception that relates to the expert evidence required.

If the case is worth less than £25,000, which potentially puts the case at risk of being allocated to the fast track (if it has not settled pre-action, including under the light or standard tracks), another factor that will be important in ensuring allocation to the multi-track will be your expert evidence.

In this chapter we shall discuss the importance of expert evidence and what we might want to consider in cases that fall outside of a multi-track.

Multi-Track Cases

If your case is likely to be a multi-track claim because of its (potential) value then there is not much additional FRC information to consider, besides the usual advice of making sure that you instruct appropriate experts to comment on liability and quantum issues etc.

If the case is a multi-track because of all other reasons, e.g. if liability is denied, then again one should not put any additional pressure on things like expert evidence.

However, as discussed in previous chapters, if it is not entirely clear whether the case might fall outside of a multi-track, then you might want to consider the information below related to expert evidence depending on what track your case might be at risk of being allocated to.

The main point that we are going to discuss in this chapter is the number of experts and their reports per case that could change the outcome of your case being allocated to certain tracks.

However, before we move on to discuss the effects of the expert evidence in each track, we would like to remind that one still needs to ensure that each expert opinion that is obtained is done so in proportion to the case and with the actual need and not so to abuse or 'game' the system.

Fast Track Cases

It is still unclear whether clinical negligence cases that would potentially be eligible to be allocated to the fast track will be subject to FRC or not. However, there is a high risk that if your clinical negligence claim can be or is allocated to the fast track then FRC will apply. If they do, then they will be significantly less than the amounts in the intermediate track (see Chapter 2).

One of the deciding facts in fast track cases which are less in value than £25,000 can be your expert evidence. The criteria are as follows:

- oral expert evidence is limited to one expert per party in any expert field; and
- expert evidence is limited to two expert fields.

That means that either you agree to joint instructions with the defendant (maximum of two experts can then be instructed), or you can cover the bases with one expert only (for both your liability and quantum evidence). As we saw in Chapter 3, this is fewer experts than in the pre-action standard track (due to come into force on 6th April 2024). However, some of these cases may have only ever required one expert each or admissions may have been made narrowing the issues to the extent that only one expert each is needed at trial. It is also possible that the court limits the amount of expert evidence required *at trial* or the defendant makes late admissions and successfully applies for reallocation (which is retrospective to the earlier stages, see Chapter 2).

If you know that you will need at least two experts and both will need to give evidence at trial, then you are officially outside of the fast track and, according to the new rules, the case would then probably automatically become a multi-track claim, unless the case value is higher than £25,000 and the case then might fall within an intermediate track.

The new rules are not specific if in these circumstances you could then argue that the claim would be subject to intermediate track, however, the rules at the same time are clear that unless certain criteria is met, they are not intermediate track claims, so it will likely be a multi-track case then.

In that case, it is likely your intention to obtain expert reports on both breach of duty and causation of damage (if they are separate), and also instruct any expert discipline to cover your quantum evidence (if necessary). It is probably not your intention to agree to a joint expert report, unless you do see a very good reason to do so, because then you risk being unable to effectively clarify that opinion and your case to be subject to FRC due to the case ultimately being suitable for the fast track. Despite your very best intentions, however, a judge hearing competing arguments at a CMC/Allocation hearing or on paper may be persuaded to impose joint experts in order to allocate the case to an 'appropriate' track for its value. Preparing to avoid this from the start of the case is likely to be time well spent.

In particular, the risk arises if you are relying on the same expert for all of your evidence (breach of duty and causation), in which case you could either try to argue that you will need more than one day for everything to be considered and so the case become too complicated for the fast track, or you attempt to instruct an expert in different discipline to comment on any issues around your client's conditions and prognosis if this is reasonable.

One thing to be aware of is that the case value could increase if you continue to investigate it. In some situations, we have to explain to our clients that if they want to settle a bit sooner then the case value might be a bit lower, and they might give us instructions to proceed without spending more time on additional expert evidence.

However, if you do want to obtain that additional evidence that is likely to increase the value from up to £25,000, to over £25,000, then you need to consider whether that is good for you or not. If liability is denied (even partially) then you are more likely to be 'safe' in pursuing allocation to the multi-track. However, in any other case you might want to re-evaluate the position and see if all that additional work will pay off, because then ultimately you are still caught by FRC and it might be disproportionate or not valuable for you to proceed with that option.

The table below summarises the position and briefly explains when you might be encouraged to obtain an additional expert's report in case you want to ensure that the case would fall outside of the fast track. This is assuming that the case value is below £25,000; additional expert evidence is unlikely to change that; and the courts reject the notion that these cases must be allocated to the multi-track. Remember, under the proposed regime for qualifying cases which *settle* under £25,000 (due to come into force on 6th April 2024), will be subject to FRC retrospectively; the claimant must beat the pre-issue neutral evaluation amount by >20% to avoid a severe costs penalty (see Chapter 3).

	Number of Expert Reports the Claimant has obtained to Date	**Status on Liability**	**Does the Claimant have any ongoing problems?**	**Would additional evidence be from an expert in a different discipline?**	**How many experts will the Claimant be relying on at a Trial**	**Likely track**
Scenario 1	1 or 2 joint reports	N/A	No	N/A	Limited to 2 joint experts	**Fast Track?**
Scenario 2	1 or 2 joint reports	N/A	Yes	No	Limited to 2 joint experts	**Fast Track?**
Scenario 3	1 or 2 joint reports	N/A	Yes	Yes	Will be 2 or more experts	**Multi Track**
Scenario 4	1 report	N/A	No	N/A	Limited to 1 expert per party	**Fast Track?**
Scenario 5	2 reports	Denied	N/A	N/A	2 x or more	**Multi Track**
Scenario 5	2 reports	Partially admitted	N/A	N/A	Limited to 1 expert per party	**Fast Track?**
Scenario 5	2 reports	Partially admitted	Yes	Yes	2 x or more	**Multi Track**
Scenario 6	2 reports	Admitted	N/A	No	1 x report (quantum evidence)	**Fast Track?**
Scenario 7	2 reports	Admitted	Yes	No	1 x report (quantum evidence)	**Fast Track?**

Scenario 8	2 reports	Admitted	Yes	Yes	2 x report (quantum evidence)	**Multi Track**

Therefore, to summarise, if you are dealing with a case that is worth less than £25,000 in value, you want to make sure that there are at least two experts that you will be relying on at the trial in order to ensure that the case does not fall within the fast track. This could be done by either ensuring that all necessary disciplines were instructed to comment on liability issues, and/or to ensure that you obtained an opinion related to quantum that could boost your chances for the case to fall back to the multi-track.

However, let's not forget that you must remain reasonable and ensure that you are not wasting your client's time nor trying to abuse the system; it all has to be based on the evidence that you have to date and not necessarily influenced by FRC.

Intermediate Track Cases

If your case value is between £25,000 and £100,000, and liability has been admitted in full, there is still a chance that your case might fall back to the multi-track. This will depend on the situation with your expert evidence.

The current rules state that the requirements for the case to be allocated to intermediate track would include the requirement of the parties not relying on oral evidence of more than two experts per party.

The fact that liability needs to have been admitted in full for the case to be allocated to the intermediate track suggests that the only reason for the case to go to trial is likely to be issues around quantum. That means that the only expert evidence you will be relying on are your quantum reports (that cover the financial implications for your client), and/or your condition and prognosis reports (that cover the nature and extent of their injuries).

In that case, in order for the case to fall outside of an intermediate track, you need to have three different experts that you are going to rely on when it comes to the issues of quantum. If there are any aspects of causation and/or your client's condition and prognosis that are still in dispute, the case should automatically fall outside of the intermediate track due to the lack of full admission. Again, there is the scope ambiguity in the rules and for cases being reallocated or reassigned to a lower complexity band if the issues are narrowed pre-trial. All of this ought to be carefully prepared for within the strict FRC straitjacket to maintain profitability.

The issues of quantum relate to any expert evidence that goes beyond the immediate injuries your client sustained, in other words it only talks about the financial implications related to your client's injuries in this case. As an example, these include but are not limited to, any standard condition and prognosis reports discussing the costs associated with your client's treatment, reports addressed directly to any past or future losses such as employment reports, care reports etc. Differentiating your case by using personalised evidence helps to demonstrate why it is unjust to lump it in with a generic and theoretical view of what a 'normal' clinical negligence case looks like.

It is easier to decide on how many reports you are going to rely on once you have attempted to settle the case and the defendant has already raised any issues with your schedule of loss. However, that does not help if you are trying to make a decision about it earlier in the case as it might not become clear until you settle the case, and/or the case is issued.

You can still attempt to predict what is likely to happen even beforehand if you understand the central issues and the evidence required to prove them. If the case has not been issued, and the case settled, arguably you can persuade the court (and defendant) that you would have relied on all the reports that refer to any financial losses that your client had to incur. This is partially if no specific comments have been made by the defendant before settling the case. Costs arguments by the defendants are likely to continue to be that the reports not served were not relied on. This is a stronger argument where a (supportive) report has not been referred to at all and its impact cannot be seen in the settlement.

What happens then if the defendants and their representatives start making very accurate comments or admissions about our offers and/or schedules of special damages or loss in order to narrow the issues? That would be a nice problem to have. If it ultimately ends up being a question of us relying on one or two instead of three reports, then we will have to be happy to see a day of the defendants being precise with their responses and coming to sensible agreements even if we might not be able to successfully argue for the case to fall within the multi-track.

The below table summarises the situation as to when the case might be eligible for an intermediate track and when the case might fall outside of the track if the expert evidence exceeds the required threshold.

	Status on Liability	**Does the Claimant have any ongoing problems?**	**How many experts will the Claimant be relying on at a Trial**	**Likely track**
Scenario 1	Denied or Partially Admitted	N/A	N/A	**Multi Track** (depending on the interpretation of the rules)
Scenario 2	Admitted	No	Less than 2 x	**Intermediate Track**
Scenario 3	Admitted	Yes	Less than 2 x	**Intermediate Track**
Scenario 4	Admitted	Yes	3 x or more	**Multi Track**

Multiple Experts

It is tempting to assume that the inherent greater complexity of clinical negligence cases will make it relatively easy to show that more than 2 experts (for cases risking entry to the intermediate track) or 3 experts (for cases risking entry to the light or standard tracks) will be required.

Advanced planning is likely to make it far more effective if you want to turn this assumption into reality regularly. Your case may genuinely require different disciplines of expert on breach and causation and one on C&P. If it looks as though the settlement value is around £25,000 at the start of the case, then it could well be suitable for the light or standard tracks. If you can settle it for more than £25,000 but liability is admitted 'early' then it could be suitable for the intermediate track.

Identifying the central allegations at the start of the case, and then keeping them under review as the case progresses, gives you as much time as possible to identify a genuine need for other experts and craft an argument likely to withstand robust challenges from your opponent and the court.

The fact that the substantive, evidential and procedural rules have not been simplified helps with this. Unless suitable early admissions are made, all of the links in the breach of duty and causation chain must be proved. A delay in diagnosing a scaphoid fracture may justifiably require expert evidence form an A&E nursing expert; an A&E consultant; a radiologist and a specialist orthopaedic hand surgeon given the right set of facts. Causation of consequential losses and condition and prognosis is likely to require the orthopaedic expert but may also require a pain management expert and a psychologist or psychiatrist. Quantification may require expert evidence in care and assistance or a forensic accountant (if the claimant is self-employed). Other specific claims have similar possibilities – a stillbirth or neonatal death case can easily require experts in paramedic medicine, obstetrics, midwifery and neonatology on breach and causation as well as psychology or psychiatry and it is worth planning this out early. In the case.

If this is your chosen strategy, bear in mind that the judge hearing the CMC/allocation hearing may simply approach this on the basis that the value of the case takes precedence. We have experienced this pre-October 2023 even where both sides agreed the case should be allocated to the multi-track. The careful planning we had implemented pre-issue eventually (after two hearings) achieved the correct outcome and avoided considerable injustice to our client.

Using Expert Evidence

Since there has been no change to the substantive, evidential or procedural rules, expert evidence still needs to be internally logical and consistent in order to be persuasive. The recommendation that the claimant's liability and quantum expert evidence be disclosed with the letter of claim in cases worth under £25,000 appears to be poorly thought out and unjust because it runs counter to the usual order in the standard directions order for multi-track cases (which applied to virtually all clinical negligent cases before October 2023). There is no overt indication that the intermediate track will depart from this either meaning that it is only cases which the government considers to be suitable for the light or standard tracks after April 2024 which are subjected to this significant change.

The issue does not arise in the intermediate track because there is no requirement that expert evidence should be served pre-action. The decision to admit liability must be taken in the normal way. Accordingly, where the anticipated settlement range reasonably straddles £25,000, it does not appear to be appropriate to automatically use the standard or light tracks pre-action.

As we have seen in Chapter 3, the underlying policy reasoning is that cases under £25,000 are so simple that the overwhelming majority will settle pre-proceedings. Our experience of such cases before October 2023 is that defendants do not share this view and persistently do not make 'commercial' settlement offers (i.e. offers based on saving money by making early admissions or recognising risk). They only make admissions where they believe that they have been negligent rather than responding to the allegations made in the letter of claim or the findings of their own internal investigations. Moreover, defendants' investigations at times appear to proceed by ignoring the letter of claim entirely.

As such, there is little reason to anticipate that this will change after the introduction of either set of the FRC rules. Disclosing all of the supporting evidence with the letter of claim allows the defendant 6 months (not 4) to obtain its own expert evidence and witness statements with full knowledge of the claimant's case. The reason why such requests should always be rejected outside of this <£25,000 FRC scheme is that experience of generations of litigators shows that the claimant's case is ignored in favour of judging it on the quality of the supporting evidence. It is therefore considered negligent to adopt this course of action before all of the facts of the case are known. This is why the standard directions order requires standard disclosure to occur before witness evidence with the simultaneous exchange of expert evidence on breach and causation occurring only after the experts have seen the finalised factual evidence.

With this in mind, there may well be cases where the risks of disclosing the expert evidence with the letter of claim objectively outweigh the benefit of a pre-issue settlement. An example would be a case where there is a genuine dichotomy of the factual evidence whereby the dispute is only likely to be resolved by the trial judge. Another would be where there is a fairly broad range of expert opinion which is only likely to be resolved wither by an experts' joint meeting or by the trial judge hearing the oral evidence. These cases do not lend themselves to the sequential exchange of expert evidence.

It is possible that that the rules for cases settling under £25,000 will turn out to be different to the government's proposals. At the time of writing, they have not been published. The central question for claimant's lawyers is whether we are obliged to disclose the expert evidence in every case.

Page 31 of the consultation response states that most cases will proceed via the standard track and the light track is suitable where it is *anticipated* that breach and causation will be admitted. This is the claimant's decision and then it is for the defendant to confirm it by making these admissions. The suggested criterion is that there is evidence to support the belief that an early admission will be made.

The difficulty is that we know that defendants often do not make such admissions. Accordingly, the first safety measure that should reasonably be used by claimants is to write a short letter to the defendant enclosing the document relied on and requesting confirmation that liability will be admitted before the decision that FRC applies is made. If liability is to be admitted, then there is evidence in favour of using the light track and the FRC notification letter can be safely sent. If not, then there is evidence that the assumption is an unsafe one at the earliest possible stage.

Once the light track is deemed unsuitable, the expectation is that the case proceeds in the standard track. *Section 5.3 (p41)* of the consultation response states that the letter of claim must be accompanied by the expert evidence on liability and quantum. However, the issue highlighted above did not form part of the consultation. *Section 5.8 (pp61-69)* covers the sanctions for non-compliance. One of the consultation questions was whether failing to provide evidence of sufficient *quality* should amount to a conduct issue justifying a 50% reduction to the claimant's FRC amount. In order to set this up, the defendant need only provide an explanation in support of its belief that the claimant's evidence is inadequate in its letter of response. Then, at a later date, the court will need to decide whether this was reasonable.

However, the government's consultation response does not state that the claimant *must* follow the standard track protocol; just that it *should*. Failing to follow it risks being found to be a conduct issue potentially justifying the penalty of a 50% reduction in the FRC amount.

Although this should not be taken lightly, the claimant does have a choice. There is a range of possible scenarios created by the complexity of the human body; differing medical disciplines and the standards of care applicable to each of them; and the wide variety of different factual situations which can arise clinically. The standard and light tracks work best for cases where these variables are easily understood and can be clearly articulated and where liability should be admitted. They work worst where these variables create complexity, ambiguity or uncertainty. We respectfully submit that no litigant should be expected to voluntarily disclose evidence which potentially undermines its position under the spectre of a costs sanction in order to 'save costs'. This must be a choice arrived at having had the benefit of receiving carefully considered, independent legal advice.

Accordingly, claimant lawyers must be able to provide that advice independently of the commercial influences of getting paid. This therefore also requires advice on the pros and cons of complying with the rules and sequentially serving the expert evidence. This is likely to depend to a significant extent on the quality of the instructions; the extent to which the expert is able to head off counterarguments; evidence of the defendant's position already being entrenched; the range of opinion; and the quality of the supporting materials. This will be a challenge within the FRC straitjacket.

Where the evidence is strongly supportive, internally logical and well supported, then there is a lot to be said for disclosing it despite the risks. Where the evidence is unsupportive, then the case ought to be abandoned. Where the evidence is somewhere in the middle, then a decision needs to be made as to whether the case should be abandoned or whether it should continue to trial without following the pre-action protocol and risk the costs sanction.

Disclosing the evidence may well result in a letter of response denying liability but you will see the defendant's evidence. A further risk assessment can then be made to inform the decision as to whether to proceed to the mandatory stocktake and negotiation or to abandon the case.

Not disclosing the evidence means preparing to ultimately persuade the court that this was reasonable on the facts of this case. The letter of claim should therefore pre-emptively explain why the protocol is not being complied with and why this is reasonable. The more that this 'failure' can be shown to be isolated to a specific set of facts and the more that the rest of the protocol can be complied with or the more uncertainty there is as to whether the case is worth less than £25,000, the more chance there is that it will be found to be justifiable. Even so, the risk that the judge finds against you can never be excluded entirely.

Alternatively, these risks can be mitigated by serving the evidence protectively. The consultation response does not state that the evidence must be served openly. Although it must be served *with* the letter of claim, it appears that this could occur by having a second letter marked either 'without prejudice' or 'without prejudice save as to costs'. The latter option would permit these documents to be considered on costs issues. The advantage of this approach would be that the expert evidence (and any documents served with it) cannot be referred to in the main part of the case allowing them to be updated later should further evidence come to light. The disadvantage is that the defendant will still be able to use the content of the evidence and so any change of opinion could still be brought to light via properly targeted *Part 18* or *Part 35 Questions* or by skilful cross-examination. Disclosing the requisite evidence protectively would still allow the defendant to respond to it as envisaged by the consultation response.

There is also a potentially significant disadvantage to the defendant basing its response on the perceived quality of the expert evidence rather than the allegations being made. If liability is denied, then the case will not be suitable for the intermediate track if negotiations break down. As the current rules appear to preclude allocation to the small or fast tracks (subject to what is said in Chapters 2 & 3), this would mean that cases worth under £25,000 where liability is disputed would need to be allocated to the multi-track. If the case ultimately settled up to £25,000 then it is likely that pre-action FRC would be imposed but this would not prevent post-issue costs being assessed on the standard basis.

On the intermediate track, *CPR 1998, Rule 28.14(3)(c)* limits the length of expert reports to 20 pages (excluding 'necessary' technical and academic papers, photographs and plans only). This page limit is likely to include the matters directly relevant to the opinion offered (please see the *CPR Committee's November 2023 Minutes* (above). Subject to this, it may not be in a particular client's best interests for an expert to slavishly comply with the page limits on their reports.

The new *CPR 1998 Rule 28.14(3)(c)* does allow the court to permit longer reports. In clinical negligence at least, it may well be that we have already received a longer C&P report pre-action before the case became suitable for the intermediate track.

This may also depend on the outcome of the *CPR Committee's November 2023 Minutes'* recommendation as to when liability has to be admitted to trigger this. If liability must be admitted in full in the letter of response, then we can direct the C&P expert to this rule. However, the issues on causation of consequential losses or quantum may not be straightforward. The substantive, evidential and procedural rules have not been simplified to accommodate this rule.

In light of the downward costs pressures inherent in FRC, situations may arise where it is considered reasonable not to serve expert evidence instead relying on criticising your opponent's expert. This was the approach adopted in *TUI v Griffiths [2023] UKSC 48* where the defendant also elected to reserve its critique that the claimant's expert had not covered his opinion on causation fully until trial (such that the claimant's expert was not present to be cross-examined). Whilst the Supreme Court has ultimately depreciated this approach, it does highlight the risk that perceived failures to follow the substantive, procedural and evidential requirements may lead to expensive delays and risk.

Furthermore, the new rules do not say whether these limits apply to breach and causation expert evidence obtained before admissions were made. Accordingly, there may be persuasive reasons (supported by evidence) why this rule was not complied with. An illustration of the potential issues can be gleaned from the multi-track case of *Beatty v Lewisham & Greenwich NHS Trust [2023] EWHC 3163 (KB)*. Due to an appropriate pre-trial narrowing of the issues, only one expert per side was required and the trial lasted one day. Nonetheless, the criticisms *Jay, J* makes of the claimant's expert in failing to properly account for the factual evidence and his adversarial style under cross-examination; the ultimate weakness of the case on causation; and the possibility that the expert evidence had not been updated for over 2 years before trial are instructive. It seems unlikely that a case proceeding under the FRC tracks will succeed if there are gaps in the substantive, procedural or evidential requirements. This requires us to find innovative ways of ensuring that this occurs in every case. *Beatty* also clearly illustrates that narrowing the issues in a multi-track case can, *prima facie*, make the case appear suitable for the other tracks and this possibility ought to be planned for.

Experts should also consider explaining in his report why their *Part 35* duty to the court has overridden this rule where that is the case.

Exchanging Expert Evidence

The intermediate track does allow a separate amount for a single conference in the pre-trial period. Accordingly, it will become necessary to make a reasoned decision whether to hold this before the expert evidence is exchanged (in order to finalise the reports) or more immediately pre-trial (after the joint meetings have occurred). If more than one conference is required, then another way of paying for this will need to be found and agreed with your client and counsel.

If you decide to have the conference later, then you will need to be confident that the reports are fully compliant and cover all of the issues. This may well take up a significant proportion of the available FRC, especially if this has not been done earlier in the case. Understanding the requirements for compliant and persuasive expert evidence is crucial and a checklist of the requirements will likely assist.

Similarly, it remains prudent to analyse the defendant's expert evidence it identify gaps in the reasoning and weak spots in its case.

Experts' Joint Meetings

The intermediate track does not allow a separate amount for counsel preparing the agendas. Regrettably, there is no evidence that FRC is likely to resolve the ongoing issues we encounter in practice in respect of agreeing the agendas. In light of the limited amount of time available under FRC, the most efficient approach may well prove to be to simply have 2 agendas or single, combined agenda setting out each side's questions if swift agreement cannot be reached.

When drafting agendas, an important decision to make is to decide whether you are better focussing in on the differences between the experts' respective opinions in light of their reports or on seeking as much agreement as possible on the pleaded issues. Whilst these will sometimes be the same, mostly they are not. Counsel, in particular, will often draft agendas based on how the case will need to be presented at trial and the vast majority of fee earners cannot do this (because they have no trial experience). Focussing on the areas of remaining disagreement based on the served reports is a more realistic goal for fee earners, especially where they fully understand their case.

However, this leaves a problem where one expert has failed to deal with an issue, fact or point. Is it wiser to leave this out or allow them a second bite of the cherry? Leaving it out is reasonable because they have not addressed it in their report. However, the trial judge may be assisted more by seeing the matter clearly dealt with in the joint statement.

On balance, there are significant risks associated with not asking trial counsel to have at least some input into the drafting of the agendas. If you are confident in your abilities as the conducting file handler, then counsel is more likely to agree to check your agendas at little or no additional cost. If you are not, then it is more likely that you will need to use some of your FRC to pay them to assist you.

If you are planning to have a pre-trial conference, then it may well be more efficient to send the joint statements to counsel as part of the conference bundle as opposed to risk a duplication of effort by reviewing them yourself first.

Conclusion

As it has become evident, the number of experts involved in each case can be the deciding factor as to what track the case might end up at. In situations where the case might fall outside of the multi-track, it is always good to double check what is the current situation and how many expert reports you think you are going to rely on or would have relied on (if the case was to go to trial).

If your expert evidence justifiably exceeds the threshold that is suited for each of the other tracks, then you might be 'off the hook' and should be able to argue successfully that your case no longer meets the requirements for it to be suitable for the multi-track. However, there is likely to need to be a genuine justification to persuade the court that you are not just trying to circumvent the FRC rules.

As highlighted above, one needs to be mindful as to how you come to this conclusion and ensure that that is not something that you are going to achieve only for the mere reason of the case not being caught under the FRC. As long as it makes sense to have that many expert reports etc, then you should be just fine.

In summary, despite no alterations to the substantive, evidential, or procedural rules, the coherence and consistency of expert evidence remain crucial for its persuasiveness. However, the constraints from FRC on ensuring that expert opinion is based upon all of the relevant evidence risks making it harder for claimants to win. The recommendation of disclosing claimant's liability and quantum expert evidence with the letter of claim (in cases worth under £25,000) seems ill-conceived and unfair, as it contradicts the usual order in multi-track cases' standard directions order. This change primarily impacts cases deemed suitable for the light or standard tracks after April 2024, with no overt indication of it affecting intermediate track cases.

This shift represents a significant change selectively applied to specific cases. It is likely fee earners will need to make difficult decisions as to when conferences are held, when to instruct counsel and on which issues. When dealing with expert joint meetings in the intermediate track, it is important to consider various factors. Firstly, there is no specific allowance for counsel to prepare agendas, and the likelihood of the court or the parties resolving agenda-related issues promptly and efficiently remains uncertain. In such cases, two separate agendas or a single combined one if quick agreement cannot be reached. If experts' fees remain outside of FRC, then this may be sufficient to exert commercial pressure on defendants to seek more agreement.

CHAPTER NINE

STREAMLINING: USE OF PROCESS MAPPING AND AI

Introduction

Given that FRC essentially limits the amount of hours that can be spent on a case, it follows that increased efficiency is touted as being the way to progress cases. This forms the mainstay of the approaches many firms have already adopted or plan to do so.

Broadly speaking, these can be categorised into using process mapping; templates; or artificial intelligence. One of the main challenges with these approaches is that the processes created tend not to account fully for the other stakeholders' actions.

Whatever combination of tools is adopted, they must be used within an overall management strategy aimed at repeatedly winning cases profitably. This may be sector-wide, firm-wide, department-wide or personal to an individual fee earner. It makes little practical sense to use these tools in isolation in an adversarial system where many stakeholders hold an interest in the outcome. Since FRC decreases the size of the available resources, every stakeholder who relies on this resource pool has less to work with.

Using Process Mapping

Process mapping is a visual technique used to represent and understand how a series of activities, tasks, or steps come together to accomplish a particular goal or outcome. It is similar to creating a map that shows the journey from the beginning to the end of a process. Just as a traditional map helps you navigate through physical places, a process map helps you navigate through a sequence of progressive actions on your cases.

In the context of clinical negligence, process mapping would involve breaking down all the steps you take, from initial marketing, risk assessing the case, gathering evidence, marshalling this into a viable whole through to settling the case, recovering costs and marketing the outcome. Each step is represented in the map, usually as a box or shape, and these boxes are connected with lines to show the order in which the steps are completed. This forms a repeatable cycle.

Process mapping is used in various fields, including business, healthcare, manufacturing, and more. In healthcare, for instance, it could be used to illustrate the steps involved in patient care, from admission to discharge. By visually mapping out the process, you can better understand the flow of events, identify potential bottlenecks or inefficiencies, and pinpoint areas for improvement.

In a nutshell, process mapping is a way to make complex processes easier to understand by breaking them down into simple, visual representations. Accordingly, process mapping can play a significant role in simplifying clinical negligence litigation by enhancing transparency, efficiency, and understanding of the processes involved. It is a valuable tool for improving efficiency, communication, and problem-solving and so avoid using up significant amounts of the FRC for each case by reinventing the wheel for each new case.

Practical examples of how process mapping in healthcare and litigation can assist in profitable case management include:

1. **Clear Documentation of Procedures:** Process mapping provides a visual representation of the clinical procedures and protocols followed in patient care. This documentation can help legal teams understand the sequence of events leading up to the alleged negligence.

2. **Identifying Key Stakeholders:** Mapping out processes helps identify the various individuals involved in patient care, from medical professionals to administrative staff. The relevant dramatis personae in the case, can then be identified more efficiently and the key personnel required for the case itself care then added in more easily. This can aid in determining responsibilities and accountabilities in the litigation process.

3. **Pinpointing Communication Flaws:** Process mapping highlights communication pathways within the healthcare system and in the litigation. In cases of negligence, this can reveal if crucial information was withheld, miscommunicated, or overlooked, leading to adverse outcomes. This assists both in identifying relevant evidence and in highlighting errors or gaps in both sides' cases.

4. **Revealing Standard Operating Procedures:** By visualizing the standard operating procedures (SOPs) followed, process mapping can help determine whether healthcare providers adhered to established protocols or deviated from them, potentially leading to errors. Likewise, if all of the fee earners within the same department are following the same processes, it is far easier to ensure that FRC remains profitable.

5. **Chronology of Events:** Process maps create a chronological representation of events, making it easier for legal professionals to grasp the timeline of actions and decisions, which can be crucial in establishing negligence.

6. **Identifying Decision Points:** Decision points in patient care and within the litigation, can be critical in determining liability. Process mapping highlights where significant decisions were made, enabling legal teams to assess whether these decisions were appropriate and well-informed.

7. **Analysing Contributing Factors:** Process maps can highlight contributing factors to adverse events, including systemic issues

such as resource constraints or lack of training. This broader understanding can contextualize individual actions and aid in apportioning responsibility. When conducting periodical departmental debriefs of concluded FRC cases, this helps to identify where process changes are most likely to be beneficial.

8. **Enhanced Collaboration:** Process mapping involves input from various stakeholders, fostering collaboration between legal experts and medical professionals. This multidisciplinary approach can lead to a more comprehensive assessment of negligence claims.

9. **Identifying Gaps in Documentation:** Incomplete or missing documentation can hinder litigation efforts. Process mapping can uncover gaps in the records, prompting the need for further investigation or substantiation.

10. **Facilitating Expert Testimony:** Clear visual representations from process mapping can be used as evidence in court. Medical experts can more effectively explain complex procedures, decisions, and actions to judges and juries.

Incorporating process mapping into clinical negligence litigation can therefore bring about a more structured and transparent approach to assessing claims. However, it is important to note that while process mapping can simplify certain aspects of litigation, the legal process remains complex and may require collaboration between legal experts, medical professionals, and other stakeholders to arrive at a fair resolution.

Using Templates

Using legal templates can offer several advantages in improving the efficiency of clinical negligence litigation. It is prudent to consider both the pros and cons of using templates.

The use of legal templates can enhance efficiency in the following ways:

1. **Consistency:** Legal templates ensure a consistent format and structure for documents, reducing the risk of errors and inconsistencies in pleadings, motions, and other legal documents.

2. **Time Savings:** Templates eliminate the need to start from scratch, saving lawyers time in drafting routine documents and allowing them to focus more on case-specific details.

3. **Faster Document Preparation:** With predefined sections and content, lawyers can quickly assemble documents by filling in relevant information, leading to faster preparation of legal materials.

4. **Accurate Legal Language:** Templates are often crafted by legal experts, ensuring that the appropriate legal language, terminology, and clauses are included in documents.

5. **Streamlined Workflows:** Templates provide a roadmap for document creation, helping lawyers organize their thoughts and arguments more efficiently.

6. **Reduced Risk of Omissions:** Templates prompt lawyers to cover essential points, reducing the chances of omitting critical information in legal documents.

7. **Ease of Collaboration:** Templates can be easily shared among legal team members, facilitating collaborative efforts and ensuring everyone follows a uniform approach.

8. **Training and Consistency for Junior Lawyers:** Templates, when kept up-to-date, can serve as training tools for junior lawyers, guiding them on proper document drafting and ensuring consistency across the firm.

9. **Focus on Case Strategy:** By expediting the document drafting process, lawyers can allocate more time to developing a robust case strategy and focusing on legal arguments.

10. **Adherence to Court Requirements:** Templates can be designed to meet specific court formatting and submission requirements, reducing the risk of non-compliance.

Conversely, care should be taken not to over-rely on them. Some of the risks associated with template use include:

1. **Lack of Customization:** Templates may not perfectly fit the nuances of each case, potentially leading to oversimplification or omission of case-specific details.

2. **Risk of Overlooking Issues:** Relying solely on templates could cause lawyers to overlook unique legal or factual issues that require tailored attention.

3. **Loss of Creativity:** Templates can stifle creativity in document drafting, leading to formulaic and less engaging legal materials.

4. **Inaccurate or Outdated Content:** If templates are not regularly updated, they might contain outdated legal references or incorrect information.

5. **'Cookie-Cutter' Approach:** Overreliance on templates might result in a generic, one-size-fits-all approach that doesn't effectively address the complexities of a specific case.

6. **Dependency on Technology:** Technical issues with template software or systems could disrupt the workflow and lead to delays.

7. **Risk of Plagiarism:** Inappropriate use of templates without proper customization could lead to inadvertent plagiarism or ethical concerns.

8. **Limited Flexibility:** Templates might not accommodate unique legal arguments or innovative strategies that could be beneficial for a particular case.

9. **Complex Cases:** Extremely complex cases may not be well-suited for templates, as they require more in-depth and tailored analysis.

10. **Inadequate Communication:** Overreliance on templates might lead to a lack of effective communication and collaboration among legal team members.

In summary, legal templates can significantly enhance efficiency in clinical negligence litigation by expediting document preparation and maintaining consistency. However, their use should be balanced with a thorough understanding of the case's specifics to ensure that crucial details are not overlooked and that the documents accurately reflect the legal arguments being presented.

Using Artificial Intelligence (AI)

There is an important caveat to be made when considering the use of AI in FRC cases. The generative large language models currently enjoying popularity effectively predict the next word in a statistical model. They do not conduct original research or have the same ethical responsibilities that lawyers do. Accordingly, if you do decide to use AI to assist with fee earning work, it is essential to check that work for accuracy. Bear in mind that the wording of the statement of truth for statements of case and witness statements are, respectively (*CPR 1998, PD 22 (paras. 2.1 & 2.2)*):

> *'[I believe][the (claimant or as may be) believes] that the facts stated in this [name document being verified] are true. [I understand] [The (claimant or as may be) understands] that proceedings for contempt of court may be brought against anyone who makes, or causes to be made, a false statement in a document verified by a statement of truth without an honest belief in its truth.'*

> *'I believe that the facts stated in this witness statement are true. I understand that proceedings for contempt of court may be brought against anyone who makes, or causes to be made, a false statement in a document verified by a statement of truth without an honest belief in its truth.'*

Accordingly, it is very likely that a statement of truth cannot be properly signed without carefully checking the document or research produced using AI and the time taken to do so may well be counter-productive when attempting to stay within the FRC limits. *Harber v Commissioners for His Majesty's Revenue & Customs (…) [2023] UKFTT 1007* and The Law Society Gazette's report *"LiP presents false citations to court after asking ChatGPT" (29th May 2023)* both illustrate the dangers of not checking the accuracy of AI-generated research.

Nonetheless, proponents of AI and machine learning (ML) often propose four main areas where these technologies can benefit lawyers:

1. Optimisation of processes and workflows in order to increase efficiency; reduce errors; and improve overall productivity. This is the most alluring to those running the firm and is the most interesting in the short-term for fee earners dealing regularly with FRC.

2. Predictive analysis. These technologies allow for large amounts of data to be analysed quickly and for useful patterns of behaviour or outcomes to be predicted. Knowledge is power and the more efficiently you can process your FRC case data and gain a competitive advantage. These predictions can then be tested against ongoing cases and refined. This proactive process forms the basis for 'data-driven decisions'.

3. Automating routine and repetitive tasks. This can legitimately be seen as a potential threat to jobs. However, we prefer to view it as using a tool which allows us to do more. Just as it is easier to chop down a tree with a chainsaw than a hand axe or quicker to travel by car than a horse-drawn carriage, time can be saved in

FRC cases by having AI/ML do the routine tasks and allowing you to spend your limited hours on progressing the case, negotiating the best deal for your client and helping with your firm's cash flow.

4. Collaborating both with your colleagues and with your opponents. With opponents, the hurdle is likely to be why your case is worth more than they believe within a relatively narrow damages band of £25,000-£100,000. As we will cover in more detail in Chapter 10 FRC works best where the case settles pre-action. If you can reach a stage where you have all of your settlement evidence ready, the need for proceedings (and the associated higher risks of working unprofitably) are greatly reduced. Within your teams, using tools which enable real-time communication and cross-fertilisation of ideas to help solve problems quickly significantly improves your chances of winning cases within the FRC limits.

Whatever system you or your firm uses, as a fee earner expected to run clinical negligence cases profitably, we recommend that you consider how it helps you with certain key issues.

Summary of Key Issues for AI & ML

AI/ML Potential Use Case	**FRC Objective**
Acceleration	Speeding up existing processes
Detection	Identifying problems before they occur
Prevention	Planning to stop problems
Delivering	Effective execution of plans
Debriefing	Maintenance of a healthy system

Acceleration

AI can significantly accelerate claims and reduce case duration for lawyers dealing with clinical negligence claims by leveraging data research and analysis. Firstly, AI can expedite the process of finding suitable experts outside of office hours. By utilizing advanced search algorithms and natural language processing, AI can scan vast volumes of expert profiles and academic databases to identify the most relevant and available experts efficiently. This not only saves lawyers valuable time but also enables them to access expert opinions and insights promptly, contributing to faster case progression and decision-making.

Secondly, AI can enhance the analysis of treatment protocols and clinical studies within the FRC limits. AI-powered tools can efficiently review experts' supporting materials and medical literature, extracting key insights and relevant information. By automating this process, lawyers can quickly identify pertinent evidence, assess its impact on the case, and make informed decisions within the cost constraints of the FRC regime. This ensures that legal professionals can expedite their work while maintaining compliance with FRC limits.

In summary, AI's capabilities in data research and analysis enable lawyers to accelerate claims and reduce case duration in clinical negligence cases. By efficiently finding suitable experts and reviewing supporting materials, AI empowers legal professionals to make faster and more informed decisions, ultimately expediting the claims process while adhering to cost limitations. This not only benefits the legal team but also ensures timely resolutions for claimants and healthcare providers.

Potential Solution	Example	Required Information
Data research to find patterns & solutions to FRC problems	E.g. Finding suitable experts outside of office hours	Court-compliant suitability criteria drawn from case law Fee structure Template approach letters
Analysis of treatment protocols & clinical studies	E.g. Reviewing experts' supporting materials efficiently within FRC limits	Clear understanding of central issues in dispute Accurate analysis of materials Human sense checking

Detection

AI can significantly assist lawyers in the detection of potential issues and anomalies within clinical negligence claims. Firstly, through early warning systems, AI can highlight anomalies in case progression data, such as predicting when fee earners are approaching a particular FRC stage limit. By analysing historical case data and fee earners' productivity, AI can provide alerts when cases are at risk of exceeding FRC limits, enabling proactive management to avoid financial penalties. This early detection not only prevents compliance issues but also helps optimize resource allocation and improve cost-effectiveness.

Secondly, AI can diagnose case issues by utilizing pattern recognition techniques. By analysing patterns in historical case data, AI can predict likely issues that may arise in similar cases. For example, it can identify common hurdles, delays, or challenges that occurred in past cases with similar characteristics. This allows lawyers to proactively address potential problems, streamline processes, and develop tailored strategies to overcome issues, ultimately improving case outcomes and efficiency.

In summary, AI's capabilities in early warning and diagnosing case issues based on historical data can greatly benefit lawyers in clinical negligence claims. By flagging anomalies in case progression data and predicting likely issues, AI empowers legal professionals to take pre-emptive actions, mitigate risks, and ensure smoother case management, ultimately leading to better client satisfaction and more successful outcomes.

Potential Solution	Example	Required Information
Early warning highlighting anomalies in case progression data	E.g. case forecasting data predicting when fee earners will hit FRC stage limit	Accurate time recording & identification of key goals within stages
Diagnosing case issues via pattern recognition	E.g. use of historical case date to predict likely issues on similar cases	Standardised GDPR approvals from clients Reliable historical case data Accurate gap analyses

Prevention

AI can be a powerful tool in preventing problems and barriers to settlement in clinical negligence claims. Firstly, by predicting the defendant's responses and likely settlement points, AI can help lawyers avoid missed opportunities. Using historical data and predictive analytics, AI can identify patterns and factors that influence defendants' decisions to settle. This allows legal professionals to make informed negotiation strategies, increasing the likelihood of reaching favourable settlements and avoiding unnecessary litigation costs.

Secondly, real-time monitoring of internal performance through AI can help lawyers improve their habits and decision-making processes. AI systems can track and analyse lawyers' performance metrics, such as response times, case management efficiency, and negotiation outcomes. This real-time feedback allows legal professionals to identify areas for improvement, adjust their strategies, and make data-driven decisions to enhance their overall performance in handling clinical negligence claims.

Lastly, adopting information accuracy through AI can help lawyers avoid failures stemming from cognitive biases. AI can provide reliable and personalized reporting of case outcomes based on objective data, reducing the influence of subjective judgments and cognitive biases. By relying on accurate, data-driven insights, lawyers can make more informed decisions, assess case strengths and weaknesses objectively, and reduce the risk of making errors due to biases that could hinder the settlement process.

In summary, AI can be a valuable asset in preventing problems and barriers to settlement in clinical negligence claims by predicting defendant responses, surveilling internal performance, and ensuring information accuracy. By leveraging AI-driven insights and data, lawyers can make more informed, strategic decisions, ultimately leading to smoother settlements and improved outcomes for all parties involved.

Potential Solution	**Example**	**Required Information**
Predicting Defendant's response to avoid missed opportunities	E.g. using data to predict likely settlement points	Reliable data inputting Clear data appoints for cases' key stages Ability to focus on those pressure points
Surveilling internal performance	E.g. real time monitoring of your own performance to improve your habits	Desire to improve Case debriefs to understand what worked and did not Learning from efficiency data

Information accuracy to avoid failure	E.g. reliable personalised reporting of case outcomes to avoid cognitive biases	Objective past reporting measures (e.g. profitability, duration & success rates) Used to inform future performance measures Allowing reliable replication of own success

Delivering

AI can play a pivotal role in developing searchable expert databases for clinical negligence cases. By leveraging natural language processing (NLP) and machine learning algorithms, AI systems can efficiently identify and categorise experts based on their specialties, availability, and past performance.

This enables legal professionals to quickly access suitable and available experts for case reviews. Additionally, AI can automate the process of updating and expanding the database by continuously analysing new data and expert profiles, ensuring its relevance and accuracy over time.

Furthermore, AI-driven chatbots or virtual assistants can streamline the initial case triage and information gathering process. These AI-powered tools can engage with claimants or legal professionals to collect standard case information, such as incident details, medical records, and potential witnesses.

By using conversational AI, these systems can ask relevant questions, validate information, and provide immediate responses, significantly reducing the administrative burden and expediting the claims assessment process. This not only improves efficiency but also ensures consistency and accuracy in the data collected, reducing the risk of errors and omissions in clinical negligence claims.

Overall, AI-driven solutions for expert databases and automated case triage offer a more efficient and reliable way to handle clinical negligence cases, benefiting both claimants and legal professionals.

Potential Solution	**Example**	**Required Information**
Responding to support needs	E.g. searchable expert databases of suitable, available experts	Current expert availability Automated search function Pre-agreed instruction criteria
Automating service provision	E.g. use of chatbots or virtual assistants to triage cases or gather standard case information	Clear idea of required information Effective information gathering Clear exit route to humans for unusual cases

Debriefing

AI can provide invaluable support in the debriefing process following the conclusion of clinical negligence claims. Firstly, AI-powered analytics can enhance lawyers' adaptability by conducting periodic reviews of cohorts of completed FRC cases. These reviews can analyse past cases to identify trends, common challenges, and successful strategies. By gaining insights from historical data, legal professionals can adapt their approach, improve case management, and enhance their overall effectiveness in handling FRC cases. AI can provide recommendations based on the analysis of past cases, allowing lawyers to continuously refine their strategies and decision-making processes.

Secondly, AI can assist in conducting a FRC 'health check' by providing real-time performance monitoring. By tracking case profitability through daily time recording and expense analysis, AI can alert legal teams to potential issues early in the process. This allows for proactive management of costs and resource allocation, ensuring that FRC cases remain financially viable. Moreover, AI can provide insights into areas where efficiency improvements can be made, helping legal professionals to optimize their workflows and maintain profitability within the constraints of the FRC regime.

In summary, AI can play a crucial role in enhancing lawyers' adaptability through the analysis of completed FRC cases, enabling continuous improvement in case handling strategies. Additionally, AI's real-time performance monitoring can identify areas for optimization, helping legal teams to navigate the challenges posed by cost constraints effectively.

Potential Solution	**Example**	**Required Information**
Adaptability	E.g. periodic reviews of cohorts of completed FRC cases	Accurate case management information on agreed pressure points Debrief review of outcomes & lessons learned Implementation of improvements for major & marginal gains
FRC 'health check' real-time performance monitoring	E.g tracking case profitability from daily time recording	Accurate time recording of case tasks Accurate profitability benchmarking Flexible pivoting as required

Management Protocols

The overarching intention should be to harmonise the approach to case management in order to encourage self-development by achieving greater self-generated success within the FRC regime.

By assisting yourself and your colleagues to innovate, you have an alternative to imposing a new way of working. This encourages teams to focus on their everyday attitudes and behaviours which form the habits which underpin performance.

A useful approach to adopt is to develop positive new habits by focussing on improving your daily attitudes and behaviours.

Understanding the small steps you can to take each day to reach your goals, you can repeat the process regularly to reach these.

The underlying concept can be visualised by imagining that every part of our job falls into one of 3 areas: legal, commercial & organisational. The goal is to find the right balance between these.

E.g.: A witness statement is needed. It must comply with the procedural requirements under the CPR 1998 and the evidential requirements of the case ('legal'); sufficient time must be allocated to it to be prepared by an appropriate colleague ('organisational'); & performing this task helps with case pro-activity, reducing case duration & increasing the recoverable time on the file ('commercial').

As an overview, an effective and practical case management protocol should be divided into three parts: top, middle and bottom.

In the top tier, the aim is to work on each case at least monthly. This allows legal issues to be addressed; permits organisation; and includes time for a brief client update, case pro-activity, data integrity, and other 'data driven' activities to be dealt with.

In the middle tier: the aim is to take a progressive step at least monthly. This moves each case towards the next pressure point ('lily pad') and so towards settlement. You can then work back to fill in gaps left by hopping back between lily pads whilst a response to the main action awaited (from the defendant, claimant, expert, the court, or other stakeholder). This is balanced by using the legal, commercial and organisational skill sets .

In the bottom tier, the aim is on the analysis of the core points needed to win each pressure point – e.g. legal issues, evidential issues or strategic issues. More generally, you use the amount of FRC intelligently on those things which take more time to do. To do so:

- Break them down into their small, constituent parts ('organisational').
- Take responsibility for solving each problem professionally yourself or delegating effectively ('organisational'). Delegation can be to a paralegal, expert, counsel, defendant or the court as needed as long as the costs are recoverable within the FRC regime.
- Solve each mini problem sequentially ('organisational') and time record fully for each piece of work ('commercial'). Under FRC, time recording helps you to directly track your profit margin for each case.
- Research solutions as needed ('legal'), remembering that this eats into your profit margin. If you want to charge your client for this, recovering costs for research is often contested so you require a clear attendance note setting out why this was an unusual situation ('commercial'). You could develop standardised precedents for this rather than reinventing the wheel each time ('organisational').
- Review solutions and the time taken to reach them. Saving this information to help improve your approach for next time ('organisational').

Litigation Stages

This can be drawn together into a structured approach to the litigation process.

1. **Initial Risk Assessment & Client Retention**

   The key habits are to produce a clear initial risk assessment in a prescribed format setting out the central allegations to help the conducting fee earner run the case and to keep new clients.

   Cases need to be either onboarded quickly to avoid losing them to your competitors or rejected with appropriate signposting. The client care paperwork needs to be templated but clear and accurate. This is best achieved as an overhead outside of FRC.

2. **Initial Investigations to 2nd Risk Assessment**

   The key habits within this stage are:

   1. Focussing investigations on the central allegations;
   2. Testing the central allegations against the initial factual evidence;
   3. Clear advice to your client; and
   4. Closing cases which do not continue to have sufficient prospects of success.

3. **Liability expert evidence to 3rd Risk Assessment**

   The key habits within this stage are:

   1. Focussing investigations on the central allegations;
   2. Testing the central allegations against the initial expert evidence;
   3. Proper instruction of experts;
   4. Clear updated advice to your client; and

5. Closing cases which do not continue to have sufficient prospects of success.

4. **Letter of Claim to Letter of Response and 4th Risk Assessment**

The key habits within this stage are:

1. Focussing the allegations on the central allegations supported by expert evidence;
2. Testing the central allegations against the defendant's response;
3. Proper analysis of letter of response;
4. Clear updated advice to your client; and
5. Closing cases which do not continue to have sufficient prospects of success.

5. **C&P expert evidence & case valuation**

The key habits within this stage are:

1. Proper quantification of cases pre-issue;
2. Testing the valuation against the other evidence; and
3. Clear advice to your client

6. **Pre-issue negotiations and settlement or 5th Risk Assessment**

The key habits within this stage are:

1. Making a protective settlement offer pre-issue;
2. Narrowing the issues to be litigated;
3. Effective stocktaking;

4. Clear updated advice to your client;

5. Settling pre-issue; and

6. Closing cases which do not continue to have sufficient prospects of success.

7. Issue & Service of Proceedings, Defence & 6th Risk Assessment

The key habits within this stage are:

1. Issue proceedings correctly and within limitation (allowing for bankruptcy, capacity, correct fees, wording, etc);

2. Serving proceedings promptly and correctly (within 4 months without needing an extension);

3. Accurate pleading of the case by both sides first time (including Replies to Defence which must be served with the DQ where matters such as fundamental dishonesty have been raised);

4. Effective use of Part 18 Questions and Notices to Admit Facts to help achieve this;

5. Clear updated advice to your client; and

6. Closing cases which do not continue to have sufficient prospects of success.

8. Case management – directions & allocation/assignment

The key habits within this stage are:

1. Accurate completion of the DQs;

2. (Rarely): Effective preparation of Replies to the Defence

3. Case management directions which proactively direct the case;

4. Allocation and assignment which are properly linked to the directions and provide sufficient funds to deal with the remaining issues;

5. Effective representation at the CMC; and

6. Clear updated advice to your client.

9. **Finalisation of evidence & 7th Risk Assessment**

The key habits within this stage are:

1. Obtaining all relevant documents for standard disclosure;

2. Conducting standard disclosure;

3. Analysing your opponent's disclosure & cross-referencing with your own evidence;

4. Conducting effective specific disclosure applications as needed;

5. Finalising your own witness statements and cross-referencing with your opponent's disclosure;

6. Analysing your opponent's witness statements cross-referencing with your own evidence;

7. Clear updated advice to your client; and

8. Closing cases which do not continue to enjoy a reasonable prospect of success.

10. Finalisation of expert evidence & 8th Risk Assessment

The key habits within this stage are:

1. Finalising all of your own expert evidence and cross-referencing with your own and your opponent's documentary disclosure & witness statements and with your own expert evidence;

2. Confirming that your own & opponent's experts' supporting materials do support those opinions;

3. Analysing your opponent's expert evidence and cross-referencing against your evidence;

4. Successful use of Part 35 questions as needed;

5. Successfully bringing or defendant an application to control expert evidence;

6. Producing clear agendas which deal with the central allegations & managing the joint meetings;

7. Clear updated advice to your client; and

8. Closing cases which do not continue to enjoy a reasonable prospect of success

11. Pre-trial 9th RA & trial or settlement

The key habits within this stage are:

1. Finalising your own schedule/counter-schedule of special damages/loss with respect to the central allegations;

2. Analysing your own opponent's schedule/counter-schedule of special damages/loss with respect to the central allegations;

3. Efficient approach to pre-trial review;
4. Correct pre-trial preparation; and
5. Effective trial management & risk management

12. Costs recovery

The key habits within this stage are:

1. Pre-emptively planning for FRC costs-recovery;
2. Successfully obtaining payments on account of costs following admissions of liability;
3. Successfully obtaining Sanderson/Bullock Orders where there are multiple defendants;
4. Successfully enforcing QOCS protection or obtaining issue-based costs orders/reductions on lost cases where possible;
5. High recovery of time recording vs recovered costs
6. Winning provisional or detailed assessment hearings when these are (rarely) unavoidable

Creating Something Better

Every case has the same general lifecycle comprising of the same main milestones. Within this, the precise steps required to reach each milestone and ultimately resolve the case may differ depending on the precise factual matrix and actions of the other stakeholders. A framework (such as the one described above) provides a structure to build your general case plan around. The use of process maps, templates and AI should then be focussed on the areas where the most efficiencies are likely to be gained. This then allows individual cases to be progressed in a more directed manner with a greater chance of keeping with the FRC amounts.

The overall goal remains the same as with multi-track cases; *viz.* to win and get paid. There is just less margin for error in FRC. Wins must be within the FRC amount. Otherwise, you have won only a pyrrhic victory. This is easier said than done because maintaining the discipline to progress each file in a similar way whilst not misinterpreting or leaving gaps in the available evidence does not come naturally to everyone. It can easily become demotivating.

By way of illustration, if we assume that a notional fee earner has a £250,000 target and aims to settle all of their FRC cases pre-action, Chapter 2 shows that their average FRC recovery is £14,300. This would mean that they have to settle 18 cases a year, or 1.5 per month. In contrast, if pre-October 2023, they averaged a proportionate £25,000 in recovered profit costs per case, they would need to settle 10 in the same period (less than 1 per month). Without these cases becoming any simpler, this notional fee earner must settle 80% more cases to meet their target. This is in addition working on cases which will be lost or otherwise do not proceed. Their pre-October 2023 action plan will not work with FRC.

Having a framework to build their strategy around is likely to help this fee earner. They, and anyone helping them, can see the main milestones to reach and what needs to be done to get there. They know if they spend proportionately more time on one milestone (say, witness statements), then they have less time to spend on others (say, negotiation). They still have flexibility in how they reach the milestones and with how much they spend on each one. Flexibility is essential when you operate in an adversarial system comprising of many different stakeholders. In simple terms, you cannot control the other stakeholders, only your own daily attitudes and behaviours.

Within the framework, some milestones are more important than others. These focus on the pressure points of the case. The two most relevant are:

(a) Obtaining a suitable admission on breach and causation (the first criteria for the intermediate track); and

(b) Settling the case (triggering the costs payment).

There are three key supporting milestones:

(i) Instructing the main liability expert (showing you have supportive factual evidence);

(ii) Sending the letter of claim (showing you have supportive expert evidence); and

(iii) Making an initial *Part 36* offer (showing you have valued the case).

The basic plan of action can therefore be simplified into an easily remembered 1:2:3 sequence:

1. Objective: Profitable wins; measured by

2. Main actions: Obtaining admissions & settling cases; achieved by

3. Key habits: Expert instructions; letters of claim; & making offers.

From this, there is no reason that the structure set out in the framework above cannot then be simplified further by taking some actions in earlier stages. Whether this is sensible in any given case depends on internal factors such as an individual's confidence; competence and motivations but also on external factors such as the clarity of the factual matrix; quality of the expert evidence; and willingness of the defendant to settle the case on mutually acceptable terms (as opposed to 'resolving' it on terms which only suit it).

This is why it is crucial to have a clear escape route for rejecting cases at each stage of the framework. The more that this is predictably based on new evidence (as opposed to an arbitrary decision point or subjective decision), then it is more likely that this will be seen as being objectively reasonable by your client.

Conclusion

The limited amount of work that you get paid for in the FRC regime greatly increases the risk that your pre-existing methods of winning cases will be unprofitable. This ultimately increases the risk of very competent lawyers leaving clinical negligence and thereby reducing patients' access to justice. This is an unacceptable outcome.

FRC also rewards efficiency but, in so doing, tends to promote a process-driven approach to clinical negligence. Even if the main qualifying criterion is a full admission on liability, it does not follow that the remaining quantum case will be straightforward. There is no 'one size fits all' and any given individual case risks being one which does easily fit into the FRC regime.

Believing that streamlining processes is the solution is often an indication that the proposer has little practical day-to-day experience of running this type of case. If they ever did, it was many years ago. Simply enforcing change management; adopting subjectively efficient new processes; obligatory template use; or relying on technological advances without understanding that the complexities of clinical negligence are unrelated to their value is a very risky strategy.

Likewise, trying to ignore these changes or hoping that you will win more cases than you lose is equally risky. Whilst focussing on proportionality and costs budgeting has helped, many fee earners remain inefficient and the law reports continue to show examples of 'poor' practice.

The middle ground lies in finding ways to fit existing best practice into the new straitjacket of FRC. Whilst this feels like fitting a square peg into a round hole, it is not impossible to achieve.

CHAPTER TEN

STRATEGIES AND GENERAL APPROACH TO FRC

Introduction

Since we are at the start of a new era in clinical negligence, there are a number of strategies which could work. As our experience with FRC grows, some of these will prove more effective than others. Some may work for a time but then become unviable once further amendments to the rules are introduced.

In this chapter, we aim to explore the available approaches against what is known about the October 2023 version of the rules and what might change by April 2024. Forecasting what is likely happen is fraught with danger and so we limit ourselves to considering the options and the practice issues they raise. What happens in practice is likely to depend on the evidence in each case and policy decisions made by the courts.

Broadly-speaking, our duty to our clients and to the court requires us to limit FRC to those cases which genuinely require it. Where there is ambiguity, this needs to be planned for as early as possible, and the plan executed vigorously. Care is required because, at least for cases settling below £25,000, FRC will apply if no letter of claim was sent before the rules for the 'lower value' clinical negligence cases come into force (perhaps as early as April 2024).

Exclusion (Don't Do FRC Cases)

Some firms have decided not to take on cases which might be worth less than £100,000 or even £250,000 since FRC were initially proposed. As such, this is a viable option. Such a decision requires you to be confident that your risk assessment process minimises the risk of 'lower-value' cases slipping through the net.

As time goes on, such fee earners risk becoming further and further removed from the FRC debate because they will have no practical experience of running such cases. In the event that they do find themselves doing FRC work, then there is an argument in favour of them referring them to a solicitor who does possess the necessary skill set enabling them to specialise in FRC cases.

A related issue is whether it is commercially viable to take over a file from another firm of solicitors. Before the implementation of the new rules, we have already seen examples of firms requiring not just a lien on their costs but a lien which splits the amount of FRC. For the receiving solicitor, this is fraught with danger. There is no reason to assume that you can rely on the quality of the work done, and yet re-doing the work makes no sense if the costs are to be shared. If the original firm terminated the CFA due to poor prospects, then it is not entitled to expect a lien on its costs, so does one wish to accept a case which has already been rejected? If the case is accepted, ask yourself whether you really need the previous file. It may be that it is better to start again.

Carry On Regardless (Don't Change)

FRC cases are still clinical negligence cases. Unless the substantive, evidential and procedural laws are simplified, our professional obligations will continue to require us to fully advise our clients. Accordingly, if you are unconcerned with working at a loss, continuing to work as if the case was under the multi-track could pay dividends and win a case others would lose.

In this approach, fee earners have less FRC planning to do and tend to rely more on costs draftsman to get the best result possible.

Back to the Future

Once FRC are in play, the incentive to review evidence in order to build up a watertight case is significantly reduced. Winning by careful preparation becomes counter-productive. If a claimant is confident that their experts have properly addressed the central allegations and fully accounted for the evidence, what is to be gained by prevarication or delay?

Following this through logically can lead to a conclusion that it is better to move as swiftly as possible to trial once pre-issue negotiations have failed to settle the case. The new FRC rules encourage this because they are intended to ensure that 'excessive' costs are not recoverable.

On this view, it is better to progress quickly through each remaining stage of the litigation. Issue and serve proceedings together; do not agree to an extension for the defence; push for a short pre-trial timetable; have standard disclosure ready; minimise updates to witness statements and expert reports; have short or even no expert agendas; and let the expert persuade the trial judge that their opinion is correct.

Once a case is distilled in this way, the alleged frippery which has driven these reforms through evaporates away leaving only the core of the case as the distillate. The substantive and evidential issues can only be determined in one of two ways: either through negotiation or at trial. If pre-issue negotiations fail to resolve the case, is it likely that a further attempt pre-trial is likely to succeed? That leaves trial as the sole method of determining the case. It makes no sense to delay this. The 'old-school' or self-confident litigator will not be afraid of this.

In this sense, we see a return to the 1980s approach to clinical negligence. The claimant's lawyer becomes a post box once again, rarely making decisions about the strength of the case or the evidence. They rely on the expert to do their job and on counsel to plead a reasonable case and to be a persuasive advocate at trial. The lay witnesses are either believed or they are not. The fee earner prepares the evidence and court documents and ensures that they comply with the relevant substantive, evidential and procedural rules. But they do not put their heart and soul into marshalling this evidence. Instead, their job is to drive the case ever forward, through all obstacles, in order to reach trial in the shortest possible time. Advice is still provided to the client but it is directed at case progression and the timescale provided to the client is adhered to until the court orders otherwise.

The place for determining whether the legal tests have been met is trial rather than correspondence. If agreement on an issue is not reached, it is left to be determined at trial one way or another. If a court application is needed, it is made quickly and detailed correspondence about it only serves to delay the determination of this issue.

In short, on this view, collaboration on anything other than final settlement is reduced, being limited to key steps only because it only serves to give your opponent more time. Since there are already extensive delays in the civil court system, your clients' interests are best served by getting in ahead of others. It would be incumbent on the claimant's solicitor to get everything right first time all the time; anything else risks losing ground to others and allowing your opponent to regroup. If this is your chosen approach, accept criticism constructively and professionally and move swiftly. A significant risk of this approach is that refusals to reasonably negotiate can trigger costs penalties for unreasonable conduct and you may find the unrecovered costs overall exceed the recovered costs.

Volume Approaches

Economies of scale play an important role when revenue decreases. NHSR only has to concern itself with itself and its small number of panel firms. It controls the way in which cases are defended and the rates it pays to a level approaching a monopoly or monopsony. In contrast, only the largest claimant firms can spread their costs over a wide enough client and employee base to minimise the impacts of change and risk management inherent with FRC.

In FRC this translates into hoovering up as many cases as possible through effective marketing strategies and then processing them efficiently. Metaphorically speaking, the factory ships trawling the world's oceans spring readily to mind. Once a case has been captured in the sales funnel, the potential claim is risk assessed, rejected or accepted and onboarded within 24 hours or so. Initial investigations follow a prescribed format and many more cases are rejected or lost than proceed. This is one reason why resolution does not always equate to getting damages or costs.

Process driving cases and high individual caseloads and targets are commonplace. Volume litigation seeks to make use of the low profit margin of each individual case to utilise the cheapest and least experienced level of fee earner. As such, the level expertise per case is relatively low and over-reliance on counsel relatively high. Supervision by more senior colleagues can only reasonably achieve so much.

In the wider marketplace, however, the volume approach leaves fewer case available to niche or medium-sized firms. The relatively high numbers of cases which do not succeed results in more clients looking for firms to take on their case after it has been rejected once. Whilst this secondary market may have been viable before FRC were imposed, it is far less so afterwards. Access to justice is thereby reduced.

Mixed Caseloads (Intermediate & Multi-track)

There is no overarching reason that fee earners cannot have both FRC and multi-track work in their caseloads. The advantage of this is that they will continue to see a wider range of case issues which creates the opportunity to justify why a given case seemingly within the FRC bands is worth more than first thought or otherwise should be allocated to the multi-track. If a given FRC case looses money, the fee earner does at least have the opportunity to offset this on their multi-track cases. Scaling this up, departments which have some fee earners doing FRC work and some doing multi-track work have the opportunity to offset FRC costs against multi-track work.

The disadvantage is that the fee earner spreads themselves too thinly and does not stay sufficiently up to date with FRC developments or alive to the risk that a experience of higher value cases can create a cognitive bias preventing the realisation that any given case is in fact one where FRC will apply. On a departmental level, care must be taken to ensure that unprofitable work does not extinguish profitable work. FRC exacerbates this risk (by decreasing the amount of recoverable costs from infected cases) and so increases the risks of cross-contamination.

Excellent Client Service

One of the biggest challenges posed by FRC is maintaining high client care service levels. If you get paid the same whether you provide a Rolls Royce or a Robin Reliant service, where is the incentive to do more? If you do, but your colleagues do not, who will settle more cases? If repeat business is unlikely (because any particular client is unlikely to ever need your services again), why go to the extra effort to provide a 'five-star' service?

Recovering the costs for providing a 'Rolls Royce' service has long been touted as problematic because it is often associated with overcharging. The paying party has not agreed in advance to reimburse you and so understandably argues that the cost is disproportionate and so delays payment safe in the knowledge that the court will likely agree on assessment and the claimant's solicitors will accept less to help with cash flow. Sacrificing quality to obtain reduced case durations and improved cash flow at a lower, more proportionate cost is seen as the desirable goal. Whilst this may be so for the lawyers, is it also true for our clients?

What is forgotten is that providing a high-quality service is a way of differentiating yourself from your competitors. When everyone is offering the same service, why should a prospective new client choose you? If nothing else, clinical negligence is likely to be more competitive as FRC beds in because (a) more firms will be trying to get the smaller proportion of cases with values in excess of £100,000; and (b) firms will be looking for ways to reduce the lost revenue and profits they had before FRC. Accordingly, and perhaps counter-intuitively, providing a high level of customer service is a much scarcer commodity within FRC and scarcity is often seen as desirable to consumers.

Whilst some firms will prefer to provide a service based on speed and price; speed and quality or quality and price are also reasonable alternatives. Trying to achieve all three consistently may well prove too much if you are to remain profitable. Larger firms risk not having the flexibility to offer solutions which do not leverage their economies of scale advantages. Smaller firms, however, do have the flexibility to pivot between different sub-categories of clinical negligence and select strategies which allow them to leverage their quality. Clients who know they have received an excellent service are more likely to be willing to pay for it (from higher deductions from damages).

How to offer such high-quality services consistently is a detailed topic taking us outside of the scope of this book. As a starting point, it is worth taking the time to think back to situations from your everyday life where you have enjoyed excellent service. What made it so great? Once you have remembered, you can start the process of implementing similar changes into your day-to-day attitudes and behaviours such that it becomes habitual and second nature.

Use of chargeable hours as a profitability check

Keeping track of the amount of chargeable work done on cases affected by FRC may well seem counterproductive. Afterall, you get paid a fixed amount irrespective of the work actually done.

However, where your approach is to attempt to maintain quality as a means of winning cases, then knowing how much time you have spent on any given task helps you to plan how much time you can spend on others. Accordingly, if you have a relatively document heavy case, you may benefit from spending more time on disclosure and less on witness statements.

Focus on Pressure Points

Those fee earners who focus on this in multi-track cases are often able to conclude them quicker than those who do not. The pressure points in a case are those areas where a significant event occurs and the case objectively progresses. Examples include instructing the breach of duty expert, sending the letter of claim, making a settlement offer or arranging ADR, serving proceedings, experts' joint meetings and trial.

Since a significantly greater proportion of recoverable costs are incurred around these key stages, it makes sense to focus on getting them right within the FRC straitjacket. Moving confidently between them is a key behaviour in FRC cases in terms of maximising your prospects of success within the recoverable amounts of fixed costs.

Accurate Quantum Valuations

A considerable amount of peace of mind comes from knowing that your case either is within or without FRC. A key component of this is ensuring that you have a case valuation which is based on a solid evidential basis (please also see Chapter 6).

It therefore makes sense to have a clear line of documentary, witness and expert evidence to support the schedule of special damages or loss. Case comparators ought to be as close as is possible to the facts of your case and a clear narrative be set out as to why the particular part of the JC Guidelines applies. Causation of consequential losses and the nature and extent of the claimant's health in any event needs to be clearly explained.

The greater the degree of ambiguity in the claimant's evidence, the greater the scope for the defendant haggling the value of the case down and thereby reducing the amount of FRC recovered.

Doing this within the amount of FRC is difficult enough without finding out too late that you are going to receive less than you had budgeted for.

Vulnerability & Capacity

Vulnerability and lack of capacity provides an avenue to get an additional amount of FRC under both schemes (albeit in different ways). However, there is no guarantee that the defendant or court will accept that this additional work was required at all or that it was required as a result of the vulnerability or lack of capacity.

Accordingly, evidence of both of these things should be kept as proof. This therefore requires an efficient system to be in place lest you either cannot recover the additional amount or the additional amount of FRC you do receive is less than the value of the additional work done.

By way of an illustration, *Section 5.2 (pp78-80)* of the government's September 2023 response to the <£25,000 consultation considers the impact of these proposals on equality, the vulnerable and those with health disparities. To summarise, the potentially adverse impact of these proposals on these areas of society is countered by an additional amount of £1,800 FRC. However, *Table 3 (p53)* shows that this applies only to children and protected parties. Adult claimants who have a disability or vulnerability but who retain capacity to litigate do not qualify despite the government identifying that they stand to lose out by being more likely to fall within this scheme (because they are likely to have lower earnings capacity) and they are likely to find it harder to find solicitors willing to take their case on.

If we adopt the approach from Chapter 2, then £1,800 allows an additional ~9.5 hours work through to the pre-issue stock-take. This is effectively the price tag placed on maintaining access to justice for children and protected parties; it is assumed that this will be sufficient to cover the additional work required for these clients. However, this in not necessarily the same work as is required for the vulnerability itself (because 'vulnerability' *per se* does not attract the FRC uplift). Indeed, the appointment of the litigation friend ought to reduce the impact of the 'vulnerability' issues.

Breaking this down further logically, it seems likely that the additional £1,800 should be used to cover the unique features of these cases first. These include the selection and appointment of the litigation friend and the application for the approval of the settlement (if it is reached pre-issue). Liaising with the court over the measures it needs to put in place for vulnerable claimants and witnesses and settling the case pre-trial should all be covered by the costs regime applicable at allocation. From a purely efficiency-based perspective, it makes no sense just to specifically record the additional work required and hope that it will be seen as an 'exceptional circumstance'. Instead, the skill and expertise will be to persuasively establish that a vulnerable adult is a protected party. If so, it is reasonable to anticipate that this will be challenged where the evidence is ambiguous and the logical point to challenge this would be the approval hearing. This means that the claimant's expert evidence would need to support the lack of capacity which, in turn, means that the medical records, witness statement and C&P examination would need to have identified this. Thus, the additional £1,800 can easily be expended dealing with building the evidence of a lack of capacity and then arguing it at court. This therefore carries with it the risk that the court will find that capacity exists (and so the additional amount is lost making the case even less profitable or a loss maker). However, you would have better evidence in support of a contention that this case amounts to a genuine 'exceptional circumstance'.

Capacity issues are not uncommon. According to this 2019 clinical paper, a conservative estimate is that 2 million adults in the UK lack capacity:

> *"Around two million adults in the UK have significantly impaired decision-making capacity. However, there are concerns that this population is under-represented in research, due in part to the challenges around obtaining consent. Under-representation of populations denies those who would have wanted to participate the opportunity to make a contribution to society, but also fails to generate results that are applicable to them. Consequently, the evidence base for their care is poorer than for other populations."*
>
> (Protection by exclusion? The (lack of) inclusion of adults who lack capacity to consent to research in clinical trials in the UK | Trials | Full Text (biomedcentral.com))

In contrast the intermediate track requires evidence of how the vulnerability has increased costs and by what amount (see *Chapters 2 & 3*). It is reasonable to anticipate defendants' contesting this in order to limit the amount of the additional costs and there is no guarantee that the judge will allow all of the additional amount being sought. Accordingly, contemporaneous disclosable evidence will still need to be produced on sub-issues including what the vulnerability is; what additional work is required by virtue of it; the value of this additional work; and attempts made to mitigate the additional costs in addition to the issues relevant to capacity where this also an issue.

It is entirely possible that cases believed to be worth more than £25,000 will settle for less than this. If so, then the standard or light track FRC will apply to the pre-action costs if no letter of claim was sent before they came into force (see *Chapter 3*). Where this occurs, the additional work done in respect of the vulnerability may well become unrecoverable.

In terms of measures which can be taken to ameliorate this risk, the usual practice of getting written authority from the client to take instructions on routine matters from another person who does not have a vulnerability may become more useful. However, instructions on important matters must still be taken from the client (because they do not lack capacity).

On balance, a clear plan of action covering what additional work is likely to be needed should be made at the start of the case. This should include what additional witnesses (or additional content in the statements) and what additional expert evidence (and issues to be covered by each expert) is reasonably required to address the vulnerability and capacity issues. This is likely to highlight (irrespective of settlement value) those cases which justifiably require allocation to the multi-track; those which justify the uplift in the intermediate track; those which justifiably require litigation friends in the standard or light tracks; and those which cannot justifiably be brought into any of these categories. The plan should focus on how the legal criteria are met (and how the judge will be eventually persuaded of this) on the facts of this particular case.

Conduct

The same is true if you believe that the paying party has put you to additional work. A further, and likely prohibitive, hurdle is that the court must agree that the conduct was exceptionally bad. As we saw in *Chapter 2*, this seems to allow for only a very small proportion of conduct issues to count.

If you are bold enough to try this, you will need to have very clear evidence to present to the court as to the egregious nature of the conduct, how this increased costs and the amount by which it did. This evidence must also withstand the paying party's attacks on it and the likely reticence on the part of the court to depart from the 'swings and roundabouts' and 'minimising costs' policy dogmas currently pervading civil justice.

Exclusions

This holds equally true if you want to rely on exceptional circumstances as a means of obtaining higher costs amounts or disapplying FRC. It is insufficient to have an arguable case on this; it must be a very strong one. The chances of succeeding on this seem to be slim. If, perchance you do manage it, then there is no guarantee that you will succeed again. If lightning strikes twice, that is one thing – more than this it ceases to seem 'exceptional'.

This is also the risk of conflict arising from the pursuit of justice for an individual claimant clashing with the policy decision to fix costs recovery. This is not a new conflict since it has arisen to a lesser extent following the introduction of proportionality. It is also not new to the law because criminal law, family law and personal injury law (amongst others) have had similar constraints imposed upon them for many years. We are yet to see objectively verifiable evidence that access to justice and fair results have been increased. In the months preceding the implementation of the FRC into clinical negligence, there was a deafening silence from the judiciary as to its views on this (including those members sitting on the Civil Procedure Rules Committee). Given this, we should any practitioner assume that a judge will look favourably on an application which has the effect of avoiding FRC?

That said, if your client (or your firm) has been properly advised of the risks and consequences of failing to persuade the court and is willing to take them, then the fear factor implicit in the rules evaporates. There are myriad circumstances where a particular clinical negligence case may not fit easily within the FRC straitjacket and our common law system develops via precedent. Accordingly, there is at least the system in place to create a clearer system of guidance as to when exceptions might apply in specific clinical negligence scenarios.

Multiple Experts

Please see Chapter 8

Multiple Witnesses and Lengthy Statements

Similarly, it is reasonable to anticipate considerable reticence on the part of procedural judges to allow multiple witnesses or statements in excess of the prescribed length. Each time this is permitted, it risks undermining the stated purpose of FRC (to limit costs). However, an independent judiciary should not act as advocates for a policy change and there is a wide range of possible factual scenarios in clinical negligence cases (arising from the complexities of medicine and the human body). It is also relevant to remember that the new rules *prescribe* rather than *proscribe*; they do not state that claims within the FRC costs limit cannot have more than 3 lay witnesses or have witness statements over 30 pages in total. Instead, they state that these limitations are appropriate for such cases. This implies that it may be necessary to apply for permission to have longer statements within the FRC tracks rather than base an application to allocate to the multi-track on this feature alone.

One size does not fit all and there may well be cases where multiple clinical witnesses and lay witnesses are justified. There is then the 'swings and roundabouts' hurdle to overcome. On average, it may seem persuasive to a procedural judge that it is fair to impose FRC on a case requiring 'excessive' witness or statement length because the correct balance is struck by all of the other cases where this does not happen. In the absence of hard evidence, such 'judicial experience' may well prove determinative. However, in the face of helpful evidence showing the reasons why the additional witnesses and pages are likely to assist the trial judge, it becomes much harder for the judge to feel justified in relaying on generalised beliefs or submissions. The old adage of writing the decision you want for the judge in your evidence and submissions is no less applicable here – you need to show them why it is 'safe' to depart from the comfort of a generalised policy on the facts of your case.

Risk Assessments

Under the FRC regime we now face, there is a school of thought which takes the view that there is little to be gained from regularly re-assessing the risk on cases. Once you have taken it on, you should have sufficient confidence to see it through to resolution and the lawyers running the cases have sufficient expertise to win more cases than they lose.

Such an approach is understandable when one remembers that the FRC amounts are not generous and do not leave much room for profitability. Any activity which does not propel the case towards a swift conclusion is eating into an already small profit margin. Subsistence level billing from a high caseload and target is best controlled by the strict adherence to an unyielding process.

An alternative view is that those running the cases are more efficient if they understand the central allegations from the outset. Once they do, their investigations are directed towards them and they are far more effective at spotting gaps and errors. There is therefore a balance to be struck between constructive case progression and risk management.

Paring this down to the FRC regimes we now face, the emphasis is on resolving cases pre-issue. The key stages are:

- 1st Risk Assessment: covering the decision to accept a case;
- 2nd Risk Assessment: covering the decision to obtain expert evidence;

- 3rd Risk Assessment: covering the decision to send a letter of claim;

- 4th Risk Assessment: covering the decision to proceed with pre-issue ADR;

- 5th Risk Assessment: covering the decision to proceed with the issue and service of proceedings;

- 6th Risk Assessment: covering the decision to proceed to trial.

Medical Records

The first key tactical decision under FRC is which medical records you require. There is a very good chance that this decision will need to be made before the defendant's position on liability is known. This is particularly prevalent where the claimant is elderly because they are likely to have a number of medical records which are not relevant.

There is much to be said in favour of obtaining those records which relate to the central allegations. This assists in directing attention to the relevant issues thereby reducing the costs.

Unfortunately, the new rules do not directly support such a logical approach. There is nothing to prevent the defendant continuing the pre-October 2023 behaviour of requiring that all records be disclosed, irrespective of the central allegations. There is little incentive to get drawn into correspondence on the issue if the defendant is simply following its own internal protocol. The claimant either obtains all records or maintains its position. Either course risks eating into the limited amount of FRC.

If, however, you are confident that you have correctly identified the central allegations and that the relevant evidence has been obtained, then that is how the case proceeds. If you are wrong, then the defendant has a better chance of successfully defending the case. The additional amount of costs allowed as part of the later stage incorporating standard disclosure can be used to contain an updated set of records. By this time, the defendant's case will have been crystallised in its pleadings.

The key behaviour here is to be able to ensure that there is sufficient evidentiary support in the records to base their opinion on. The simple expedient of asking the expert to confirm in their report if they consider they have seen all of the relevant records helps to support your position. Since you do not want to expend your already limited resources on obtaining further records, it is important to get this right first time.

There is a further risk that needs to be accounted for. If the defendant, however unreasonably, maintains that insufficient records have been obtained to allow it to deal with the disputed issues, then this reduces the chances of pre-issue ADR resulting in a mutually acceptable settlement. There are likely to be some cases where the defendant's concerns are justified, but there are far more where they are not. The choice is largely between basing your position on the evidence of each case or on a desire to achieve settlement by collusion. The risk of the former is that settlement either does not occur or occurs at a lower value than you believe is fair. The risk with the latter is that once you give ground once, further concessions will be sought because your opponent knows that settlement is valued more highly than trial. Whatever your decision is, it is far better to make it early in the initial investigations and to stick with it.

The second key tactical consideration is to decide whether to outsource the sorting and pagination of the medical records and whether a chronology is required (and, if so, who does this). Some experts insist on preparing their own which would create duplication. Preparing the chronology inhouse eats into the limited amount of FRC without necessarily progressing the case. The decision is complicated by the ongoing uncertainty as to whether the medical agency fees are recoverable in full if they include an element of uplift. It does not necessarily follow that the fee will be considered reasonable. If it is not, then that reduces the already small profit margin further. Again, this decision which will often be taken before the defendant's liability position is known. As such, it is best made based on what is known about the nature and extent of the claimant's injuries and obtaining only the records needed to cover the central issues.

An illustration of these issues is provided by *Northampton General Hospital NHS Trust v Hoskin (Unreported, E74YX378, Manchester County Court, 22nd May 2023). HHJ Bird* (hearing an appeal and submissions from the parties' respective senior counsel), held that it was necessary to distinguish between the amount charged by the expert and the amount charged by the agency to enable the judge hearing the detailed assessment to have all of the information required by *CPR 1998, PD47.* One consequence of this is that paying parties make lower offers on expert fees pending the outcome of the Court of Appeal's decision c. September 2024. If agency fees are unrecoverable, then claimant firms will need to bear those costs out of the limited FRC amounts. It should be noted that HHJ Bird sits on the CPR Committee.

Witness Statements

An interesting dichotomy arises between intermediate track cases and other cases. Traditional best practice is to take preliminary witness statements as part of the initial investigations, send them to the breach and causation experts and to update them as more evidence comes to light. Separate quantum statements may be taken later.

The light and standard tracks require the claimant's witness statements to be disclosed with the letter of claim and so the defendant has the benefit of seeing them before having to disclose its own position. This circumvents the traditional (just and reasonable) simultaneous exchange of witness statements under the usual directions order. It is much closer to the requests made by NHSR during the pre-action period which are usually justifiably refused by prudent claimants' solicitors in multi-track cases.

Accordingly, once these rules for lower-value cases are introduced , the expectation is that 'finalised' witness statements will be disclosed. Experience strongly informs us that defendants are likely to base their letters of response on the perceived quality of the evidence served on them rather than on the strength of the legal arguments. Moreover, the risk of having previous inconsistent statements means that enforcing such disclosure effectively prevents witness statements being updated in light of the defendant's case and as further evidence comes to light. The evidential rules regarding previous inconsistent statements have not been relaxed to accommodate this fundamental change in the procedural rules.

It should also be borne in mind that witnesses are not permitted to add substantially to their evidence in their evidence-in-chief at trial. However, they can expect to have their evidence thoroughly tested under cross-examination. The trial is unlikely to be contemporaneous with either the events in question or with the date the statement was made. On top of this, the courts tend to find witnesses more credible when their evidence is corroborated with documentary evidence.

As a minimum, therefore, these witness statements should clearly and succinctly cover the central allegations on breach of duty, causation of damage, causation of consequential losses, quantum matching as closely as possible what is in the medical records and other documentary evidence. However, the records were not written by the claimant but by busy clinicians who are often either having their treatment impugned or are employed by the Defendant. This means that a reasonable explanation for any fact not contained in the records is desirable in order to maximise the chances of proving liability at trial. Thus, quantum enquires also need to be completed before the letter of claim is sent. The time taken to obtain loss of earnings evidence and to properly understand the claimant's prognosis needs to be included in your case management planning.

In contrast, there is presently no requirement for intermediate track cases have the witness statements served. As such, there is a reasonable argument for not taking the witness statements until the defendant's position on liability is known. If liability has been admitted, then there is no need for a witness statement covering this and quantum issues can be focused on. If liability is not fully addressed, then you know this is needed.

Ultimately, witnesses must still be credible and be prepared to attend trial to have their credibility robustly challenged under cross-examination. The case law on witness credibility remains challenging for claimants in clinical negligence cases because the trial judge is faced with difficult questions of fact. Clinicians are still likely to be given considerable leeway by trial judges (because they see large numbers of patients everyday) and have the advantage of referring to the contemporaneous medical records they made.

What can be done about this in cases afflicted with FRC? One approach that is often overlooked in pre-October 2023 cases is that defendants do not usually call the clinicians whose treatment as not been impugned. However, the impugned clinicians who do give statements often cite medical records prepared by their colleagues as incontrovertible fact. In the right case, it is advisable for the claimant to insist on taking witnesses from these other clinicians in order to properly test the defendant's factual evidence. This is far from straightforward to accomplish despite there being no property in a witness. The costs and time involved in tracing these clinicians and persuading them to give statements followed by the need to interview them properly mitigate against doing this before the letter of response has been served. If their evidence remains relevant at this stage, then the risk not recovering the costs of pursuing this avenue of investigation may be worth taking. In some cases, this may make a case suitable for the multi-track irrespective of its value. As long as the defendant has been given the chance to make admissions on the facts relevant to his witness, the trial judge ought to be assisted by hearing this specific evidence at trial in order to properly assess any disputed entries in the medical records.

It is important to think ahead to the directions hearing and to remember to ask yourself whether the witness and page limits in the FRC tracks are reasonable for your case. Consider getting the directions order to stipulate what is needed (names, issues, length) and plan for this eventuality by building the evidence up as you go.

Expert Evidence

Please see Chapter 8

Letters of Claim & Response

In respect of the intermediate track, allocation will not have occurred when the letter of claim is sent. It is possible that liability has been admitted earlier following a duty of candour investigation or inquest. If it appears that liability should be admitted, then it is sensible to send a request to the defendant to admit liability in order to avoid those costs being incurred. If liability is admitted, and the case appears to be one where the value will be between £25,000 and £100,000, then you can say in the letter of claim that the case appears to be suitable for the multi-track.

Otherwise, the earliest indication is likely to be where the defendant admits breach and causation in the letter of response. Assuming that the rules are changed in line with the *CPR Committee's November 2023 Minutes'* recommendation, it will be mandatory for the defendant to admit liability in full at this stage for the intermediate track to apply. Until then, and remembering that the cause of action must arise after 1st October 2023, there is no particular incentive for the letter of response to make suitable admissions. There is also likely to be scope for disagreement over what precisely needs to be admitted. The remainder of the pre-action period should include attempts to narrow the remaining issues under the *Pre-Action Protocol for Resolving Clinical Disputes* in any event. If the case does not settle outright, then ADR could be used to reach a clear agreement as to whether the intermediate track ought to (or ought not to) apply at allocation. An open agreement can be adduced at the allocation stage whereas as confidential one can nevertheless be reflected in the way the statements of case plead the case. The aim is to make it clear for the in the statements of case whether the pre-action admissions are regarded by the parties as being sufficient to trigger the imposition of the intermediate track and FRC.

Although the light and standard tracks are not expected to come into force until at least April 2024, they are already influencing case decisions. The government's September 2023 consultation response for cases worth under £25,000 recommends that existing cases will be excluded from this scheme where notification in the form of a letter of claim has been sent before the implementation date. At present, there is no suggestion that the cause of action has to arise after the commencement date of these rules.

If the actual rules do not change this, then it makes sense for cases to be managed so letters of claim are sent before the implementation date. As long as these are compliant with the *Pre-Action Protocol for Resolving Clinical Disputes* and have sufficient evidentiary support for the allegations made, then there ought not to be an issue. This may not be the case where letters of claim are sent at the last minute or otherwise appear to have been sent in order to circumvent the new rules.

It may also be the case that having provided sufficient information in an early notification letter will prove sufficient notice. Until the new rules are published, we can only say that the recommendation specifically names letters of claims as being the proposed method. Strict adherence to this also raises the possibility that cases which have enjoyed an admission of liability without a letter of claim being necessary could fall into the new scheme. Evidence that the admission was made in light of a reasonable understanding of the facts should be sufficient to avoid this. Accordingly, a similar approach to that taken where defendants attempt to resile from pre-action admissions would assist (i.e. what information was the admission based upon?). Bear in mind that the desired outcomes are different, however. When resiling, defendants want to be able to contest liability and pay nothing. For cases worth under £25,000, the objective would be to limit pre-action costs to those fixed for the Light or Standard Tracks.

In the period between 1st October 2023 and 1st April 2024 (or whenever the commencement date is) there does not appear to be much incentive to send an early notification letter in any case which might conceivably settle for less than £25,000: rather a compliant letter of claim is preferable.

Pre-Issue Negotiations

This is likely to be the key area in FRC. The intermediate track is suitable for cases where only damages need to be assessed. As long as suitable admissions are made pre-action, then the parties' focus should be on finding the middle ground on quantum between £25,001 and £100,000. If this cannot be done via exchanging *Part 36* offers or picking up the telephone, then some form of joint meeting or mediation should resolve it.

Where some admissions have been made, falling short of full admissions, then there is still scope for settling the case. These cases are more likely to require a recognition by the defendant (as the paying party) of the risks it faces. It remains to be seen how the incentive of paying FRC influences defendants' behaviour.

Even cases where no admissions have been made can be settled pre-action. This usually requires disclosure of evidence to demonstrate the risks but this is not obligatory. Ultimately, properly prepared cases with well-timed *Part 36* offers and effective negotiation should still be capable of settlement pre-action. Accordingly, the numbers of clinical cases actually requiring allocation to the Intermediate track may prove to be relatively modest.

Cases worth under £25,000 have a significant incentive to settle under FRC. Once the parties have exchanged evidence under the new pre-action protocol, there should be a very clear understanding of each side's case. Ultimately, it will require defendants to want to settle. If the claimant's supporting evidence is not *persuasive*, then the defendant's response may well be an entrenched denial. Although there is still the chance to reach settlement pre-issue, the stocktake has just as much chance of achieving resolution by abandonment.

If a reasoned decision has been taken not to disclose all of the requisite evidence with the letter of claim, then there is a risk that liability will be denied simply because 'insufficient' evidence has been disclosed. One the one hand, it is correct that not all of the *required* evidence has been disclosed. On the other hand, have they had less information than was provided in other tracks? As long as the answer is 'no', then the defendant was provided with sufficient information to instruct its own expert(s) and respond. The issue then becomes one of the consequences of the claimant failing to comply with the new rules and whether they are likely to be penalised in costs. The defendant could still admit liability, settle the claim and seek the 50% costs penalty 'notwithstanding' the claimant's failure to disclose evidence. There may be situations (albeit very rare) where the claimant's solicitor still makes a profit in these cases. If so, they may readily agree this. In the majority of these cases, it is more likely that it will be necessary to request a court hearing and prove that the reason for non-compliance falls short of the test for 'unreasonable conduct'. This is likely to require persuasive evidence as to your thought process and attempts to avoid the non-compliance (as set out above). If nothing else, it should not be assumed that the requisite disclosure is required to provide a constructive letter of response. If the defendant *chooses* not to, it should also expect to justify this choice in more detail.

Counsel

The use of counsel is significantly reduced under either scheme but there is potentially more flexibility under the intermediate track.

Ongoing cases which can be safely excluded from both schemes can proceed as per your usual practice. However, as FRC become more embedded and infect more clinical negligence cases, continuing to instruct counsel beyond the limits of FRC becomes progressively less economical. A benefit of this may prove to be that clinical negligence fee earners become more effective and self-sufficient. A disbenefit may prove to be that the core issues are consistently not dealt with properly.

Using counsel sparingly means fee earners need to take responsibility or risk losing money through losing winnable cases, paying the shortfall in counsel's recoverable fees or dealing with complaints and/or professional negligence claims.

Instructions to counsel also need to be clearly focussed on the central issues and evidence and limited to work which is recoverable under the applicable FRC scheme. In some cases, it may be reasonable to agree that counsel will do additional work. This will need to be paid for out of the amount of FRC recovered from other stages; from the success fee; or from the amount of any shortfall in recovered costs that the claimant has agreed to pay.

Counsel has the same issue as fee earners do as regards hourly rates: charging their usual hourly rates effectively reduces the amount of time that they can do in drafting the pleadings or advising in conference. It is crucial to be clear on what counsel will and will not do before instructing them in order to avoid underestimating the amount of work required or overestimating their ability to do it within the FRC amount. Whilst individual barristers or sets of chambers may be willing to certain tasks as loss leaders, hoping that this will always be so is a recipe for disaster.

Likewise, it may seem tempting to dispense with counsel and draft the particulars of claim inhouse thus claiming the additional amount. Firstly, this additional amount is reserved for counsel or specialist legal advisors. This does not necessarily mean that the conducting fee earner or colleague is entitled to this additional FRC amount. You could do the work, perhaps brilliantly, only to find that you do not get paid for it (thereby reducing your profitability on the file). Secondly, drafting pleadings in house could come back to haunt you. It will be clear that counsel has not been used and, however unfairly, this can create the impression that something important has been missed. Even where it has not been, unhelpful and avoidable points may be taken in the defence. Where they have, you are more likely to face Part 18 Requests and applications, strike out applications and other attempts to clarify your client's case which are aimed at undermining it.

This, and other ill-prepared actions, can lead to counsel refusing to take the case on under a CFA. If so, then you are faced with either paying their fees privately or spending time shopping around to find someone wo will act under a CFA. Depending on the urgency and importance of the situation, this may work out well, but there is no guarantee that it will. Prevention is better than cure and so best practice requires a clear grasp of the central allegations and using the limited amount of available time you have to prevent these problems arising.

Issuing Proceedings

Everything else being equal, commencing proceedings at the last minute is even more risky under a FRC regime than it was traditionally. There is less recoverable time to spend on ancillary matters. Where inexperienced fee earners have high caseloads, more chance of things going wrong. This also applies to more experienced fee earners who are unfamiliar with the process required for the mandatory use of the Damages Claims Portal. For example, failing to give the defendant 14-days' notice of your intention to issue proceedings can resulting costs penalties outside of the FRC regime. The online portal is not without its user problems and it cannot be safely assumed that the claim form will be issued first time. Moreover, the relevant date for limitation purposes is the date when the claim form is issued on the system, not the date it was 'delivered' to it.

Under either regime, there is likely to be less 'need' to issue because there are clear incentives to 'resolve' cases instead. This also risks creating a mindset that cases will not be issued. Perhaps counterintuitively, experience shows that preparing a case for negotiations rather than trial, tends to leave gaps which undermine settlement.

Accordingly, part of the limited work that can be recovered under FRC, needs to be reserved for issuing proceedings safely.

Serving Proceedings

Here counsel's fees for drafting the particulars of claim are a separate recoverable amount. Where suitable admissions on breach and causation have been made for potential intermediate track cases, the particulars of claim should be limited to pleading causation of consequential losses and quantum. The court is likely to be assisted by a clear paragraph stating whether the case is or is not suitable for the intermediate track and doing so requires the defendant to plead a response. If they do not, then there will usually be a catch all provision that anything not pleaded to is denied. Whatever the response, it is sensible to write to the court promptly after the defence has been received to confirm whether the case is or is not suitable for the Intermediate track. Whilst not required by the new rules, it decreases the risk of the court officer misunderstanding the position.

Subject to seeing the new rules, there is potentially greater flexibility for the light and standard tracks. The proposed FRC regime is apparently limited to the pre-action period. Once the case has been issued it is subject to the allocation rules which came into force in October 2023. The rules certainly appear to intend that cases must be allocated to the multi-track if they are not suitable for the intermediate track (but see Chapter 2). There may be no anomaly here if liability has not been admitted. Where it has, then we can reasonably anticipate defendants or district judges wanting to consider whether these cases should be allocated to the fast (or even small) tracks. This is where having a full understanding of what the qualifying criteria are for those cases is crucial.

It needs to be remembered that all of the usual rules about the service of proceedings (including time limits) apply; neither FRC regime has relaxed them. Cases which have failed to settle because breach and/or causation are denied, are far less likely to be suitable for these lower tracks. Quantum-only cases may be but the key question with these will be to understand why they have failed to settle before allocation. The quantum issues may well be more complicated than the value indicates. One example could be where case law needs to develop to allow a particular head of loss to be recoverable (such as an unmarried cohabitee claiming the same heads of damage as are permitted for spouses in dependency claims).

Whilst it is tempting to think that obtaining default judgements will be more useful under FRC, it remains the case that procedural judgements are often easily overturned. This is likely to eat into the amount of FRC recovered. However, this is not always the case and, in *Buckingham v Elneil (2022) (unreported, 15th July 2022 per Leslie Keegan at 7 Bedford Row)* the lack of a draft defence and lack of evidence that there was likely to be a cogent basis for defending the claim were sufficient to maintain the judgement once it had been proved that proceedings had been properly served.

Allocation & Assignment

Please see Chapter 2 for the issues discussed there. It seems likely that the directions and pre-trial timetable required to deal with disputed damages-only issues under the intermediate track will be shorter than for multi-track cases.

Care and doggedness are likely to be required, however. The more that the parties and the courts permit breach of duty or causation of damages issues to contaminate causation of consequential losses and quantum issues, the more the CMCs, directions and pre-trial timetables will look like those found in multi-track cases. Accordingly, care should be taken with the wording of any agreed directions order to ensure that it does not permit such issues to be allowed in by ambiguous wording or wording taken from the multi-track model directions order. This is not to say that the multi-track model directions should not form the base for the intermediate track – they should because they have stood the test of time. The reason that care should be taken is because experience shows that it is often hard or impossible to persuade the court later that an apparent breach of the order amounts to such in the absence of very clear wording.

The County Court at Central London seeks to address this by stating the *disputed issues* which an expert is entitled to report on within their sphere of expertise. This is a useful approach to adopt, especially given the 20-

page limit on expert reports (see above). Accordingly, part of the limited time available under this stage of the FRC should be spent ensuring that the directions order properly protects your client and, if not, ensuring that this is properly analysed at the CMC.

There is also a significant risk that the county courts will be unable to list a trial within a reasonable timescale. It would be prudent to use part of the FRC amount under this stage to get the court's availability before the CMC. This can be easier said than done and may require numerous attempts or waiting in a call queue. Another practical issue is that the case needs to have been transferred and accepted by the trial court from the CCMCC in order for this information to be given at all. The initial allocation decision may be made whilst the case is still at the CCMCC and so this also needs to be taken into account.

The risk, especially to the claimant's legal team, is that delays in getting the case to trial can significantly eat into the amount of FRC and so reduce or extinguish profitability. Disagreements over the dates when the remaining steps need to be taken, agreeing the 'usual' 28-day extensions to these; the time, expense and relative uncertainty of interlocutory applications and a long gap between the last date in the timetable and the trial itself all risk causing this. Accordingly, the claimant's legal team need to proactively and efficiently minimise these risks, especially where they want to deduct a shortfall in recovered costs from the claimant's damages. Claimants are entitled to expect the vigorous prosecution of their case where they have to pay for it and where the value is anticipated to be relatively modest.

For case in the sub-£25,000 range, there are likely to be further considerations. The challenge is likely to be to successfully combine a proportionate set of directions covering the remaining issues in dispute with the (perhaps erroneous) view that the case is simple by virtue of its modest value with the amount of work that can be done within the FRC straitjacket. As indicated above, there needs to be a persuasive explanation as to why the case has been issued. This should be provided by the reason for the case failing to 'resolve' pre-issue. The issues in dispute should be clear from the parties' respective statements of case. The directions should, therefore, be those which reasonably and proportionately assist the trial judge in deciding these issues.

However, submissions are encountered which are aimed at persuading the judge that the value of the case mandates elevating costs saving measures above issue-based directions; in essence these seek to divorce case management from the issues in dispute. This may appear to be very reasonable until one remembers that the claimant must prove their case. If the defendant has elected to maintain the dispute over the issue, then it should not be permitted to also prevent that issue being determined justly. This is likely to remain a contentious issue so planning for this by using part of the available FRC to gather the evidence needed to win it is prudent.

Claimants need to be alive to the possibility that the court may try to allocate the case to the fast track (see Chapter 2 and above). Unless the *CPR 1998* is amended to make it clear that clinical negligence cases cannot be allocated to the small or fast tracks, this risk remains a possibility. Accordingly, one area of dispute is likely to be in trying to get the case allocated to the multi-track even though the October 2023 rules at first glance make it clear that cases must be allocated to this track unless they are suitable for the intermediate track (see Chapter 2).

Seeking to divorce the case management decisions from the remaining disputed issues in the case on grounds of case value have even greater significance in lower value cases. Accordingly, it is necessary to have a very clear idea of what these are, what evidence is likely to assist the trial judge in determining them; what the most proportionate and reasonable method of adducing this evidence is pre-trial; and tailoring your directions to these. Again, being able to present the supporting evidence and knowing the case are key.

Disclosure

The disclosure of the relevant documentary evidence has the potential to cause dispute between the parties and so erode the profitability of cases subjected to FRC.

1. **Pre-action Disclosure**

Voluntary disclosure of the relevant documents is the most efficient method under either FRC regime. As we have seen above, it is required under the proposed regime for cases worth under £25,000 but it may not always be in your client's best interests to do this.

Under the proposed regime for cases worth <£25,000, the claimant is obliged to gather, review and disclose both liability and quantum evidence for disclosure with the letter of claim. In essence therefore, the claimant must go to the time and expense of obtaining this evidence and is likely to experience similar delays as experienced before FRC came into force. Any gaps in this evidence are likely to be highlighted by the defendant when preparing its letter of response. It remains to be seen whether defendants routinely seek to request additional documents from the claimant as a condition precedent for sending the letter of response. It is likely to be asserted that the defendant cannot respond to the letter of claim without this and this will be raised if the claimant does not agree to an extension for providing the letter of response or exiting the light or standard tracks. The claimant will then be faced with the option of expending additional time trying to comply with the defendant's request or proceeding without having seen the defendant's response or evidence. This will require a careful re-assessment of the case's prospects of success and the risk of the court making a finding of unreasonable conduct.

Cases which might be eligible for the immediate track proceed under the pre-existing *Pre-Action Protocol for the Resolution of Clinical Disputes*. As such, the initial investigations can proceed largely as they would for multi-track cases. Care is required, however. Spending too much time on gathering the documentary evidence may not be fully recovered if either Intermediate track costs apply at settlement or if the case settles for less than £25,000 and light or standard track costs apply.

We should also bear in mind that QOCS applies and so the courts tend to interpret the availability of this protection as mitigating against as meaning that pre-action disclosure applications should only succeed where the documents sought are genuinely core. Otherwise, they can be left to standard disclosure and, if the case fails after issue, QOCS applies to protect the claimant. For the core medical records, it remains the case that they are usually disclosed between the application being made and the hearing. Although some fixed costs are recoverable (see Chapter 2), is this worth the trouble? For cases <£25,000, a reasonable alternative may be to send a letter of claim making it clear that the missing evidence precludes you from disclosing the other evidence. If so, then it may still be possible to disclose some of the other evidence rather than seek to justify a blanket refusal to adduce any of it.

2. Standard Disclosure

There is a fairly strong argument in favour of believing that fewer documents will be required to be disclosed under both FRC regimes. For intermediate track cases, assuming that these are limited to 'damages-only' cases, then the documents should be limited to those which have some bearing on these issues. For cases which have been in the standard or light tracks, the intention is likely to be that only very limited disclosure will be necessary.

However, at present, there is nothing authoritative to show what this will be. Going back to first principles, the documentary evidence needs to relate to the issues in question. The medical records will show evidence relevant to pre-existing medical conditions, co-existing morbidities and life expectancy as well as care needs and effects of the avoidable injury on employment. Personnel, occupational health and employment records are likely to be relevant for employed claimants whilst the accounts are likely to be needed for the self-employed. Benefits and tax records, expenditure receipts, diaries and utility records could all be required. This list is not exhaustive. All of these records ought to be sorted and analysed before the schedule of special damages is finalised and disclosure occurs.

It may also be the case that these are considered to be irrelevant to the claimant but the defendant maintains that they are relevant. Dealing with such disputes will eat into the limited amount of FRC.

In some cases, the answer will lie in the prognosis expert evidence and in the likelihood that cases worth up to £100,000 will have a predictable and limited period of loss. A substantial proportion of cases will do so. However, others will not. Defendants remain entitled to test out the claimant's evidence and are unlikely to accept your case valuation at face value. All things considered, it is advisable to allocate a reasonable amount of the limited FRC to ensure that you have obtained the correct evidence in support of your client's symptoms, losses and expenses and that standard disclosure is correctly dealt with by both sides.

In cases where you are trying to prove that the claimant should be awarded more than £100,000 there is an added risk that gaps in the evidence will pull the case value down and into the FRC bracket. If so, you may find that the work done is ultimately irrecoverable and it is prudent to plan for this eventuality.

3. Specific Disclosure

Similarly, there is no significant commercial incentive for claimants to pursue specific disclosure in the majority of FRC cases. Where the defendant is genuinely delaying disclosure of updated medical records or some other relevant piece of evidence, then it may be reasonable to pursue this. However, a reasonable alternative may be to maintain evidence of a reasonable series of requests and the application to be dealt with at the pre-trial review. There are pros and cons of adopting this approach and it partly depends on how much time there is until the PTR and how much time there is between it and the trial.

4. Third Party Disclosure

Since this almost always requires the claimant to pay the third party's costs of complying with the disclosure request, this will reduce the profitability of the file. The costs should be weighed against the benefits to be obtained and careful advice provided.

In many cases, this may well result in a decision not to proceed with this line of enquiry. It may be possible to persuade the defendant to make the request but the costs consequences of this (both in terms of paying for the disclosure and the potential effect of having to wait for disclosure of the evidence from the defendant) need to be carefully considered.

5. Accidental Disclosure

Accidentally disclosing documentary evidence is rarely a good thing. In FRC cases, the additional costs of trying to remedy the error risks reducing or extinguishing the amount of recovered costs.

Accordingly, a proportion of the limited time you can spend on FRC cases, should be spent on ensuring that sufficient checks and balances are in place to avoid this problem arising.

6. Late Disclosure

Neither FRC regime disapplies the parties' ongoing duty of disclosure. Accordingly, there is the possibility that documents may come to light later in the case which change the risk profile of pursuing the case to trial. This is particularly relevant where *Part 36* offers have been made and the additional disclosure makes a previously unprepossessing offer appear reasonable.

A subset within the range of possible scenarios is where social media or surveillance evidence is served late in the pre-trial either with or without an allegation of fundamental dishonesty. The lateness of the disclosure is likely to be outweighed by its probative value and the risks to the claimant are likely to drive a wedge between them and their legal team.

A practical preventative measure is to advise your client at the start of the case of the consequences of being honest, not exaggerating the effects of their injuries on them and of understanding the factual evidence being presented on their behalf. Additionally, it is reasonable to inform them at the start of the case that publicly available social media posts can be bought into evidence.

Exchange of Witness Statements

There is likely to be a temptation to not update your witness statements prior to exchange in light of any change in the way the defence has been pleaded, additional disclosure or a change in your client's circumstances or prognosis. Not doing so risks undermining their case or credibility and potentially increasing the risk of an allegation (and finding) of fundamental dishonesty.

Likewise, FRC does not obviate the need to re-risk assess the case in light of the defendant's witness evidence (even if this has been disclosed pre-action for cases worth <£25,000). Not doing so risks missing changes in the evidence being relied upon.

It also remains prudent to send the served statements to your experts so they can finalise their reports in light of them.

Exchange of Expert Evidence

Please see Chapter 8

Experts' Joint Meetings

Please see Chapter 8

Pre-Trial Preparation

At this stage, the ideal position to have reached is that there are no outstanding issues and the limited amount of additional FRC for this stage can be spent on properly preparing and agreeing the trial bundle; securing the experts' and witnesses' attendance at trial; ensuring that the court has made suitable accommodation for vulnerable witnesses; preparing for and attending the PTR; making a final attempt at negotiating a settlement; and providing final advice to your client.

If a pre-trial conference is required, then allowance must be made for organising this; preparing the bundles; attendance at the conference; and dealing with any issues and risk that arise from it. Where counsel has not been involved since the pleadings were drafted, the risk of additional work being required is significantly higher and increases further if a different barrister is used.

Schedules & Counter-Schedules

The intermediate track does not allow additional sums for counsel to prepare or finalise these documents. Accordingly, fee earners either need to do these themselves or agree to fund this some other way.

The work to be done here includes avoiding the risk of fundamental dishonesty; the proper investigation and analysis of the supporting evidence; reviewing and advising on the counter-schedule; understanding the likely ranges of damages awards and settlement; and correctly identifying any surprises arising at this stage. It is worth reiterating that fee earners should be objectively asking themselves why the case has reached this point if it is worth under £100,000 as many cases ought to have already settled.

Trial Listing

It is important to know and diarise when and how the trial listing will occur. Do not forget to check that the experts and witnesses scan make the proposed dates before it is listed and to issue witness summonses to ensure no other case takes precedence over yours. Likewise, make sure trial counsel's booking has been secured and properly diarised in chamber's booking system. Although this organisation time eats into FRC, it is far better to be safe than sorry.

Trial

The additional costs allowed in the intermediate track are limited but do allow for counsel's attendance supported by an employee of the instructing solicitor. There is also a separate amount allowed for attending the handing down of reserved judgements. Accordingly, claimants will at least have the option of having support and counsel will theoretically have someone to deal with witness and client queries.

As with any trial, it remains prudent to have the conducting fee earner available remotely to answer any unforeseen questions and for the person attending in support to have a clear understanding of the file and all relevant contact details. Travel and accommodation expenses are not included in the FRC amounts and this may well influence the decision to attend trial.

It is also relevant to note that there is always the risk that the court will adjourn the trial at short notice due to a lack of available judges. This is not something which can be accurately predicted or guarded against. As well as being hugely inconvenient for the parties, no additional FRC is allowed to cover the costs incurred in the preparation and that will be needed to be incurred to prepare for the new date. This is especially problematic where the experts charge cancellation fees. There is no absolute guarantee that these will be recoverable inter parties.

Finding a Balance

Whatever mix of strategies is adopted, the ultimate goal is to maintain a profitable caseload in the short, medium and long terms. The essence of negotiation is often considered to be that both parties give up something of value in order to reach settlement. For cases which are likely to be suitable for the intermediate track, this 'sweet spot' appears to be in the part of the pre-action period between service of the letter of response and the issue of proceedings. Although the case has not yet been allocated, settlement on more cases could be achieved by agreeing that stage 1 FRC will apply. The claimant wins their case whilst the defendant achieves resolution pre-action with the certainty of FRC. If this becomes habitual, then both sides achieve a more certain long-term position which is mutually beneficial.

This can also be used to resolve cases with a potential settlement range which straddles the £25,000 limit for the light/standard and intermediate tracks. Compromising the claim at slightly more than £25,000 removes the risk of the claimant getting lower fixed costs and the risk to the defendant of the case being allocated to the multi-track in addition to the aforementioned risks.

To illustrate this, it is helpful to consider a notional cohort of 100 cases which have settled pre-action:

Sample Profit & Loss Table for 100 Intermediate Track Cases (£25,001 settlement, All Stage 1, Average incurred costs = FRC)

Win Rate	FRC (Win)	Loss Rate	Lost Costs	Profit/Loss	Success Fee	Profit/ Case
100%	£1,130,000	0%	£0	£1,130,000	£312,500	£14,425.00
90%	£1,017,000	10%	£113,000	£904,000	£281,250	£11,852.50
80%	£904,000	20%	£226,000	£678,000	£250,000	£9,280.00

70%	£791,000	30%	£339,000	£452,000	£218,750	£6,707.50
60%	£678,000	40%	£452,000	£226,000	£187,000	£4,130.00
50%	£565,000	50%	£565,000	£0	£156,250	£1,562.50
45%	£508,500	55%	£621,000	-£113,000	£140,625	£276.25
40%	£452,000	60%	£678,000	-£226,000	£125,000	-£1,010.00

In this scenario, you incur the exact amount of FRC on every case.

So, if you adopted a strategy of using all of the available FRC amount (e.g. either to maximise your chances of getting admissions in the defence and withdrawing then if liability is disputed; or because the defendant has forced you to do more work than you wanted), then each case you win is offset by each you lose. This could be offset somewhat by the amount of the success fee.

If we assume that you get a 25% success fee and the amount of applicable damages is half of the £25,000 settlement, then each successful case would add another £3,125 to your profit costs per win. This would be enough to remain (barely) profitable with a 45% win rate.

If you had very low overheads, your firm might be prepared to adopt such a very marginal strategy.

It will be noted that a 60% win-rate gives a modest profit of £4,130 before overheads are taken into account. If your fee target is £200,000 p.a., you would need to win 48-49 cases to meet this (or 1 per week allowing for holidays). Accordingly, the case for being organised and streamlining your cases is fairly clear.

Sample Profit & Loss Table for 100 Intermediate Track Cases (£25,001 settlement, All Stage 1, Average incurred costs = 60% FRC)

Win Rate	FRC (Win)	Loss Rate	Lost Costs	Profit/Loss	Success Fee	Profit/ Case
100%	£1,130,000	0%	£0	£1,130,000	£312,500	£14,425.00
90%	£1,017,000	10%	£67,800	£949,200	£281,250	£12,304.50
80%	£904,000	20%	£135,600	£768,400	£250,000	£10,184.00
70%	£791,000	30%	£203,400	£587,600	£218,750	£8,063.50
60%	£678,000	40%	£271,200	£406,800	£187,000	£5,983.00
50%	£565,000	50%	£339,000	£226,000	£156,250	£3,822.50
45%	£508,500	55%	£372,600	£135,900	£140,625	£2,765.25
40%	£452,000	60%	£406,800	£45,200	£125,000	£1,702.00
35%	£395,000	65%	£440,700	-£45,700	£109,375	£636.75
30%	£203,400	70%	£474,600	-£271,200	£93,750	-£1,774.50

In this scenario, you are more efficient and incur only 60% of the FRC amount on each case.

If you are able to maintain a system where you can either settle or withdraw in stage 1 incurring 60% of the FRC amount, then you could in theory still be marginally profitable with a 35% win-rate. This illustrates that doing more work is not necessarily the correct approach to making a profit under FRC.

Sample Profit & Loss Table for 100 Cases (£100,000 settlement, All Stage 1, Average incurred costs = 60% FRC)

Win Rate	FRC (Win)	Loss Rate	Lost Costs	Profit/Loss	Success Fee	Profit/ Case
100%	£1,730,000	0%	£0	£1,730,000	£312,500	£20,425.00
90%	£1,557,000	10%	£103,800	£1,453,000	£281,250	£17,344.50
80%	£1,384,000	20%	£207,600	£1,176,400	£250,000	£14,264.00
70%	£1,211,000	30%	£311,400	£899,600	£218,750	£11,183.50
60%	£1,038,000	40%	£415,200	£622,800	£187,000	£8,098.00
50%	£865,000	50%	£519,000	£346,000	£156,250	£5,022.50
45%	£778,500	55%	£570,900	£207,600	£140,625	£3,482.25
40%	£692,000	60%	£622,800	£69,200	£125,000	£1,942.00
35%	£605,500	65%	£674,700	-£69,200	£109,375	£401.75
30%	£519,000	70%	£726,000	-£207,000	£93,750	-£1,132.50

In this scenario, you are able to settle cases at £100,000 and so this may be an incentive to settle cases which straddle this settlement value. You are once more efficient and incur only 60% of the FRC amounts win or lose.

Accordingly, cases settling at £100,000 increase the amount of FRC received but do not change the profitability threshold. This indicates that attempting to run cases more efficiently is a better strategy than trying to increase the case value (everything else being equal).

Conclusion

When choosing your mix of tactics for your caseload, the bottom line is to maintain profitability. If you cannot do so, then there is likely to be someone else who can or, at the very least, who might be able to do it better. If so, then the quality of your work will be less relevant.

This does not mean that quality must be subsidiary to quantity. It just means you must be confident of striking the right balance. Cases cannot be won without a certain level of quality work being done. Once you are able to complete the work needed to win cases consistently, then you can focus on improving your results.

Profit margins will be increased by winning more cases and by keeping your incurred costs below the FRC limits for each stage. Where you cannot do this, then the success fee provides a safety net. Once you are obliged to deduct some of the shortfall in costs from your client's damages, you have already lost money on that file and are trying to reduce the amount lost. This is not a realistic long-term strategy and is likely to decrease client satisfaction and your marketability.

FRC is undoubtedly a challenging new environment and there are many things which can cost you money. As such, the key habits to develop are litigation efficiency and your negotiation skills.

CHAPTER ELEVEN

NEGOTIATIONS AND SETTLEMENTS

Case Value

We have already discussed case value, its importance particularly with FRC, and how to value your cases in previous chapters. However, just to emphasise its importance when it comes to negotiations, there are a few things to note.

With some cases being potentially borderline and being treated as an intermediate track claims instead of multi-track ones, one not only needs to establish the maximum value of the case (i.e. what you think the claim is worth if you add everything into consideration) but you also need to carefully consider how strong your case is and what the defendant's position regarding the same is. This will help to avoid any surprises and will help you with your negotiations too.

If you are about to enter into settlement negotiations, it is more likely than not that you will have an understanding of the defendant's position on both liability and quantum. To remind ourselves, if liability is in dispute then you need to worry only about the cases that are below £25,000 that might well be caught by FRC from 6th April 2023.

Nevertheless, it is always good practice to understand your opponent's position. This will also help you to manage your client's and your own expectations when it comes to case settlement. We should also not forget the new QOCS rules that will put even more pressure on any defendant *Part 36* Offers being made, which makes it even more essential to be as realistic as you can about the case value and any settlements. On top of this, are the proposed rules for cases which settle for £25,000 or less which require the claimant to get more than 20% of the pre-issue neutral evaluation. So, claimants may face having to beat both of these if they want to go to trial.

If the defendant has already provided you with some comments, and/or if there has been an offer made by them, then you know what ultimately the minimum case value is. It is always encouraged to take these comments into account and again advise your client about the same too.

If, however, due to many other reasons, you do not know what the defendant's position is, then you need to look at any other triggers that might result in the case value going down from your original valuations. These can be related to your own liability evidence, your own expert(s) not being sure about certain things, the client not having full proof of certain facts, etc. All of those things can help you to understand what could be a minimum case value or otherwise so called 'bottom line'.

If you know your potential 'bottom line' then you can also estimate the risk of the claim being caught outside of the multi-track. However, this will most likely be important for claims that are just below £25,000 or those cases where the defendant has admitted liability in full and the case value is borderline over £100,000. It is worth repeating that FRC creates commercial incentives to defendants to minimize the value of cases and the artful negotiator will seek to avoid these if they cannot gain an advantage from them.

Negotiations

Negotiating effectively is like a form of art which is difficult to perfect. Tips can be given on how to approach ADR and what should be taken into account; the rest, we are afraid, lies with people themselves to practice with confidence so they can do the job right.

Negotiations can take place at any stage of the claim in many different situations. Therefore, we cannot always control the time, circumstances and/or with whom you might be negotiating (although you should try to). However, what you can control is how well prepared you are.

Negotiation tactics are influenced by game theory. To have fair chances in the 'game', one needs to know your case value and why you are trying to claim as much. In order to know the ins and outs, you need to know the facts of your case very well. To know your case value, you also need to know your bottom line (as discussed above) as it will help you to know how far you can take your negotiations. To know this, you need to understand your evidence and the relevant quantum law.

No matter what the new rules on FRC are, the decision *when* to start negotiating is not always within our control and sometimes you will have to trust the process. You can control building the pressure to negotiate and understand the ways in which the new rules combine with the pre-existing ones to promote settlement, but the decision to give in to this is down to the individual client. However, the below are a few additional things to note when it comes to negotiating, especially in situations where you know the case value could reach the trigger point of the case falling out of one and falling into another track that might help (and you know the defendants will be pushing hard to get there).

- Ensure that your comments are backed up by either factual evidence (e.g. medical records) or your own expert evidence.

- Be prepared to refer to any case law or guidelines that would strengthen your arguments; at the end of the day, the opponent cannot ignore the law.

- Consider why the case, even if you settle for less, might not be eligible for any other track but the multi-track, in which case it might prompt the defendant to accept your position.

- If there is a chance for the defendant to suddenly change their position on e.g. on liability, act quickly and strategically to avoid that from happening – do not leave time for things to escalate or a become a problem.

- Be helpful to the defendants without giving in too much, especially if they are not providing you with any helpful comments/information in reciprocation; it might be that they are just testing the water or adopting delaying tactics.

- Ask defendants to support any offers they make with some further comments so that you can get back to them with more accurate answers; refuse to participate in any further discussions if they do not back up their offers – they could be bluffing.

- Always bear in mind how much of the FRC for the stage your case has reached remains so that you know how much time you can spend in negotiation in order to remain profitable. There is a risk that a savvy opponent will be able to justify requiring additional work to be done before settlement and this may persuade your client to agree to accept lower sum.

If, at the end, you are left in a position where you need to either accept the defendant's offer (which will mean that your case will be either caught by FRC or within a lower level of FRC) or persuade them to accept your slightly higher offer. Whenever you can, then we suggest that you push for it for your client's benefit.

If the defendant sees that behaviour from enough of us, then it will ultimately become much 'cheaper' for them to settle for a bit more than to drag the case on for much longer. Ultimately the solicitors and/or insurers on the other side will have to advise their clients (defendants) that this case needs to settle and that the risks of being later held to have unreasonably continued to push for a settlement within the FRC limits outweighs the benefits. Having confidence in your case valuation is crucial for this to work. However, only practice will show us what to expect from the other side and what will be the best way forward long term.

Pressure of FRC

Going through all the things that we have discussed above, while essential to consider, can be time-consuming. Unfortunately, with cases that are (likely) going to be caught by FRC, we risk not being able to afford to spend as much time as we used to on each case; on deciding what the case value is (both maximum and minimum); and on preparing for negotiations and taking informed instructions. Sometimes just remembering some of the things we discuss above might be enough, as long as you are complying with all the principles and have not undervalued the claim.

Therefore, what should we do then if the case is caught by FRC, but we still need to do our job right to ensure that the best settlement is achieved for our client and the firm.

Despite everything, you should roughly know at the start of the case whether you are going to work as if the case is going to be caught under FRC or not. If you are unsure and/or do not want to risk being caught by FRC later, then as we recommend in the previous chapters, it is better to assume that it will. You can choose to treat any case in value below £250,000 as potentially being caught by FRC, unless you are sure about things like liability status and litigation risk.

If the case is unexpectedly caught by FRC, then there is not much that you can do beyond maximising the complexity band it is assigned to and so you might be required to limit your investigations, and/or details in your preparations for negotiations or settlements. The good news is that a fair proportion of cases which will be worth less than £100,000 are easier to value and/or negotiate so hopefully you will not be required to go beyond your skill set or the FRC amounts each time you come to quantum investigations and settlement.

However, if you follow the steps above and get into a habit of doing those tasks, you might naturally become quicker and more accurate at valuing your cases and preparing for negotiations are you go along. If you train your staff to follow the same principles, then you might also be able to rely on others to do a job for you, especially your junior staff to help you out when needed.

Other things to consider to save some time while negotiating/trying to settle are as follows:

- Get on board with your client and seek preliminary instructions on e.g. what is the bottom line, and can you accept any offers that would fall within a certain bracket without contacting your client further.

- Provide the client with accurate information on deductions right at the start, so that you do not have to, if the above approach is adopted, to contact them during your investigation to explain this over and over again.

- Ask for help from your junior colleagues on tasks such as doing research, obtaining information from your clients on quantum etc.

- Use templates and approved letters/forms for your offers instead of trying to invent something new each time; be wary of all the rules so use most up to date precedents to avoid further hassle later on.

- Ask your opponent when negotiating to have full instructions from their clients, instead of waiting for them to get back to you each time you speak; whilst this might not always work, it will not hurt to try.

- Consider calling an opponent and having that conversation over the telephone – this might speed up the process and allow you to pressure or persuade them to settle.

- Make time sensitive Calderbank offers, especially before any important task that both sides need to comply with.

- Equally, do not waste time negotiating if the parties are too far apart.

Following *Churchill v Methyr Tydfil CBC [2023] EWCA Civ 1416*, the court has the power to stay proceedings to allow the parties to engage in 'non-court-based dispute resolution' (probably equivalent to ADR). However, the court declined to offer clear guidance as to when it is appropriate to do so and the parties can still refuse to negotiate during the stay. The refusal by one party to reasonably engage in ADR already covers costs risks and these are increased under the FRC regimes. As such very good reasons need to objectively exist to justify refusing to enter into any form of ADR in clinical negligence cases without incurring adverse consequences.

Settlements

With FRC costs now being in place, our duty might not only be to achieve the best possible outcome for your client, but also for yourself/your firm by ensuring that your case is not, where possible, caught by FRC. In most cases that means that you will try to settle the case for more, so you should still be acting in the best interest of your client.

If liability is denied, the only cases you need to worry about are the cases where the value is below £25,000. Unfortunately, a lot of us have a lot of cases that fall into this category.

For many reasons, these types of cases until now have been considered not 'fit' for the fast track. Sadly, the new rules which may be coming in April 2024, indicate that there will be even more pressure to settle cases worth up to £25,000 pre-action at low FRC levels. While we might be able to currently rely on the fact that any settlements below £25,000 might give us our incurred costs back, we should be careful because the defendants will start pushing for these to be considered as caught by FRC where letters of claim have not been sent.

If liability is admitted in full, then you want to ensure that your case settles for more than £100,000, otherwise, it is more likely than not that it can be considered as suitable for the intermediate track.

To confirm, no matter how much you value your case to be worth, the 'marker' which will determine what the case value is will be how much it settled for. Therefore, it will be important to get those numbers right; it will not matter, however, how much the client will be left with after all deductions have taken place.

If at the end you need to make a decision to settle vs issuing proceedings, then there might be a chance for you here yet.

If the defendant is not going to settle for more just because they want the case to be caught under FRC, you might want to consider issuing proceedings. In that case, if you are happy with the evidence that you have and your own case valuations, it could be a good idea.

If you decide to issue, you become in control of how you want the case value to look like. Therefore, at least temporarily, within reason, you get control of how to present your case, which can ultimately help the judge to decide on the track that the case should be allocated to. The rules are currently silent on whether the drop in case value after allocation would always mean that the case would be reallocated. There could be a few variations, however, in practice, it might be that if the case reaches a certain stage of proceedings, it would not be practical to do so, and that means that your case would get a chance to stay in a multi-track. The defendant may decide that it is not worth the risk of making the application.

In addition, in that case, the defendant might be pressured or otherwise persuaded to settle quickly and for more too, as again it will be 'cheaper' for them than going all the way to trial and/or trying to still arguing the toss over a few thousand pounds.

However, each case needs to be looked at individually. It would still be recommended to choose this route only if you are very sure about your case valuations and the evidence you have.

If settlements are being achieved this way, the defendants change their strategies to avoid issuing and actually compromising for more, which would result in cases not being caught by FRC this way.

While we do not want to over discuss QOCS new rules related to Defendant's being able to recover their costs if they beat their own *Part 36* offers, it would be advisable to make any strategic moves that are backed up by evidence to minimise such risks falling onto the clients. What we do not want is overvaluing cases and then settling for way more not only to be caught by FRC but for also paying the defendant's costs in addition.

Conclusion

It is difficult to predict what approach will be taken by the defendants and how the rules will work out in practice. However, if we are prepared and know what we want to happen with our cases, then we should be successful in settling cases for the sums that would guarantee the spot in a multi-track. Perhaps that is just going to result in tougher negotiations and better settlements for our clients.

To make it even easier to remember what we might want to do, the table below summarises main trigger points and what to consider in each situation.

Case Value	Liability Status	Expert Evidence you will rely at Trial	Things to Consider	Likely Track	Caught by FRC?
<£25k	N/A	More than 1 x	N/A	Multi-track	Risk of a case being caught by FRC is **low.**
<£25k	N/A	Less than 1 x	Perhaps worth considering if any other expert evidence is needed, and/or if there is any other reason why the case should be reallocated to multi track.	Fast Track	Risk of a case being caught by FRC is **high.**
£25-100k	Denied	More than 1 x	N/A	Multi Track	Risk of a case being caught by FRC is **low.**
£25-100k	Denied	Less than 1 x	How likely it is that the case might settle for less than £25k, and/or are we sure there is no need to involve any other expert(s) here.	Multi Track	Risk of a case being caught by FRC is **medium.**
£25-100k	Admitted	Less than 3 x	Are we sure there is no need to involve any other expert(s) here to comment on quantum.	Intermediate Track	Risk of a case being caught by FRC is **high.**

£25-100k	Admitted	More than 3 x	N/A	Multi Track	Risk of a case being caught by FRC is **low.**
>£100k	Denied	N/A	N/A	Multi Track	Risk of a case being caught by FRC is **low.**
>£100k	Admitted	Less than 3 x	How likely it is that the case might settle for less than £100k. Perhaps one of the cases that might be worth issuing.	Multi Track	Risk of a case being caught by FRC is **medium.**
>£100k	Admitted	More than 3 x	N/A	Multi Track	Risk of a case being caught by FRC is **low.**

ABRIDGED INDEX

MORE BOOKS BY LAW BRIEF PUBLISHING

A selection of our other titles available now:-

'A Practical Guide to the Independent School Standards – September 2023 Edition' by Sarah McKimm
'A Practical Guide to Estate Administration and Crypto Assets' by Richard Marshall
'A Practical Guide to Managing GDPR Data Subject Access Requests – Second Edition' by Patrick O'Kane
'A Practical Guide to Parental Alienation in Private and Public Law Children Cases' by Sam King QC & Frankie Shama
'Contested Heritage – Removing Art from Land and Historic Buildings' by Richard Harwood QC, Catherine Dobson, David Sawtell
'The Limits of Separate Legal Personality: When Those Running a Company Can Be Held Personally Liable for Losses Caused to Third Parties Outside of the Company' by Dr Mike Wilkinson
'A Practical Guide to Transgender Law' by Robin Moira White & Nicola Newbegin
'A Practical Guide to 'Stranded Spouses' in Family Law' by Mani Singh Basi
'A Practical Guide to Residential Freehold Conveyancing' by Lorraine Richardson
'A Practical Guide to Pensions on Divorce for Lawyers' by Bryan Scant
'A Practical Guide to Challenging Sham Marriage Allegations in Immigration Law' by Priya Solanki
'A Practical Guide to Digital Communications Evidence in Criminal Law' by Sam Willis
'A Practical Guide to Legal Rights in Scotland' by Sarah-Jane Macdonald
'A Practical Guide to New Build Conveyancing' by Paul Sams & Rebecca East
'A Practical Guide to Defending Barristers in Disciplinary Cases' by Marc Beaumont
'A Practical Guide to Inherited Wealth on Divorce' by Hayley Trim
'A Practical Guide to Practice Direction 12J and Domestic Abuse in Private Law Children Proceedings' by Rebecca Cross & Malvika Jaganmohan

'A Practical Guide to Confiscation and Restraint' by Narita Bahra QC, John Carl Townsend, David Winch
'A Practical Guide to the Law of Forests in Scotland' by Philip Buchan
'A Practical Guide to Health and Medical Cases in Immigration Law' by Rebecca Chapman & Miranda Butler
'A Practical Guide to Bad Character Evidence for Criminal Practitioners by Aparna Rao
'A Practical Guide to Extradition Law post-Brexit' by Myles Grandison et al
'A Practical Guide to Hoarding and Mental Health for Housing Lawyers' by Rachel Coyle
'A Practical Guide to Psychiatric Claims in Personal Injury – 2nd Edition' by Liam Ryan
'Stephens on Contractual Indemnities' by Richard Stephens
'A Practical Guide to the EU Succession Regulation' by Richard Frimston
'A Practical Guide to Solicitor and Client Costs – 2nd Edition' by Robin Dunne
'Constructive Dismissal – Practice Pointers and Principles' by Benjimin Burgher
'A Practical Guide to Religion and Belief Discrimination Claims in the Workplace' by Kashif Ali
'A Practical Guide to the Law of Medical Treatment Decisions' by Ben Troke
'Fundamental Dishonesty and QOCS in Personal Injury Proceedings: Law and Practice' by Jake Rowley
'A Practical Guide to the Law in Relation to School Exclusions' by Charlotte Hadfield & Alice de Coverley
'A Practical Guide to Divorce for the Silver Separators' by Karin Walker
'The Right to be Forgotten – The Law and Practical Issues' by Melissa Stock
'A Practical Guide to Planning Law and Rights of Way in National Parks, the Broads and AONBs' by James Maurici QC, James Neill et al
'A Practical Guide to Election Law' by Tom Tabori
'A Practical Guide to the Law in Relation to Surrogacy' by Andrew Powell
'A Practical Guide to Claims Arising from Fatal Accidents – 2nd Edition' by James Patience
'A Practical Guide to the Ownership of Employee Inventions – From Entitlement to Compensation' by James Tumbridge & Ashley Roughton
'A Practical Guide to Asbestos Claims' by Jonathan Owen & Gareth McAloon

'A Practical Guide to Stamp Duty Land Tax in England and Northern Ireland' by Suzanne O'Hara

'A Practical Guide to the Law of Farming Partnerships' by Philip Whitcomb

'Covid-19, Homeworking and the Law – The Essential Guide to Employment and GDPR Issues' by Forbes Solicitors

'Covid-19 and Criminal Law – The Essential Guide' by Ramya Nagesh

'Covid-19 and Family Law in England and Wales – The Essential Guide' by Safda Mahmood

'A Practical Guide to the Law of Unlawful Eviction and Harassment – 2nd Edition' by Stephanie Lovegrove

'Covid-19, Brexit and the Law of Commercial Leases – The Essential Guide' by Mark Shelton

'A Practical Guide to Costs in Personal Injury Claims – 2nd Edition' by Matthew Hoe

'A Practical Guide to the General Data Protection Regulation (GDPR) – 2nd Edition' by Keith Markham

'Ellis on Credit Hire – Sixth Edition' by Aidan Ellis & Tim Kevan

'A Practical Guide to Working with Litigants in Person and McKenzie Friends in Family Cases' by Stuart Barlow

'Protecting Unregistered Brands: A Practical Guide to the Law of Passing Off' by Lorna Brazell

'A Practical Guide to Secondary Liability and Joint Enterprise Post-Jogee' by Joanne Cecil & James Mehigan

'A Practical Guide to the Pre-Action RTA Claims Protocol for Personal Injury Lawyers' by Antonia Ford

'A Practical Guide to Neighbour Disputes and the Law' by Alexander Walsh

'A Practical Guide to Forfeiture of Leases' by Mark Shelton

'A Practical Guide to Coercive Control for Legal Practitioners and Victims' by Rachel Horman

'A Practical Guide to the Law of Driverless Cars – Second Edition' by Alex Glassbrook, Emma Northey & Scarlett Milligan

'A Practical Guide to TOLATA Claims' by Greg Williams

'A Practical Guide to Elderly Law – 2nd Edition' by Justin Patten

'A Practical Guide to Responding to Housing Disrepair and Unfitness Claims' by Iain Wightwick

'A Practical Guide to the Law of Bullying and Harassment in the Workplace' by Philip Hyland
'How to Be a Freelance Solicitor: A Practical Guide to the SRA-Regulated Freelance Solicitor Model' by Paul Bennett
'A Practical Guide to Prison Injury Claims' by Malcolm Johnson
'A Practical Guide to the Small Claims Track – 2nd Edition' by Dominic Bright
'A Practical Guide to Advising Clients at the Police Station' by Colin Stephen McKeown-Beaumont
'A Practical Guide to Antisocial Behaviour Injunctions' by Iain Wightwick
'Practical Mediation: A Guide for Mediators, Advocates, Advisers, Lawyers, and Students in Civil, Commercial, Business, Property, Workplace, and Employment Cases' by Jonathan Dingle with John Sephton
'The Mini-Pupillage Workbook' by David Boyle
'A Practical Guide to Crofting Law' by Brian Inkster
'A Practical Guide to the Law of Domain Names and Cybersquatting' by Andrew Clemson
'A Practical Guide to the Law of Gender Pay Gap Reporting' by Harini Iyengar
'NHS Whistleblowing and the Law' by Joseph England
'Employment Law and the Gig Economy' by Nigel Mackay & Annie Powell
'A Practical Guide to Noise Induced Hearing Loss (NIHL) Claims' by Andrew Mckie, Ian Skeate, Gareth McAloon
'An Introduction to Beauty Negligence Claims – A Practical Guide for the Personal Injury Practitioner' by Greg Almond
'Intercompany Agreements for Transfer Pricing Compliance' by Paul Sutton
'Zen and the Art of Mediation' by Martin Plowman
'A Practical Guide to the SRA Principles, Individual and Law Firm Codes of Conduct 2019 – What Every Law Firm Needs to Know' by Paul Bennett
'A Practical Guide to Adoption for Family Lawyers' by Graham Pegg
'A Practical Guide to Industrial Disease Claims' by Andrew Mckie & Ian Skeate
'A Practical Guide to Conducting a Sheriff Court Proof' by Andrew Stevenson
'A Practical Guide to Vicarious Liability' by Mariel Irvine
'A Practical Guide to Applications for Landlord's Consent and Variation of Leases' by Mark Shelton
'A Practical Guide to Relief from Sanctions Post-Mitchell and Denton' by Peter Causton

'A Practical Guide to Equity Release for Advisors' by Paul Sams
'A Practical Guide to Financial Services Claims' by Chris Hegarty
'The Law of Houses in Multiple Occupation: A Practical Guide to HMO Proceedings' by Julian Hunt
'Occupiers, Highways and Defective Premises Claims: A Practical Guide Post-Jackson – 2nd Edition' by Andrew Mckie
'A Practical Guide to Financial Ombudsman Service Claims' by Adam Temple & Robert Scrivenor
'A Practical Guide to Running Housing Disrepair and Cavity Wall Claims: 2nd Edition' by Andrew Mckie & Ian Skeate
'A Practical Guide to Holiday Sickness Claims – 2nd Edition' by Andrew Mckie & Ian Skeate
'Arguments and Tactics for Personal Injury and Clinical Negligence Claims' by Dorian Williams
'A Practical Guide to Drone Law' by Rufus Ballaster, Andrew Firman, Eleanor Clot
'A Practical Guide to Compliance for Personal Injury Firms Working With Claims Management Companies' by Paul Bennett
'RTA Allegations of Fraud in a Post-Jackson Era: The Handbook – 2nd Edition' by Andrew Mckie
'RTA Personal Injury Claims: A Practical Guide Post-Jackson' by Andrew Mckie
'On Experts: CPR35 for Lawyers and Experts' by David Boyle
'An Introduction to Personal Injury Law' by David Boyle

These books and more are available to order online direct from the publisher at www.lawbriefpublishing.com, where you can also read free sample chapters. For any queries, contact us on 0844 587 2383 or mail@lawbriefpublishing.com.

Our books are also usually in stock at www.amazon.co.uk with free next day delivery for Prime members, and at good legal bookshops such as Wildy & Sons.

We are regularly launching new books in our series of practical day-to-day practitioners' guides. Visit our website and join our free newsletter to be kept informed and to receive special offers, free chapters, etc.

You can also follow us on Twitter at www.twitter.com/lawbriefpub.

www.ingramcontent.com/pod-product-compliance
Lightning Source LLC
LaVergne TN
LVHW050301210926
848481LV00014BA/346

* 9 7 8 1 9 1 6 6 9 8 1 8 5 *